EPISODES

SCENES
FROM

LIFE, LOVE,

AND
AUTISM

BLAZE GINSBERG

SQUARE
FISH

ROARING BROOK PRESS
NEW YORK

SQUARE
FISH

An Imprint of Macmillan

With the exception of the members of the author's family and certain public figures, the names and identifying characteristics of the people and schools mentioned in this book have been changed to protect their privacy.

Library of Congress Cataloging-in-Publication Data
Ginsberg, Blaze.
Episodes : my life as I see it / Blaze Ginsberg.
p.   cm.
Summary: Blaze Ginsberg creates titles and categories for the different periods
and moments in his life, creating a list of episodes that exist in various stages
of production as his life progresses and the days of his existence roll on.
ISBN 978-0-312-65943-1
1. Ginsberg, Blaze, 1987–. 2. Autistic youth—Biography. 3. Autism in adolescence—
Case studies. 4. Teenagers' writings, American. I. Title.
RJ506.A9 G565 2009   616.858820092   2010278442

Originally published in the United States by Roaring Brook Press
First Square Fish Edition: November 2012
Square Fish logo designed by Filomena Tuosto
Book designed by Scott Myles
macteenbooks.com

10 9 8 7 6 5 4 3 2 1

AR: 6.4 / LEXILE: 850L

For my family, my friends, and for my mom

by debra ginsberg

When Blaze was about ten years old, he gave me a perfect description of how his mind worked. Actually, it was more of a description of the way everyone's mind worked — at least from his perspective. We were out walking one day and he was offering a rare (for that time anyway) explanation as to why he was sensitive to loud noises, especially fire alarms. There were different colored wires present in everyone, he told me, that controlled such things. There was a blue wire that controlled emotions and a red wire that controlled a variety of non-emotional things like playing, talking, and, according to him, "all flying things." When people had problems with their blue wires they cried often. But then there was the yellow wire, which he told me controlled simply "hearing" and this was where his problem lay. His own yellow wire had been too short, he explained, and so it had "snapped" at birth and was now broken.

This made perfect sense to me. "Hearing," especially in Blaze's case, is about much more than sound. For Blaze, hearing meant processing—taking in all the information from the world around him and putting it in some kind of order that made sense. And, of course, if one's mechanism for doing that—the yellow wire—was missing or faulty, it would create some definite problems every time there was a fire drill or a dog barking. His theory was a very direct—and very visual—way of explaining that he was just wired differently. It wasn't anything we didn't know—Blaze was a kid who had been having school problems of one sort or another since his first day in kindergarten—but it was surprising to me that he was able, at least at that moment, to articulate it so clearly.

Since he was so forthcoming about the whole issue, I asked Blaze how we could go about fixing his yellow wire problem, and he told me that there was a repair wire for such things—the white wire—but when I asked where or how we could get this white wire and patch it in, he was stumped. And then the window closed and he was finished with the conversation altogether.

I mulled this information for a long time and, later, tried to coax Blaze into explaining it further—perhaps even for the benefit of his teachers and other professionals who were evaluating him and trying to figure out a less metaphoric diagnosis for his differences. But Blaze had moved on and was unwilling—or unable—to elaborate further. The next few years were rough. There were more school problems and more attempts at diagnosing where these problems were coming from—all of which ended in more or less dead ends. It would take many years before Blaze was finally given a definitive diagnosis of high functioning autism. During his middle school years, however, he did not have the luxury of this explanation for his differences and gradually retreated into a personal space inside his own head where he was comfortable. At that time there was little anyone could say or do to convince him that the outside world was any better.

Finally, when he was fourteen, Blaze was accepted into a school that would end up changing his life in a very positive way. The Surrey School, which he writes about with such fondness in these pages, is a very small, very special (and I mean special in a good way here) school whose student population just hasn't been able to thrive in public school for a number of different reasons. Not everyone wanted to be there. There were students who felt that being in a "special" school made them outcasts or who weren't comfortable in such a small school where there were always eyes watching what they were up to. But many more students were like Blaze, hungry for a place where they were accepted for who they were and allowed to learn in an environment that encouraged them to achieve and grow.

Almost immediately, Blaze started coming out of his protective shell and interacting with other people (students, teachers, counselors) in a meaningful way. Instead of just shutting down when someone asked him a question or called him on weird behavior, he was forced (gently, of course) to actually respond—to share his thoughts and feelings—and to take responsibility for his actions. For the first time in his life, he was forming relationships with people who weren't his own family members—he was inside a social circle instead of wandering around the periphery looking in.

At around the same time, Blaze started writing in earnest. He'd always enjoyed making lists, writing songs, and jotting down stories, but now he was starting to write about himself and what was going on around him. I'd always encouraged him to do this so he was never shy about showing me what he'd written or asking me for feedback on what I read. Now, I know that there is no way I can ever be completely objective about Blaze but, after a lifetime of reading, writing, and reviewing all kinds of books, I do have a good sense of what is quality writing. So when Blaze showed me some very early drafts of what would later become *Episodes*, I knew immediately that it was something unique and wonderful. It was different from anything I'd read before yet somehow very familiar. Best of all, it made me laugh out loud.

Blaze had struck intuitively on a concept for filtering his thoughts, feelings, and the events in his life that seemed so clever and clear and yet I would never have thought of it even if I'd tried for years. All of our basic human stories are essentially the same, and so the challenge for any writer is to wrap them up and present those stories in a way that is somehow different enough to be interesting, but familiar enough to be relatable. Many of the events and experiences in Blaze's life were much like anyone else's his age: the desire for friends, crushes on girls, struggles with schoolwork, getting a first job, family gatherings. How he saw and understood all of these events, though, was unusual, and this hearkened back to that original yellow wire problem—that different way Blaze had of seeing and processing the world around him and his inability to communicate that vision to anyone else. With *Episodes*, Blaze had found a way to do just that.

In this book, Blaze has taken some of the most important events in his life and made them into TV series in which he is a recurring actor. Some of these events (his crush on Hilary Duff, for example) have a limited run and are canceled after two or three seasons, not to be revisited (except perhaps in the YouTube of his memory). Some (like family gatherings at Thanksgiving) are a continuing series of specials and can be counted on to continue airing. Some (like his friendship with two close buddies) are no longer airing but will live forever in syndication. Like all of us, Blaze has favorite episodes in his life and some that he wishes he could forget. To an extent, I believe this is something we all do. We're all the stars of our own shows. Our lives have permanent cast members and those who provide critical guest-starring roles. Many of the events that define us wind up in permanent syndication where we view them repeatedly on our own mental TV screens.

Although the events in Blaze's episodes are mostly typical, the details within them are not. For example, in none of the Thanksgiving specials does Blaze ever mention food. In the "Games" series (which is about school field trips to basketball and softball games), which is one of Blaze's favorites, there is no description of plays or scores. Most of the time, Blaze can't even remember who won. For him, those weren't the important details. What were important were the different buses he took, what happened on the bleachers during the games, and the conversations he had with his schoolmates and bus drivers. Wandering through his episodes, I learned a great deal about what Blaze thought and how he saw the world around him. The landscape was very familiar but, through Blaze's eyes, I was able to see it from a completely different angle: the periphery, where Blaze had spent most of his life. I knew that Blaze had pulled off that difficult writer's task— presenting the usual in an unusual way—and I knew others would see it that way too. And that was when I realized something else. This funny, touching, quirky, and always honest book is Blaze's white wire. He'd finally found that magic patch for his snapped yellow wire; a way of processing the world with all its confusions, contradictions, and sudden jangling noises and putting it in an order that gave it meaning and sense. But *Episodes* is much more than a guide to understanding Blaze's world or even Blaze himself. It shines a light on all the little places in our own lives that we may overlook while we focus on the usual or the big picture. Just as each television show gives us a unique perspective on family drama, situation comedy, or reality, *Episodes* offers a brand new way of looking at school, teen life, and growing up.

It's true that Blaze is unique, but so is every one of us.

This is Blaze's world. But it's our world too.

main cast biographies:

blaze: self

Born in Oregon but moved to California when I was a year old. Close to my grandparents, my three aunties, and my uncle, who all live nearby. Interested in PBS Kids shows, music, writing stories, and finding a girlfriend.

mom (debra): mother

Is an author. Wrote the book *Raising Blaze* all about me and my school problems and our family. Takes her work very seriously. Does not drive. (No offense to her, but if she suddenly started driving, I don't know if I would be okay with that.) Is a good mother to me.

maya: aunt

Plays violin and tutors students. Appeared on *Jeopardy* in 1998 as a contestant.

déja: aunt

Is an actress. Has appeared in multiple plays such as *The Crucible, The Visit*, and more. Moved to Pasadena in November 2004 and moved back to San Diego in November 2005.

lavander: aunt

Sells real estate. Has had a lot of cars. On December 28, 2004, was involved in an accident in her BMW but was not injured. While her car was getting fixed in the shop, it got infested with rats. She traded that car in for a Lexus.

bodine (bo): uncle

Invented "The Jewish Triathlon" in March 2006 (the Jewish Triathlon is an exercise that involves the hot tub, sauna, and swimming pool), which we do every weekend. Also took charge of my diet in November 2006. He said I must have two pieces of fruit every morning and one vegetable every night. Also said I cannot have more than one soda a week.

nana: grandmother

Has moved across the globe several times and has five children. Starting in 1990, we've been picking her up and going out for a "Saturday Groove" where we go to stores and have tea. Is the funniest person I know.

papa: grandfather

Owns a baseball school. Plans all family trips. Gives me many rides and talks to me about how to function in the world. Taught me how to play Dominoes and poker. In February 2001, he helped to home-school me. Has gone to almost every one of my IEP* meetings at school with Mom. In November 2005, taught me how to shave. In late summer 2005, he gave me my first-ever lesson on how to talk to a girl. He said to ask girls about themselves and not to talk to them about my crazy shit.

gabe: mom's boyfriend

Has been Mom's boyfriend since July 2001. Works for HarperCollins. Has two children, Amanda and Jonathan. Lives in Los Angeles. Is giving me driving lessons and assisting me in how to communicate with girls and how to be with people.

*IEP STANDS FOR INDIVIDUALIZED EDUCATION PROGRAM. THE IEP MEETINGS ARE WITH PARENTS AND TEACHERS OF KIDS IN SPECIAL EDUCATION CLASSES TO GO OVER GOALS FOR LEARNING.

on chronology and structure

Some of the episodes in this book may seem like they are out of chronological order. For example, "Government Offices 1" begins in 2005 with Episode 1 and then Episode 2 is in 2006. But the bulk of the episodes occur in 2007 so this is where the series is placed in the book. My reason for doing this is because you can't have an entire season be just one episode. Also, there are sometimes series in this book that occur simultaneously but are separate series. This is because even though they may be happening at the same time, the series focus on different themes. For example, "My Freshman Year" and "Blaze, Courtney, and Amber" both happened in 2002, but they are about different things. This is like a regular television season where on any given night, there can be several totally different TV shows happening at the same time.

I am terribly sorry if this is confusing. I really hope you enjoy this memoir anyway.

Later,

Blaze Ginsberg

additional details
genres: comedy / drama / family / more

my freshman year of high school I (2002)

(A.K.A. ONE OF THE BEST SCHOOL YEARS EVER I)

series: **2002–2003**   release date: **SEPTEMBER 3, 2002**
genre: **FRESHMAN FOOLISHNESS**   status: **ENDED**

cast:

blaze ginsberg: himself

courtney: friend
Friend of mine and for a short time, a possible girlfriend. I met her in the summer of 2002. Is an only child. Left our school, Surrey, in the summer of 2003 because she hated it and was throwing tantrums about it like Dudley Dursley from *Harry Potter*. Also had a lot of crying cases in **My Freshman Year of High School**. Liked Marvin Gaye and pretty much agreed with me about everything. If there was anything I did not like, she did not like it either.

amber: friend
Played herself in 2002's **My Freshman Year** as a girlfriend (not romantic) of mine. Later played herself in the series **Blaze, Courtney, and Amber**. Claims she rescued me on my tenth birthday in 1997 when I ran away from home.* In September 2002 I reunited with her and we became buddies instantly. Is very sensitive to how people approach her.

wendy: teacher
Was one of my teachers at Surrey. She and her boyfriend went to high school with my uncle Bo, and they are still friends with him. She is pretty strict with her students and does not have a high tolerance level for bad behavior. One day in class she made us put our heads down like we were in kindergarten because of our bad behavior.

*THE INCIDENT WHEN I RAN AWAY FROM HOME OCCURRED AFTER I HAD AN ARGUMENT WITH MAYA. I WENT OFF WALKING BY MYSELF AND HALF THE NEIGHBORHOOD ENDED UP LOOKING FOR ME.

mr. kent: english teacher
Mr. K is also serious with his students about their behavior and whatnot. Mr. K really goes into detail when reading a story, like when we read **The Body** by Stephen King. I asked Mr. K why a character was crying over something small in the book and Mr. K told me it was because he (the character) never cried when his brother died. Mr. K got me interested in reading certain books like **The Perks of Being a Wallflower.** He is very into literature.

ms. kennedy: speech therapist
Speech therapist at Surrey. Very nice and caring, and she always wants everything to be the best it can be. She and I met when I was having a problem with another teacher one day and we became friends from there.

jane: occupational therapist
The Surrey School occupational therapist. Was very close to me. I liked her from very early on because of her personality. She really liked the stories I wrote when we were working together. She also had kind of a low tolerance level for bad/insubordinate behavior.

dr. r: counselor

various friends: themselves

---

series summary

My first year at The Surrey School (a.k.a. *My Freshman Year of High School*) may be number 1 in my top two best school years to ever exist in human civilization (for me that is). The Surrey School is a special school for kids with learning differences/those who are not able to function in a regular school. The classes are very small (only about ten kids per class) and there are only about 100 kids altogether in the school. I was at The Surrey School for many reasons, but mostly because middle school was a total disaster. In my other schools before this there were very few teachers who cared and were willing to work with people like me.

At Surrey, things really made a big turnaround from the way school used to be. This year was something unforgettable and legendary beyond conceivable knowledge because it really changed the way school had been for me for the past ten years. Prior to this year, I never really liked school too much, and most of the time I didn't really want to be there. Freshman year changed everything. Even though I had teacher issues and got sent out/was in trouble a lot, this was a good year because I was slowly starting to become a grown-up, hanging out with homies, talking to girls, and thinking about my future. Also this was a good year because I was starting to interact with other people more than I had in the past. Although I didn't realize it at the time, the ten years of school before Surrey were kind of depressing because I was really too much inside my own self and not relating to other people. So even though my interactions with people during my freshman year at Surrey were sometimes negative, at least I was *having* interactions.

Episode List

title: **PILOT**   air date: **SEPTEMBER 3, 2002**

summary

It is my first day of high school and it is somewhat nerve-racking. I enter the school before class starts. I see Courtney but turn away from her because I am feeling shy. Later on I report to class. My day starts off with Physical Science. I am a bit spacey because I have not had to sit and listen in class for quite some time. It ends all right. After that I report to Math and I need a VTO (voluntary time out) because I am antsy and need to walk around. I am allowed ten minutes and then I go back. The teacher has an aide named Rebecca; I work with her on the math. Later I go to class for RL (reading/language). It is not too great because I have been struggling with the teacher since the summer session. (I had taken Summer School at Surrey in June as a trial period to see if I would be able to go there or not). Then it is time for English. I feel a bit anxious (or, as I call it, "tight") because it's still the first day of school, but nonetheless it's fine. Then I go to lunch. After lunch, I report to PE. We play football, run laps, and it is pretty fun. Later I report to Tutorial and it is fun, although I do not do any of my homework which is what tutorial is for.

quotes

me: "Can I get a VTO, please?"

(Teacher writes one up)

me: (seeing that the VTO paper says "Student Referral"): "What? I'm in trouble?"

teacher: "Oh no, that's just what it says. It's fine, it's a VTO."

trivia

A VTO is when you get ten minutes to leave class and walk around the school or sit on the bench to chill yourself out. You get one VTO per class per week. If you abuse the privilege, by staying out of class for too long, you get sent to the office and get your VTOs temporarily suspended.

soundtrack listing

"Bird of Beauty" by Stevie Wonder (*Fulfillingness' First Finale* 1974)

This song plays because it goes really well with running laps. I like the way it makes me feel.

Episode 2

title: **FIRST COUNSELING SESSION**   air date: **SEPTEMBER 5, 2002**

summary

Today I have my first counseling session of the year with my counselor, Dr. R. I tell him I am mad at Courtney for not saying good-bye to me when I was on the bus yesterday afternoon. He tells me about the school policy where you can leave campus at lunchtime if you are approved for it and don't take advantage of the policy by not coming back.

notes

Dr. R was my first counselor at Surrey. I saw him once a week for counseling, other times as needed if I was having a problem with something. His attitude was very calm but jokey. We played board games such as Sorry! etc. to help me with social skills.

quotes

me: "Can you actually walk down to the beach when you are at school?"
dr. r: "Yes, but you can't go in the water."
(Later, as we arrive back on campus)
me: "I'm mad at Courtney."
dr. r: "Why?"
me: "Because I yelled 'good-bye' to her and she didn't respond."
dr. r: "She probably didn't hear you."

soundtrack listing

"Kings of the Highway" by Chris Isaak (*Heart Shaped World* 1989)
This song plays because it has a sad, cloudy sound and it reminds me of the weather that day and how Courtney didn't hear me when I called her.

Episode 3

title: **OLD UNKNOWN TIMES**   air date: **SEPTEMBER 2002**

summary

In Tutorial I meet a girl named Amber who says she knew me from earlier when I was in kindergarten. I don't remember this. We get to know each other pretty well this period. She reminds me that she used to live across the street from me.

notes

Amber and I used to go to school with a girl in a wheelchair who Amber did not like because the girl always honked her wheelchair horn, was bratty, and ran over Amber's toe.

trivia

Some episodes do not have an exact air date, just the month and year when they aired. This is because I don't always remember the exact date of some of these episodes (even though I am generally really good with dates).

Episode 4

title: **IT'S A YOUNG HIGH SCHOOL WORLD**   air date: **SEPTEMBER 13, 2002**

summary

My OT Jane and I are scheduled to have our first meeting today. It goes really well. We play Ping-Pong, then we go to the computer lab to write two stories called *The Boy Who Hated Bagels* and *The Girl Who Hated Turnips*. Jane gets a kick out of it and we become friends.

notes

I met Jane at my middle school in the spring of 2001.

An OT is an occupational therapist. The OT does exercises, strength tests, and computer skills to improve my fine motor skills and gross motor skills. Mostly we work on fine motor skills and typing. Jane wanted me to practice "home row" on the keyboard and I did it, but reluctantly because I thought it was too hard for me.

The Boy Who Hated Bagels was based on a real-life incident from years ago that was still bothering me that day.

trivia

The real-life bagel incident happened one day in 1994 when I was having a bagel for breakfast. Mom said that unless I finished eating the bagel, I would not get a ride to school. I did not end up finishing the bagel, and so I had to walk to school and was miserable about that. The misery of this incident suddenly came back to me in 2002 and I kept thinking about it.

soundtrack listing

"Is It Love" by Play (*Play* 2002)

"Forever Young" by Alphaville (*Forever Young* 1984)

"Is It Love" plays during the scene where Jane and I are playing Ping-Pong because of the great bond between us. "Forever Young" plays because I am happy when I am writing my stories and it shows how silly I am.

Episode 5

title: **LIFE IS TOO SHORT**   air date: **SEPTEMBER 18, 2002**

summary

Geoff Z and I are having lunch together today. Geoff Z and I are just becoming friends. He is friendly and he always goes along with me when I get silly. We make up stories about the Brady Bunch and other topics. It is really fun but gets out of control when Geoff says he turned Marcia into spaghetti.

notes

Geoff Z likes me to say his full name over and over because he likes the way it sounds. He also says "Classic" every time I say his name.

quotes

me: "One day I went to Vons and my grandmother was driving and she took the exit I don't like out of the parking lot. Has anything like that ever happened to you?"
geoff: "My grandmother ran my mother over."
me: "No way, man."
(A few minutes later)
me: "Once upon a time Jan and Marcia Brady were run over by a bus."
geoff: "I cut Marcia Brady up and made spaghetti out of her."

trivia

I don't always know whether people are joking or not. I speak to Déja when I get uncomfortable about this.

soundtrack listing
"All My Love" by Led Zeppelin (*In Through The Out Door* 1979)

Episode 6

title: **FIRST TEST**   air date: **SEPTEMBER 2002**

summary
I have a test in Physical Science today. It goes fine, but it is a little stressful.

notes
The test was on positive and negative charges of atoms.

I did not pass.

Episode 7

title: **COURTNEY'S FIRST CRYING CASE**   air date: **OCTOBER 3, 2002**

summary
There is another test in Physical Science today. We are preparing to take it. Mr. Heart, the teacher, is absent today. Courtney and another student named David keep feuding like five-year-olds and it does not stop. They keep digging and the hole between them starts to go deeper. Finally, David blows up and hits Courtney's hat and she hangs her head on the table. I nervously (because Courtney may start crying, which she did) go to find Coach Brian. I go outside to the bench to take the test and then I see Courtney in tears, walking with a speech therapist (not Ms. Kennedy).

notes
David also kicked Courtney's desk a few times and made it rock. Courtney and David had a very complex relationship. There were times when David would be yelling at Courtney and Courtney would be trying to get his attention.

quotes
david: "Hey, shut up!" (Kicks her desk)
courtney (crying): "Life is just like this. Nobody likes me these days."

trivia

Courtney seemed to get under people's skin. She wasn't very popular.

Crying was definitely a theme for this episode: Lauren, a senior, also had a crying case (from hunger) that day.

soundtrack listing

"More Than You Know" by Anita Baker (*Compositions* 1990)
This song plays because I have been through a lot with people crying and I feel the same way as Anita does in her song when she says she is wasting her time.

Episode 8

title: **THE REPORTS**   air date: **OCTOBER 7, 2002**

---

summary

Mr. Heart has returned to see how the class was while he was away. Obviously he will not be getting a very good report because of the incident that occurred between Courtney and David.

quotes

courtney: "You hit me and I cried."
david: "I hit your hat."

trivia

Mr. Heart flies hot air balloons. He told the class that he has a balloon and takes it out for flights and takes other people along with him. I am hoping that he will take me out in his balloon but worry that Mom won't sign a permission slip to let me. When I was twelve, I started to really want to go up in a hot air balloon. We see them all the time as they take off near our house. Mom said that if I ate a sandwich (which I don't like), she would go in a hot air balloon with me. But I could not agree to the deal and still have not eaten a sandwich. So I was concerned that if there were ever a hot air balloon field trip, she would not let me go.

Episode 9

title: **FIRST SEND-OUT**   air date: **OCTOBER 2002**

---

summary

Today in Science I am very talkative and not behaving very well. I get my three warnings. Finally Mr. Heart has to send me out because I am disrupting class. I report to the office and I cry about it briefly then go for a walk with Jesse the TA. I also talk to the camper staff about life.

notes

My friend Julia noticed me today.

trivia

The camper is in the parking lot. That is where the high school exit exam is given, where IEP meetings are held, and where the staff sometimes have lunch. The camper staff is anyone who is on duty in the camper for the day.

soundtrack listing

"Complicated" by Avril Lavigne (*Let Go* 2002)
This song plays because this was my first ever send-out and the first time I was ever in this tight situation.

Episode 10

title: **COURTNEY'S SECOND CRYING CASE**   air date: **OCTOBER 16, 2002**

summary

We are in Science Lab today as we are every Wednesday. We are doing our routine as usual when Courtney starts crying. I do get a little bit weirded out when I hear what she sounds like. She goes to sit in front of the office.

notes

This time Courtney was crying because of home problems.

trivia

Courtney's crying had a lot of moaning in it, which eventually rose to screaming.

quotes

mr. heart: "Courtney, go sit in front of the office."
(Later, outside the office)

me: "Courtney, why were you crying?"
courtney: "Stuff going on at home."

title: **CHEATING**   air date: **OCTOBER 2002**

summary

I go to visit the Lower School during lunchtime (this is a routine I
have now developed). Lower School is grade 5–6 at the south end
of the campus. I've started going down there to explore the school a
little more when I am finished with all the other stuff that I do during
lunch, such as eating and talking to Courtney. I greet the students
and hang out in their classroom on their rocking chair and eat some
candy. There are students working or playing on the computers in
the room. I see a fifth grade student I know who is on the fifth level of
Bugdom. I congratulate her. She tells me there is a cheat code to get
past the levels.

notes

We owned Bugdom back in 2000 until the computer we had it on
crashed.

quotes

me (talking to fifth grader): "I'm proud of you."

soundtrack listing

"Art Decade" by David Bowie (*Low* 1977)
I don't have a problem with uncontrollable change (which is when
something happens that has never happened before), but sometimes
I do have a problem with sudden change (which is when something
expected happens in a different way than usual). When that happens,
I get the vibe of this song. I didn't realize that anyone could get past
level 3 on Bugdom without working through it. This was the change.

Episode 12

title: **THE GAME**   air date: **OCTOBER 2002**

summary

I am in Tutorial playing a game on the computer where you are a green car, load up on ammo, and shoot at your enemies, the red cars. I really sink into this game.

notes

They had this game at my elementary school.

trivia

This game is nothing like Grand Theft Auto.

Episode 13

title: THE BALLAD OF THE BOX   air date: **OCTOBER 2002**

---

summary

In Computer Graphics (I have now been moved to computers from reading/language because RL was too easy for me), I am hanging around not really doing anything. Courtney is there as well. Mr. P, the teacher, and I make a box with a "Do Not Open" sign on it. Courtney opens it and that does not make me happy.

notes

This was the second "Do Not Open" box I have made.

quotes

me: "I said do not open it!"
courtney: "Blaze, be quiet."

trivia

My "Do Not Open" boxes were inspired by an episode of Mr. Rogers' Neighborhood where in the Neighborhood of Make-Believe there is a flying box that says "Do Not Open" on it.

This was the last box I made in Computer Graphics. I only played games on the computer from then on.

Episode 14

title: MENTOR   air date: **OCTOBER 2002**

---

summary

Mr. Heart has been gone for two days due to his having to fly his hot air balloon. We have a possible new student, Lucinda (she is just visiting for two days), and a new sub named Wendy. Later on I eat lunch with Lucinda and we talk about school.

notes

When a possible student visits, someone shows that person around the school for the whole day. When I came on my visit in April 2002, a student named Robert showed me around. He took me to classes and chatted with me. It's a good policy because it makes students feel comfortable at the school. I did not show Lucinda around, but I was told by my speech therapist to sit and have lunch with her.

quotes

me: "Hey, I'm Blaze."
lucinda: "Hi, I'm Lucinda."
me: "Nice to meet you. What is your other school like?"
lucinda: "It's okay, but I don't have a lot of friends there."
me: "This is my first year here."

Episode 15

title: **A NO-SHOW**   air date: **OCTOBER 31, 2002**

summary

Today it is Halloween. I start off going to see Ms. Kennedy (my speech therapist) and we play a game of Sorry! I do not win and that makes me really mad so I knock the board over and get into trouble. Also at pumpkin patch time* I do not participate in the games.

notes

Mom considered punishing me for my behavior at school.

I was banned from playing games at school for a while.

I had been punished back in July for threatening a teacher. I had tried to get out of it, but, no sir, that time it did not work.

---

*PUMPKIN PATCH TIME INVOLVES CARVING PUMPKINS (EVERYONE IS ASSIGNED A CERTAIN PUMPKIN).

trivia

Losing games was very difficult for me for a long time. I hate the feeling of not winning.

Episode 16

title: **COURTNEY'S PESTILENCE MOVE**   air date: **NOVEMBER 1, 2002**

summary

I am in Physical Science. Courtney is blowing kisses to everyone but then just stares at me without blowing a kiss or saying anything. It upsets me. I am even still angry about it when I go to Math. But then we talk it out in Computers.

notes

I don't think Courtney was intentionally trying to annoy me.

soundtrack listing

"Come Get to This" by Marvin Gaye (*Let's Get It On* 1973)

"The Apartment Song" by Tom Petty (*Full Moon Fever* 1989)
In the song, Tom Petty talks about how he used to live in a two-room apartment and the neighbors would bang on the wall day after day. Courtney kept repeating the same pattern over and over again (staring at me without blowing a kiss), which is why this song plays.

Episode 17

title: **BUDDIES COMPANY IN TROUBLE**   air date: **NOVEMBER 8, 2002**

summary

Another student Max and I are not behaving too well during Physical Science. We are kind of talking a lot and then finally Mr. Heart just sends us out and we have to go talk to the Dean of Students.

notes

Max is also a freshman and once in a while he would do things like imitating balloons popping (which he knew bothered me) to get a reaction out of me.

quotes

the dean: "Mr. Heart is trying to run a class, and you can't be talking in the middle of class."

Episode 18

title: THE BEST DAY EVER   air date: **NOVEMBER 15, 2002**

summary

I start off my day with Jane, writing a story about kids who do not like sunsets (see trivia). Later on, in English, my AlphaSmart (a portable keyboard, sort of like a laptop) is not functioning. I kind of become a pain to Mr. Kent and he sends me out. When he does, I refuse to go. He goes to get the Dean, but I throw a fit so he gets Ms. Kennedy and Jane. At this point I am having a major spin-out. In tears, I go for a walk up to the field with Jane. We talk. Ms. Kennedy calls Mom to make everything okay. I eat lunch with Jane. Later in PE, Coach Brian keeps catching me sitting down and threatens to send me out himself, but I just walk laps. Later, at the end of the day, I hug Jane for the first time.

notes

This was my third send-out of the year.

Later, I felt like a complete idiot for my behavior, but at the time I couldn't stop myself.

This winds up being the best day ever because I work it all out with Jane.

quotes

mr. kent: "If you don't go, you're going to get suspended. I'm going to get the Dean."
jane: "You're overworking yourself. Take deep breaths."
me: (crying)
jane: "Let's climb the jungle gym."
(I climb the jungle gym all the way to the top)
jane (puts her arm around me): "It's okay, we'll fix this."
(in PE)
coach b (firmly): "Blaze, don't sit down. Walk laps."
(At the end of the day)

me: "Hey, thank you."
jane: "You know what? No problem."
(We hug)

trivia

The Kid Who Hated Sunsets
by Blaze Ginsberg

Once upon a time there was a kid and his sister who loved to play during the daytime.

Whenever it was sunset they would never like it and would always cry to their mother about it.

One day they contacted a wizard named Mr. Spooks and he promised to take sunsets away forever.

"I see you don't like sunsets," Mr. Spooks said.

"No, we don't," the sister said.

"I shall take them away forever," Mr. Spooks said. He contacted his crystal ball and then sunsets were gone and the kids celebrated. But then they realized why they needed sunsets. When the sun never sets, it never becomes nighttime and nobody gets to sleep.

The brother and sister lived tiredly ever after.

soundtrack listing

"These Three Words" by Stevie Wonder (*Jungle Fever* 1991)

"Mad About You" by Sting (*Soul Cages* 1991)
This song has an intense energy—the singer doesn't want to lose the person he's singing to and that is the same energy as this episode.

Episode 19

title: **BLAZE AND AMBER**   air date: **NOVEMBER 19, 2002**

summary

Amber and I are hanging out in Tutorial today. We go outside to be alone with each other and she asks me to do impressions. I do one of Martin Luther King Jr. getting shot, which is my idea. I tell her about the Bagel Incident of 1994 and turn it over to her to do what she wants with it. I ask her if she would burn the bagel to the ground if it was her.

notes
"Burn the bagel to the ground" was our new motto.

quotes
amber (repeated line): "I'd burn the bagel to the ground."

trivia
Amber really liked impressions. In 2005 she asked me to do a Nazi salute, which I did because I didn't know what it meant at the time. She said she would be my friend again if I did it, so I did and ended up getting in quite a bit of trouble.

At this time, I considered possibly having Amber for a girlfriend and maybe living with her in the future, but it didn't work out that way unfortunately.

soundtrack listing
"Head Over Feet" by Alanis Morissette (*Jagged Little Pill* 1995)
This song plays because of the bond between me and Amber.

Episode 20

title: **AMBER'S SEVERE CRYING CASE**   air date: **NOVEMBER 21, 2002**

summary
When I rush down to Tutorial from PE, I arrive there to see the tutorial teacher and the Dean of Students talking to what seems like a computer guy, but I am also startled to see Amber in tears. The Dean pulls me away to go help find Dr. R. But we have no success. I am then taken aside by Robert (another student) who suggests we go play Bugdom in Mr. K's room while Amber talks to her friend Amy. I do not have a problem with that at all. Later on, at the end of the day, Amber sits on the bench by herself.

notes
Kathy, a student, called Amber a bitch, which is why she was crying.

Amber's crying was very squealy and her face was all dark and ashy. It was scary.

Kathy had called Amber a bitch after Amber had done something to piss her off and they got into a fight.

quotes
the dean (firmly, not wanting me to upset amber more): "You do not ask Amber what's wrong."
(Later)
amy: "May I talk to Amber?"
tutorial teacher: "Sure."
(Later)
me: "Are you okay?"
amber: "Yeah, I'm fine."
(Later)
amber: "Burn the bagel to the ground."

goofs
When Amber was crying, I thought I heard the word "forbidden" coming from her, but I was mistaken, she was just crying and making noise.

soundtrack listing
"Zeroes" by David Bowie (*Never Let Me Down* 1987)

"Mary Jane's Last Dance" by Tom Petty and the Heartbreakers (*Greatest Hits* 1993)

"Hold On" by Sarah McLachlan (*Fumbling Towards Ecstasy* 1993)

"Good Love" by Anita Baker (*Giving You the Best That I Got* 1988)

"Hold On" plays because this was the first time in the nine years (according to Amber) I have known her that I have seen her cry.

"Mary Jane's Last Dance" plays because of the energy of me and Amber talking after she was crying. In the Anita Baker song, there is a verse where she sings about being a man that reminds me of this day.

"Zeroes" plays because of my running from PE mood and at one point the way I feel when I see Amber cry goes the same way in the song.

Episode 21

title: **MADNESS UPON ME**   air date: **NOVEMBER 22, 2002**

summary
Today I am hanging around school and I am kind of mad at Amber. I do my usual thing: go to my classes and all that. At lunchtime, I finally confess to Amber that I am mad at her.

notes

This was the first time that Amber and I had a problem where I was mad at her.

I was mad at Amber because her crying messed me up so much I couldn't stop thinking about it. I never really got around to realizing that this was not her fault.

quotes

me: "I'm mad at you."
amber: "Why?"
me: "Because of your crying yesterday."
Amber: "Oh, really?"

Episode 22

title: TESTS WITH OTHER PEOPLE   air date: **NOVEMBER 25, 2002**

---

summary

Today I am taking my first assessment tests with a proctor. She tells me what to write and I do it. I look at the paper and write descriptions for the pictures. The proctor is a pretty nice woman and we get along okay.

notes

In the auditorium, there are three rooms. One is the Reading teacher's room, one is Ms. Kennedy's room, and the third is the Dean's office. There is a fourth door that is always locked—that is the proctor's room. The proctor's room is the only one that is always locked.

Episode 23

title: STORY   air date: **NOVEMBER 26, 2002**

---

summary

In Tutorial today, Amber's friend Amy writes two stories for me. One is about how she crashed a car once. The second is about Amber's crying case and how I felt about it. For the car-crashing story, Amy composes the whole story because it really happened to her. With the Amber story, I tell her what to say and she writes it down and adds her own interpretation.

notes

Amber's crying case is now an official obsession.

trivia

When Amy was driving with her instructor, she crashed the car into a wall.

soundtrack listing

"The Girl from Yesterday" by The Eagles (*Hell Freezes Over* 1994)

Episode 24

title: **SECOND HUG WITH JANE**   air date: **DECEMBER 5, 2002**

---

summary

I am testing again with the proctor. I see Jane and I go to give her a hug for happiness benefits. Then I go back to test with the proctor and get on with the rest of my day.

notes

The next year, my sophomore year, hugging became forbidden between me and Jane. There was apparently a policy about contact between staff and students which we didn't know we were violating at the time. The next year, Jane told me about it when I attempted to hug her a few times. It took me a while to finally just live with it.

quotes

jane: "Get back in there."
me (saying the date to mark the occasion in history of hugging jane): "Thursday, December 5, 2002. Thursday, December 5, 2002."

soundtrack listing

"Your Unchanging Love" by Marvin Gaye (*Moods of Marvin Gaye* 1966) This song plays because of the way it was to hug Jane. We had been best friends since early on in the year.

Episode 25

title: **COURTNEY'S SEVERE MELTDOWN**   air date: **DECEMBER 9, 2002**

---

summary

I am doing my usual routine today when Courtney has a severe crying case that gets progressively worse. After talking to her counselor, she decides going to the bathroom will help. But no sir, it does not. She then collapses to the floor, screaming. Her counselor tries to reason with her and scolds her. After about half an hour of crying herself out of sync, she finally stops in Computers. As usual, she is crying about home problems.

notes

I later heard from another student that something happened with Courtney's mom and her uncle but I didn't really get what it was. This is the last episode where Courtney cries over home problems.

quotes

courtney's counselor: "Courtney, cut this out."
(Courtney screams and cries)
(Later)
me: "What were you crying about? Let me guess, home problems."
courtney: "Correct."

Episode 26

title: **INVITATIONS**   air date: **DECEMBER 12, 2002**

summary

One day in Computers, Courtney and I chat. She then invites me over to her house for dinner. I am not particularly comfortable with this idea because it has been at least three years since I hung out with a friend outside of school.

trivia

My only serious friend in elementary school who I hung out with outside of school was a girl named Fernanda. She moved back to Mexico in 1999. I have not seen or heard from her since.

quotes

me: "I don't know, I don't really want to get between you and your home problems."
courtney: "Oh no, the home problems are all cleared up."

Episode 27

title: **WORKING TOGETHER**   air date: **DECEMBER 18, 2002**

summary

Ms. G is out because her son has a doctor's appointment. Wendy is subbing. I go to class and do have a bit of a hard time with the math. Later on after I have taken a VTO it still only gets worse. I finally snap. Wendy begins getting a send-out slip ready for me, but I start crying about it. She then comes over and gives me a hug and I go to talk to my counselor, Dr. R.

notes

Ms. G was my math teacher. She was fun and very nice. Her son was two at the time and really cute—she brought him into class once. When I had a severe problem with not liking "remainder 2," and refused to do division problems that had remainders of 2, Ms. G took the paper with remainder 2 on it and ate it. That got me to do remainder 2 problems because I wanted her to eat them again.

The send-out was canceled. It was Wendy's choice to cancel my send-out.

This is our only hug in the series.

trivia

This was absolutely the only time it was a teacher's choice to cancel a send-out in this series and the other three years of my time at Surrey. However, in May 2004 another teacher was about to send a student out for inappropriate language. I backed him up when she thought he said fuck when he actually said frick. His send-out was then canceled.

Episode 28

title: **WINTER BREAK**   air date: **DECEMBER 20, 2002**

summary

The school is getting ready for winter break. It is a short day. Courtney continues to ask me about hanging out and I finally just say yes. I give her my phone number and she calls me later on. Also I give Amber my first hug. And to conclude the first season of one of the best school years ever, the bus was really late to pick us up.

notes

Even with all the crying cases and the send-outs, this was one of the best school years ever because it was the first time I had friends and I really liked having friends at school.

trivia

During the school year, I dreamed three times about hugging Amber.

thanksgiving special 2002

special: **ANNUAL**
genre: **FAMILY**

status: **CONTINUING**

cast:

blaze ginsberg: himself
mom : mother
maya: aunt
déja: aunt
lavander: aunt
bodine (bo): uncle
nana: grandmother
papa: grandfather

guest stars:

ryan: déja's boyfriend (now ex)

plot summary

Every year, we go to Nana and Papa's house for dinner. Papa goes
around the table and makes everyone say what they are thankful for

and then we eat. Most often, we then play a game afterward. Some of the games we have played are:

Outburst
Pictionary
Apples to Apples
Bookology
Scene It?
Monopoly
Taboo
Clue
General Knowledge

Many of the games have been blacklisted over the years because we cannot play them without a fight happening. In 1996 I made up a game called Card Gazetteer, which I've tried to play again at every Thanksgiving afterward.

I have always enjoyed Thanksgiving because I enjoy spending time with my family. It became my favorite holiday in 1996. I started liking it even more after 2001, which was my last year trick-or-treating on Halloween (which used to be a favorite holiday and now is not because other people are getting candy and not me).

---

title: **THE DEBATABLE ISSUE**   air date: **NOVEMBER 28, 2002**

---

summary

Thanksgiving is at Lavander's house again. This is a new tradition started last year. Lavander lives right across the way from Nana and Papa's house, so it's almost like it's at their house. There was originally a deal that I was to eat at the table. This was a family discussion because I never eat with everyone else because I am grossed out by the food. While this discussion is going on, Bo, Ryan, and I have a little dispute over the remote when I want to watch *Clifford the Big Red Dog*. That ends up going on for a while. Ryan keeps hiding the remote and Bo helps Ryan with this somewhat. Later, with my magic powers (a.k.a. debating), I manage to pull off not sitting *at* the table but near it. No games are played this year. We sing karaoke for the second consecutive year.

quotes
lavander: "Next year he has to sit *right at* the table."

notes
Usually on Thanksgiving my PBS shows would not be on. This is the first year that this has occurred. I am fifteen and still watching PBS Kids shows. I was teased about watching *Sesame Street* once in seventh grade by a bunch of stupid kids. Also, my aunt Déja often said, "Aren't you too old to be watching these shows?"

major events in 2002
I met Courtney, my first ever-possible girlfriend (I pictured that I could get married to her), in June, although I wasn't really sure how a romance would work.

I graduated middle school and started at Surrey, which was the school where I felt like I belonged.

I started writing stories.

trivia
The first Thanksgiving I remember is 1994 when I was seven years old. Mom, Maya, and I went over to Nana and Papa's house. There was a big table of food, and I remembered that I had practiced this at school with the food table in my first grade classroom where we practiced touching fake food.

soundtrack listing
"Clocks" by Coldplay (*A Rush of Blood to the Head* 2002)

blaze, courtney, and amber (2002)*

*(A My Freshman Year spin-off series)

series: **2002–2003**   release date: **DECEMBER 22, 2002**
genre: **BOY VS. GIRL**   status: **ENDED**

cast:

blaze ginsberg: himself

mom: herself

courtney: blaze's friend

amber: courtney and blaze's friend

maureen: courtney's mom

maya: aunt

courtney's grandparents: themselves

series summary

This series, a spin-off of *My Freshman Year of High School*, lasted only one season. It became its own series because all the episodes are about me, Courtney, and Amber and our trio-hood.

I met Courtney in June 2002 in summer school. Meeting her was one of my first experiences at The Surrey School—my new school I was transferring into. I was nervous about starting at this school because I'd never been there before. In math class, two boys were picking on Courtney. I told them to leave her alone and stood up for her. She was in the same grade as I was—going into ninth grade—and I was older than her by eleven months. Courtney was very pretty. She had long dark brown hair and would occasionally wear a hat. Throughout the following school year she and I did lots of stuff together at school. I had English and Physical Science with her, and we ate lunch together most of the time.

Amber was older than me by thirteen months. She had brown hair dyed blonde and wore tank tops a lot, even though she usually stuck with the dress code, which was to wear a collar shirt.

Courtney made friends with Amber and then all three of us were friends together. One day in December, Courtney invited us and our parents to dinner at her house and that's where the trio was launched. After that we hung around school and were somewhat rebellious.

Episode List
EPISODE 1

title: **PILOT**   air date: **DECEMBER 22, 2002**

summary

I go over to Courtney's house for dinner with Mom and Maya. I am somewhat apprehensive on the car ride over there (as in nervous). I haven't been to a friend's house since 1998 when I visited Fernanda, my friend from kindergarten through fourth grade. Courtney answers the door. She is wearing a pink furry sweater and black shiny shoes. She looks cute. I take a tour of her house. We then go hang out in her room and wait for Amber to arrive. Half an hour later, Amber arrives and our trio-hood gets going from there.

It's time for dinner. I have spaghetti with garlic. I don't think there is salad at this dinner, which I am glad about because I do not like salad. We talk about life around the table. Mom talks about her books. Courtney's mom and Amber's mom talk about the different schools Courtney and Amber have gone to. Amber brings up another neighbor we used to have when we lived on the same street. After dinner I'm expecting tea. I whisper in Mom's ear asking her if there will be tea. Courtney offers to make it for me when she overhears me. There is a lot of soda at Courtney's house. I am allowed to have a Diet Coke, which I'm usually not allowed to have. The soda does not take its usual effect (to make me crazy) because it's diet, which is good because I want to stay on my best behavior for my friends.

After dinner, we start making videos with Courtney's video camera. In one of them I speak in a French accent. Courtney tries to kiss me after dinner. She and Amber blindfold me and kiss me in Courtney's room. Later I do a weird directing job on one of the videos. I yell "Cut!" and order Amber to cry for the camera and act as if she is angry at Courtney. A commotion occurs when I don't want to see the replay of the video and I try to leave the room and they don't let me. They block the door and then pull me away from it. Then after about three to four minutes it settles down. We listen to Marvin Gaye. Later we go downstairs and talk about movies like *Titanic* and *Mrs. Doubtfire*. Four hours later, it's time to go. I have enjoyed myself very much.

notes
This is the only episode filmed at Courtney's house and the only appearance of her grandparents.

soundtrack listing
"Sexual Healing" by Marvin Gaye (*Midnight Love* 1982)

"Island in the Sun" by Weezer (*Weezer, Green Album* 2001)

trivia
Courtney owns *Mrs. Doubtfire*.

Courtney has several cats, one of which died a year before this episode.

Courtney, her mom, and her grandmother have all read Mom's book about me. Last summer, when I met Courtney, we talked about *Raising Blaze*. Courtney liked the book and she even quoted from a scene where Papa scolded me about my behavior, causing me to flash back to that time. Courtney thought the book was cool.

quotes
courtney: "What's your all-time favorite video?"
me: "I don't know."
me: "Tell Courtney what happened on November 21st."

amber: "I had a crying attack."

courtney (saying the lyrics to "Old Macdonald" to test my patience because i don't like that song): "Old Macdonald had a farm, ee i, ee i o."

mom: "Let's go. We've been here for four hours."

goofs

I was walking around Courtney's house by myself and went into a room where her grandfather was. He thought I was her.

Episode 2

title: **THE WILD TRIO**   air date: **JANUARY 12, 2003**

---

summary

Courtney and Amber come over to my house with their moms. Courtney is wearing pretty much all white and some lace and long socks. Shortly after they get here we have a little appetizer. Maya and Mom have made some food. Then karaoke begins. Maureen, Courtney's mom, is a wild karaoke fan. A little while later there is some silliness and a chase commotion occurs when Amber and I go play my video game Formula One 99 without Courtney. Courtney chases us around the house and begins grabbing my foot, making it impossible to move. Courtney later calms down. Her wild mode modulates into a hug-a-thon that goes on for a while after she calms down to the end of the day. We are in Maya's room when she suddenly hugs me. The commotion had gotten started when I had originally not liked Amber's singing voice. When it was Courtney's turn to sing I take off as fast as a driver in a police chase because I'm afraid that she will sound as bad as Amber. Courtney chased me into Maya's room singing. However, when Courtney and Amber both sing "Like a Virgin" by Madonna, I am all right with it. Toward the end of the day we take a group photo together. I give Amber a hug as she leaves, and then I walk Courtney out.

notes

This is the most fun episode to ever exist in the history of my friendship life.

The next day and throughout that week Courtney and I did not have the same attitude toward each other. She didn't seem excited to see me and we didn't talk as much. This turned around at the end of the week when she hugged me after I got sent out of class.

Courtney had several crying cases the week after this episode. Her counselor pulled her from class to talk to her about why she was upset.

quotes
me (when courtney is chasing us): "Run Amber, run. Run Amber, run."
maya: "Blaze, don't tell Maureen karaoke."
me: "Maureen karaoke."

trivia
Once I say *karaoke*, Maureen does not stop singing because she loves karaoke. Maureen did not stop singing until almost the end of the day.

goofs
Amber does not have a good singing voice.

soundtrack listing
"My Rival" by Steely Dan (*Gaucho* 1980)

Episode 3

title: **THE ATTENTION OF ANOTHER STUDENT**   air date: **MARCH 3, 2003**

summary
One day at lunch EJ, another freshman, is the center of Courtney's and Amber's attention. This really makes me mad. I try to talk to Courtney but she does not respond when I say her name. Then Courtney does something that really sets me off; she kisses EJ. I really get furious about that.

notes
This is the first and only episode to center on another boy.

EJ is on my afternoon bus. Sometimes he is annoying. For example, he'll say things like "pumpernickel" over and over again just to irritate me. He even threw my headphones out the bus window one time. He has some issues. But sometimes we are friends. He bought me a new pair of headphones to make up for the ones he threw out.

quotes
me: "Do you like EJ more than me?"
courtney: "No, he's just an acquaintance."

goofs
Courtney gets lipstick all over EJ's cheek.

soundtrack listing
"Almost Gothic" by Steely Dan (*Two Against Nature*, 2000)
This song plays because it is about a crazy girl who's always bugging the singer and wanting attention.

"Love You to the Letter" by Anita Baker (*Compositions* 1990)

Episode 4

title: **FIRST KISS**   air date: **MARCH 21, 2003**

summary
One day during seventh period I'm hanging with Courtney and Amber. We chat while Courtney is ditching her music class. After a few minutes I pick up her hand and smooch it. Courtney says, "Aww" loudly and almost cries with joy.

notes
This is a touching episode.

Episode 5

title: **FESTIVAL OF ARTS**   air date: **APRIL 10, 2003**

summary
It's the Festival of Arts celebration at school. There is a barbecue. Courtney and Amber are supposed to be here. They arrive after a long while. Nana meets Courtney and that goes nicely. We hang around the school, then I go home.

notes
I ate a lot of sugar at the celebration: cookies, soda, and cupcakes.

quotes
nana: "I'm Blaze's grandmother."
(Later)
nana: Courtney seems like a nice girl. She has a very interesting fashion sense.

trivia

I was really pleased when Nana met Courtney because I had wanted Nana to meet Courtney and Amber for a very long time.

soundtrack listing

"Let It Whip" by The Dazz Band (*Keep It Live* 1982)
This song plays because it has a fast disco beat, and that is how this day has been.

Episode 6

title: **THE PRETEND WEDDING**   air date: **MAY 12, 2003**

summary

It is lunchtime and we are in the math teacher's room, where we are not supposed to be without adult supervision. Courtney and I pretend to get married. We hug. Courtney stands in one corner of the room while Amber wheels me around in a chair and sings "The Bridal March." Courtney wants me to wear her jacket so the rest of the school can see it, but I don't want to. That standoff goes on for quite some time. I end up not wearing it.

notes

During lunchtime you are not allowed in any classroom without adult supervision, but that changed somewhat since there are often events like Movie Club in the classrooms during lunch.

quotes

courtney: "Amber, be the priest."
amber: "I now pronounce you husband and wife. You may hug."

soundtrack listing

"The Bridal March" by Wagner (1850)

"The Gift" by Annie Lennox (*Diva* 1992)

Episode 7

title: **MAKING UP**   air date: **MAY 2003**

summary

Courtney, Amber, and I have been kind of out of it today. We've been fighting a lot. I am probably driving them crazy. Courtney has also been on fire with crying and screaming (as loud as a 1990 Gillig Phantom bus) episodes during school. A teacher sends for them to come meet me on the bench because it is really bothering me that we are fighting. We sit on the bench and talk and make up. They have a magazine and I grab it and accidentally rip it. Courtney and Amber get upset because they have to return the magazine and now they are worried about what's going to happen when they bring it back all ripped. But they don't get angry at me.

notes

The magazine that Courtney and Amber read belongs to Ms. Jenkins, who has many positions at the school.

quotes

courtney (screams): "Aaaaaagh that magazine belongs to Ms. Jenkins!"

trivia

A Gillig Phantom bus is a city bus that is also sometimes used as a school bus. The ones in San Diego Transit are extremely loud.

Episode 8

title: **YOU AND ME**   air date: **MAY 26, 2003**

summary

Courtney comes over to my house. She brings strawberries. I don't like strawberries so I just have crackers. Courtney then brings up *Raising Blaze* and how my old friend Julia had always been crying. I don't remember this being in the book. We leave a fake argument-message on our answering machine. Then later Courtney wants to listen to Marvin Gaye. That lasts a while. Later we go off and do our own thing. The hug-a-thon makes a reappearance but is not as long as it was last time. However, we do stand and hug like a couple. Later on Courtney's mom comes to pick her up. She sits down and talks to us for a while. Then it is time for Courtney to leave.

notes

Amber does not appear in this episode. This is the first and only episode that she does not appear in. Her absence was due to me giving her no notification that Courtney and I were hanging out today. She was somewhat bitter about her lack of appearance in this episode the following day. This was a very boyfriend-and-girlfriend–like episode for me. This is the second of two episodes that take place at my house where we listen to Marvin Gaye.

quotes

mom (as i am getting cracker crumbs on courtney's lap): "You are making a mess all over Courtney."
me: "Let's leave an argument on the answering machine."
courtney: "Let's just listen to Marvin Gaye."
courtney and me (leaving argument message): "I did not do those things! Oh you're so sure of yourself! Whatever!"

goofs

Our argument message gets a little bit erased later when the answering machine got full because I kept calling and hanging up.

trivia

In this episode Courtney is wearing all black. In "The Wild Trio" she is wearing all white.

soundtrack listing

"You're a Wonderful One" by Marvin Gaye (1964)

Episode 9

title: **SUMMERTIME SILLINESS**   air date: **JUNE 12, 2003**

---

summary

It's the last day of school. There is a field trip to Fifteenth Street beach. On the bus before we leave it is somewhat chaotic. Lucinda (the girl I had lunch with when she was visiting Surrey and who is now a student there) gets her toes smashed (as in stepped on). Courtney ends up crashing on my shoulder (fake sleeping), which she is not supposed to do. She does it twice. Later on there is a commotion (which has become a recurring theme with our trio): Courtney and Amber want me to take my shirt off. They end up pulling it off for me. I play cool with it and put it back on later. We run over to Powerhouse Park, but it is closed. So we go back down to the beach.

notes

I was invited to Amber's birthday party that day. She was going to turn seventeen on the 22nd.

No swimming in the ocean was allowed during the field trip. However, Courtney and Amber wore their bikinis.

Unexpectedly, this was the series finale of "Blaze, Courtney, and Amber" due to the following conditions: (1) Courtney's departure to another school, and (2) Amber stabbing me in the back on the second day of school the following school year. (See Post Season Special 2.)

In the four hours the three of us were together on that day, at no time did any of us give any indication that this would be the series' last episode. This was not even intended to be the season finale, let alone the series finale. We had been expecting another episode of going to Amber's birthday party, but I did not attend due to me not setting it up in advance (meaning, I didn't talk to Mom about it, make plans, or set up rides). Had there been any viewers they would have expected us to come back for more. I was hoping to keep my friendship with Amber rolling till she graduated in 2005 and have her take the place of Courtney, but no such thing happened. That was the main cause of my sophomore year being such a train wreck. It is unfortunate that this series was over after only one season. In the end, Courtney and I were the only ones who appeared in every single episode.

trivia

Fifteenth Street beach has a "powerhouse" and a park with a swing set and is right next to the old Del Mar train station, which the train does not stop at anymore.

The powerhouse is a private building for weddings and awards, etc.

Courtney's bikini was black and white. Amber's was gray. I put Courtney's street clothes in my backpack.

quotes
lucinda: "Mr. Kent, Courtney has got her head on Blaze's shoulder."
courtney: "The man should let the woman rest on him."

lucinda: "Courtney has got her head on Blaze's shoulder again."

mr. kent: "Courtney, don't do it again."

courtney (after a ninth grade boy put a great big spider on her): "Aaaaa aaaaaaaaaaaaaagh!!!!!!!!!!!!"

soundtrack listing

"Why Is It So Hard?" by Madonna (*Erotica* 1992)

"I Can't Wait" by Hilary Duff (*Lizzie McGuire Soundtrack* 2002)

"I Can't Make It Alone" by Dusty Springfield (*Dusty in Memphis* 1969)

Post-Season

Special (Dream) 1

title: **SUCH A GOOD FRIEND**   air date: **AUGUST 8, 2003**

summary

In this dream, Courtney, Amber, and I are at the Fifteenth Street beach. I've apparently been such a good friend. As a treat they mix some water for me with a water mixer (which doesn't exist in real life).

notes

The water mixer is black and looks like a regular mixer except it has a different motor. This dream happens when I am in Petaluma on vacation with my family. I wake up to the alarm clock ringing. This aired on the fifteenth anniversary that Nana and Papa moved into their house that they now own.

Special 2

title: **STABBED IN THE BACK**   air date: **SEPTEMBER 3, 2003**

summary

It's the second day of sophomore year. Courtney is no longer attending Surrey, and I haven't seen her since the end of summer session. I see Amber walking to class with Nick and say hi to her twice, but she doesn't respond. I go to PE feeling rejected. Coach B and I have words about this.

notes
Amber continued to ignore me and continued to hang out with Nick, which I took to be a complete rejection of me and I considered this to be her stabbing me in the back. Shortly after this, I expressed my anger by writing "Don't vote for Amber, she's a loser" on paper and carrying it around even though she wasn't running for anything. I also started an "I hate Amber" club a month after this episode. That pretty much got the feud going permanently.

trivia
I never really got over how bad this made me feel, and my relationship with Amber was never the same.

quotes
me: "Amber's cheating on me; she's hanging out with other boys and doesn't like me anymore."
coach b: "Hey, she has other friends besides you."

Special 3

title: IT'S MAUREEN   air date: FEBRUARY 24, 2005

summary
Mom has a book gig in Coronado. We see Maureen, Courtney's mom, who comes to the book signing. We talk about Courtney and having a possible reunion. So we exchange phone numbers, and I get Courtney's cell number. Maureen says Courtney is very busy.

notes
The reunion did not end up happening because I never contacted Courtney.

Special (Dream) 4

title: WE'RE TOGETHER FOREVER (a.k.a. "The Wild Trio 2")   air date: MAY 28, 2005

summary
In my dream, I'm back in "The Wild Trio" episode. We do almost everything we did that day when Courtney and Amber came over to my house. Only at the end we run away, out around Carmel Valley, and have a bathtub and float in it in the sky at sunset. Also, in

addition to that there is a look back to 1993 when I was six and when Aretha Franklin was singing "Chain of Fools" in Patty Griffin's voice, singing the same wrong line over and over again (this memory did not really happen).

notes
This episode took place when I was asleep on a Saturday morning.

quotes
aretha franklin (in patty griffin's voice): "Chain, chain, chain, fool of fools even though it's hard to break the rules."

goofs
In the flashback part of the dream I'm scared of something, which is wrong because I'm supposed to be happy.

soundtrack listing
"Speed of Sound" by Coldplay (XY 2005)

"Carry Me" by Patty Griffin (*Flaming Red* 1998)

my freshman year of high school 2 (2003)

(a.k.a. One of the Best School Years Ever 2)

cast:

See Cast, **Freshman Year of High School 1**

also featuring:

drew z: friend
Drew Z was a friend of mine. Drew was in my PE class. We hugged each other about 26 times a day. She was a train student (meaning she came to school on the Amtrak). She left Surrey in 2003 along with many other friends of mine. Drew cursed a lot but never cried during her role in *My Freshman Year*. She was originally planning to stay at Surrey till she graduated in 2005, but due to certain circumstances, she left Surrey when *My Freshman Year 2* ended.

Episode 29   Season 2

---

title: **WELCOME BACK FOR IT ALL**   air date: **JANUARY 6, 2003**

---

summary

Amber and I are hanging out in Tutorial, doing our normal thing, and we talk about making plans and we both agree we will get together on Sunday.

quotes
amber: "When should we hang out?"
me: "I know when."
me and amber (at the same time): "Sunday!"
amber: "Hug!"
(We hug)

soundtrack listing
"Little Voice" by Hilary Duff (*Metamorphosis* 2003)

"Stranger on the Shore of Love" by Stevie Wonder (*In Square Circle* 1985)

Episode 30

---

title: **COURTNEY'S SECOND TANTRUM**   air date: **JANUARY 10, 2003**

---

summary
Dr. G, Courtney's counselor, comes and takes her for a session. Later at lunch she is in tears.

She starts screaming and crying and carrying on, etc. It is even worse than last time. She screams and cries and it upsets me terribly. Later Amber goes to talk to her. In PE I am very mad at Courtney and I talk to my friend Matt about it.

notes
This is the first episode to include my friend Matt, although we did meet each other a couple of months back.

I was mad at Courtney because she made me feel terribly uncomfortable with her crying.

quotes
me: "If Amber gave Courtney a tissue I'm not inviting her to karaoke."
me (to matt): "It's like a ship that starts off good one day then gets out of control."

trivia
For more about Matt, see *Blaze, Matt, and Danny* series.

That I didn't want Amber to give Courtney a tissue was part of my own *mishegoss*. (*Mishegoss* is Yiddish and means nonsense, crazy things.)

soundtrack listing
"I Ain't Going to Stand for It" by Stevie Wonder (*Hotter Than July* 1980)

Episode 31

---

title: **SERIOUSLY**   air date: **JANUARY 13, 2003**

---

summary
It's been one day since my second out-of-school hangout with Courtney and Amber. Courtney is at school, but I haven't talked to her very much today. I am very out if it because I miss all the fun and pleasure of having Courtney around. I can't really focus today because my mind is too beaten from having her around all day yesterday. Courtney brings a lot to the table as a friend and she has a very high energy. It's overwhelming, but in a good way.

notes
My mind had as much wear and tear on it as a three-year-old bus because of focusing so much on Courtney.

soundtrack listing
"Happy Birthday" by Stevie Wonder (*Hotter Than July* 1980)

"Mexico" by James Taylor (*Gorilla* 1975)

Episode 32

---

title: **RUN IT OUT**   air date: **JANUARY 15, 2003**

---

summary
Courtney, Dominique (another student), and I are hanging out at lunch and they are planning to chase me around the school. I will count down the seconds till it's time. I get away very quickly, then they find me.

notes
Dominique was the only one who was not into the whole kissing thing. Courtney and Amber liked to kiss me. I didn't really appreciate the kissing at that moment because I was not ready yet, but later I saw this as a missed opportunity.

goofs
Courtney and Dominique walked right past me even though I was standing in front of their faces.

soundtrack listing
"The Call of the Wild" by David Byrne (*Rei Momo* 1989)
This song is wild, and we were wild people.

Episode 33

title: **DOWNERS**   air date: **JANUARY 17, 2003**

summary
I am in Mr. K's class for English. My friend Max and I are being noisy, and he sends us both out. I try to get Ms. K (my speech therapist) to do the same deal as last time, which is to call Mom and have her work it out, but no siree, this time she doesn't.

notes
When I get back to class, Courtney hugs me like she did when she came to my house.

trivia
I do not get punished at home.

quotes
me: "Why do I have to be sent out? It's not fair."
max: "Mr. K's class is run like a family."

soundtrack listing
"Chemical Love" by Stevie Wonder (*Jungle Fever* 1991)

"When Am I Going to Make a Living?" by Sade (*Diamond Life* 1984)

Episode 34

title: **FAMILY HANGOUT**   air date: **FEBRUARY 7, 2003**

summary
I am hanging out at Nana and Papa's house tonight for dinner. I watch

a movie on TV. Later on Nana pounds on the wall because her next
door neighbor is drilling. This has been a problem since the neighbors
moved in. I overhear Mom saying something about meeting at
Denny's. I want go there for breakfast.

notes
In the case of a natural disaster or tragedy, our family plan is to all meet
at Denny's, or the place that used to be Denny's if it gets wiped out in
an earthquake or fire or flood.

goofs
There is a drill involved in this episode but I didn't hear it, which
disappoints me even though I don't really like the sound of drills. I like
to know what goes on around me, especially if it involves a drill.

Episode 35

title: **COURTNEY'S AWAY PLANS**   air date: **FEBRUARY 10, 2003**

summary
Courtney's aunt is having a baby. She will be going away to the East
Coast to visit and see the baby be born. We talk about it.

notes
I was envious that I didn't have my own cousins.

quotes
courtney: "I won't be here next week."
me: "Where are you going?"
courtney: "To Massachusetts. My aunt is having a baby."
me: "Cool."
courtney: "The baby is a girl."

Episode 36

title: **DROWN**   air date: **FEBRUARY 12, 2003**

summary
I am at school and it is not the same as it would be with Courtney. Amber

and I talk and hang out. I just hang around and do my usual thing.

notes
This is the second and last attachment-to-Courtney episode.

quotes
amber: "Blaze, what are you doing?"
me: "I don't know."
amber: "Do you, like, miss Courtney?"

Episode 37

title: **FAMILY AT DENNY'S**   air date: **FEBRUARY 15, 2003**

---

summary
Mom, Maya, Lavander, Nana, and I go to Denny's for breakfast. It
is nice. I get oatmeal and I am glad to finally have breakfast with the
family at Denny's. Unfortunately, Mom and I get into a fight later over
my project on the Unknown (see trivia) and she threatens to ban me
from hanging with Bo tomorrow. I crash out on my bed for an hour
and a half.

notes
Bo and I have had our Sunday routine since November 2002. The
punishment did not happen. Bo came and picked me up and even
made a funny comment.

quotes
bo: "I don't know about the unknown."

trivia
The project on the Unknown was a piece of poster board and we had
to put on pictures about the unknown, as in space aliens, life after
death, and things like that. I was resistant to work on it because it was
a big project and I didn't necessarily want to be doing it. I got an A on
the project later.

Bo, not knowing about the unknown, meant that the unknown was
unknown to him, which was funny. Bo makes funny comments like
that all the time. For example, when Mom got a new gnome for the
backyard, he said, "Don't you *gnome-me*? I'm a *gnome*."

Episode 39

title: **THE DEVIL'S WORK IS NEVER DONE**   air date: **FEBRUARY 2003**

summary
In Mr. Kent's class we are watching the movie *What Dreams May Come*. I watch it but I do end up getting disturbed over it. I get so angry I kick a chair and it falls onto Lauren D's foot. I get sent out.

notes
This was my fifth send-out all year long.

I apologized to Lauren.

What Dreams May Come basically starts where a couple's dog dies, then their children and then the dad are killed by a car, then the mother kills herself. The movie was disturbing because everyone in it was dying. Robin Williams plays the dad, and he goes into life after death. We had to watch it because it related to the Unknown.

soundtrack listing
"Beautiful Homes" by Chris Isaak (*San Francisco Days* 1993)
This song plays because of my angry mood.

trivia
Chris Isaak's music and my freshman year were a big association. It even carried over a bit to my sophomore year but was officially ended after I heard "Except the New Girl" for the first time on September 27, 2003, when I was very lonely. At that point the song started to remind me too much of Amber and was too depressing to listen to.

Episode 39

title: **NOTHING BUT A COMMENT**   air date: **FEBRUARY 24, 2003**

summary
I am in Tutorial doing the usual thing, hanging around, when suddenly Tom (a senior) opens the door to Mr. Heart's room and shouts out "Mr. Fart!" It makes me laugh hysterically. I even tell Mom what happened.

notes

Tom got in a lot of trouble over this. He got community service, which is where you have to sweep leaves, pick up trash, etc., when you violate the rules. Tom is another buddy of mine.

Episode 40

title: THE DRILL   air date: **MARCH 10, 2003**

summary

I am in art class and everything is fine until the drill comes on, and that upsets me a lot. I go outside and wait for the drilling to stop and then I come back in.

notes

Computer Graphics was replaced with Art. For some reason it was difficult for me to find a good class for this period. This was my third and final class rearrangement in the series.

The drill, which is used in the classroom to drill through clay or wood for projects, makes a type of high-pitched sound that hurts my ears. I ended up getting over the sound of the drill because I would always pull the trigger and drill at nothing, even when the battery was charging.

I got in trouble once for playing with it.

goofs

I could still hear the drill from outside.

trivia

Art was useful. I actually used the drill a few times later. I also made some magic stones from clay that got fired in the kiln. Mom put them over the fireplace.

soundtrack listing

"Jungle Fever" by Stevie Wonder (*Jungle Fever* 1991)

"Clean Heart" by Sade (*Stronger Than Pride* 1988)

"Living for the City" by Stevie Wonder (*Innervisions* 1973)

This is a very musical episode because there was a lot of sensory action in it with the drill, the clay, and the movement in the class.

Episode 41

title: **GIRLS ARE TROUBLE**   air date: **MARCH 13, 2003**

summary
I do my thing at school today, the usual routine. At the end of the day, I see Courtney talking to other guys and it makes me really mad at her. At home I talk to Bo on the phone about it.

notes
Bo and I went to Los Angeles on the train the following day. We rode two hours to L.A., got off for five minutes, then got right back on the train and came home. It was all about the ride.

This episode originally aired on Matt's sixteenth birthday.

This was the second and last time Courtney did something to make me mad in the series.

quotes
(On the phone)
me: "Courtney was hugging Matt W and it made me mad."
bo: "She has a right to hang out with other guys if she wants to."
me: "Is Courtney allowed on the train tomorrow?"
bo (joking): "No, you have to have a penis to go on the train."

soundtrack listing
"Almost Gothic" by Steely Dan (*Two Against Nature* 2000)

Episode 42

title: **HELLO THERE**   air date: **MARCH 17, 2003**

summary
At home in the evening I watch *Kramer vs. Kramer* on TV with Mom and Maya. I remember seeing it on TV a while back when I was not feeling well. I got really scared when the Dustin Hoffman character picked his son up so suddenly and ran with him across the hall.

notes
This movie really influenced me. The situation of the movie really

stunned me; that the mother could leave her son and that the dad was too hard on his son. But in the end, he got to keep the kid.

This is the last outside-of-school episode.

goofs
You can't see the kid remove the spoon from his mouth when Dustin Hoffman grabs him, which I consider a goof, but which is not an actual goof in the movie.

quotes
me (to mom): "You remember that scene from that movie where that man physically attacked his son? Well I have a terrible feeling I'm going to see it again."

Episode 43

title: **THE AFTERMATH**   air date: **MARCH 18, 2003**

summary
At school I talk to everyone about what I saw on TV and I obsess about it. I write a story with Jane called *The Rescue Mission* about some travelers being stuck inside the *Kramer vs. Kramer* movie set during that one disturbing scene and a helicopter has to come and get them.

notes
This story is partially based on the end of 1972's *The Poseidon Adventure*, where people are rescued by helicopter.

goofs
I did not list the current year on my story (which I usually do).

quotes
jane: "Ha, ha, they were stuck inside a movie."

trivia
The Rescue Mission
by Blaze Ginsberg

Once upon a time there were seven people stuck inside the movie set of *Kramer vs. Kramer*. They had been on a museum field trip, but then realized they were stuck in the scene where the dad picks up his son and throws him onto the bed. They needed to be rescued.

The helicopter crew opened up the shaft.

"Hurry up Elizabeth," a boy named Jake said. The rescue men took her up but nearly dropped her. Jake went next, then their bus driver who was also in this situation was taken out next. They all got into the helicopter and the workmen locked the shaft and they took off two seconds before the scene had started. They all got home safely.

Episode 44

title: **YOUNG GIRL**   air date: **MARCH 2003**

summary
Today my friend Drew and I go around school talking to each other, and we start our hugging each other 26 times a day deal.

notes
Drew is shorter than I am and has straight black hair. She's cute.

According to what Drew says, we had been friends since about last November. However today is the earliest time that I remember from.

Drew is about three months older than I am.

Episode 45

title: **COURTNEY GOES WILD**   air date: **MARCH 2003**

summary
I am hanging with Courtney at lunch. She asks me to the prom and I don't necessarily want to go. She hugs me again and again. I suddenly get uncomfortable and go hide in the Lower School until she finds me.

notes
I didn't want to go to the prom because it was new, something I'd never done before, and that made me uncomfortable. Trying new things was difficult for me then and now.

quotes

courtney: "Will you go with me to prom? It's on the last day of school."
me: "I don't want to."
me (in the office): "When's the last day of school?"
jan (the school secretary): "June 13th."
(In Lower School)
courtney: "Blaze? Oh Blaaaaze?"
me: "Oh good lord."

goofs

Courtney managed to find me even though I was in one of the greatest hiding spots.

soundtrack listing

"Mickey's Monkey" by Smokey Robinson and the Miracles (*Doing the Mickey's Monkey* 1963)
This song plays because it's another episode where Courtney is wild, like a monkey.

Episode 47

title: **I'M THE MAN**   air date: **APRIL 2003**

summary

In Art today, I decide to create a project. My friend Elizabeth and I make a book we call "Index." We always sing the *Sesame Street* "count to twelve" song, so we write that in the book. We also say that we don't like Abigail Adams (see notes). We go pretty crazy with our own creativity and expressing our feelings in the book.

notes

I had a funny dream about Abigail Adams after I watched the show *Liberty's Kids*. That is the reason I have a dislike for her.

If Elizabeth had been around longer, she might have protected me from the mean girls I met a few years later. Mean girls couldn't get away with shit with Elizabeth. But Elizabeth left the school after the year was over.

soundtrack listing

"Party Up" by Hilary Duff (*Metamorphosis* 2003)
This song plays because I am in a very partying mood.

"Dude Looks Like a Lady" by Aerosmith (*Permanent Vacation* 1987)
This song plays because Elizabeth is acting somewhat not ladylike, as
in talking to me as if she is one of the guys.

Episode 47

title: **ELIZABETH'S FIRST CRYING CASE**   air date: **APRIL 2003**

---

summary
On my way to math class I see Elizabeth in tears. I talk about it with
her; I go and get her a tissue. She feels better after I speak with her.

notes
Now Elizabeth is having family problems.

soundtrack listing
"Lead Me into Love" by Anita Baker (*Giving You the Best That I Got* 1988)
This song plays because of the energy coming from Elizabeth.

Episode 48

title: **FUN, FUN, FUN AFTERSCHOOL EVENTS**   air date: **APRIL 10, 2003**

---

summary
There is a Festival of Arts at school today. I go with Mom and Nana.
There will be a barbecue as well today. I hang around, drink soda, and
talk to my friends. I am also hoping Courtney and Amber will arrive. I
like afterschool events.

trivia
Courtney and Amber did arrive about an hour after I got there.

soundtrack listing
"In the Heat of the Jungle" by Chris Isaak (*Heart Shaped World* 1989)

Episode 49

title: **BLOWN UP**   air date: **APRIL 2003**

---

summary

Drew and I are walking laps in PE. Everything is fine until I try to get her attention and talk to her. After not responding twice, she backfires at me and I get upset over that. When I cry she hugs me and we make up.

notes

Even though I do not have a girlfriend, I now think of this episode as preparation for what could happen one day when I do. I was very much in the boyfriend-girlfriend mode even though Drew was Joey's girlfriend and not mine.

trivia

The boyfriend-girlfriend mode meant that we were close, we hugged 26 times a day, and one day she started to do things that made me upset—like girlfriends do.

soundtrack listing

"Going to California" by Led Zeppelin (*Led Zeppelin* IV 1971)
I was listening to this song later that night when I was thinking about Drew.

Episode 50

title: **ROCKING FIELD TRIP**   air date: **APRIL 25, 2003**

summary

Mr. Kent is taking us on a field trip rock climbing to an indoor rock wall. I talk to Jane about how nervous I am about falling. Later we load up the bus and start getting ready to go. My day is made when we take Miramar Road (see trivia). We arrive there and the rules are as follows: no helping other students up the walls, etc. I go up a few times but I don't do so well. Later we go to Burger King for lunch, and when I have no money for food, I throw a cup down in my anger and Mr. Kent scolds me about it. Then Chris offers me some of his fries.

notes

I did not have money because the permission slip said nothing about lunch.

When I got back to school, I tried to get some sympathy from Amy and was successful.

I did not get up very high, but I did not fall.

quotes
mr. kent (yelling): "You're going to go wait on the bus! Do you want me to call your mom?"
me: "I'm sorry I did that."
(Back at school)
me (to amy): "I almost had a crying case today."
amy: "Why?"
me: "Because I didn't have money to buy soda and fries at Burger King."
amy: "You shouldn't let something like that ruin your day."

trivia
In January 1999, I traveled on Miramar Road with my visiting cousins and I had a blast for reasons unknown. Ever since then, I've been trying to relive that fun by going on Miramar Road whenever possible.

soundtrack listing
"Learning to Fly" by Tom Petty and the Heartbreakers (*Into the Great Wide Open* 1991)

Episode 51

title: **BREAKER**   air date: **MAY 2, 2003**

summary
In PE I see my friend Jesse's Slinky and I want to play with it. I like it so much I keep playing with it until it breaks and now I have to buy him a new one.

notes
I ended up keeping the broken Slinky.

Jesse stayed mad at me because the new Slinky was not as good as the old Slinky.

Mom bought me my own good Slinky, which I ended up totaling as well.

soundtrack listing

"That's the Way" by Led Zeppelin (*Led Zeppelin* III 1970)
This song plays because the singer in the very beginning of the song
says something about not being able to play with his friend, the boy
next door. Also Jesse was a friend of mine and now our friendship is
in jeopardy because of the Slinky. Also Led Zeppelin's music and my
freshman year are an association.

Episode 52

title: **THE BALLAD OF WENDY**   air date: **MAY 5, 2003**

summary

Wendy is subbing for Mr. Kent. We go to the computer lab and I do
not behave right (not doing my work), so she sends me out and I go to
talk to Dr. R about it.

notes

This is the last appearance of Dr. R in the series, and it is also my last
crying case.

quotes

dr. r: "She's a good teacher."
me: "I hate her."

Episode 53

title: **BUSTED**   air date: **MAY 2003**

summary

Drew is in giant trouble today. She has called another student a very
derogatory term. I hear about it when I am with Ms. K for speech. I
find out later that Drew called Isaac the N word. For that she will have
to sit in Ms. S's office all day.

notes

There was a hole in the door between Mrs. G's and Mr. K's room
because Isaac was so mad about what Drew said that he punched right
through it.

quotes
me (repeated line): "What did Drew call Isaac?"

Episode 54

title: COMMUNITY SERVICE BEFORE MOTHER'S DAY air date: **MAY 9, 2003**

summary
I have community service for an incident involving a physical altercation with another student, EJ, at lunch. I am upset that I have to do community service before Mother's Day.

notes
The community service was picking up trash.

This was my first, but not last, community service at school.

EJ was saying that Courtney was another student's girlfriend, riling me up, and then I punched him.

Episode 55

title: THAT DOG air date: **MAY 16, 2003**

summary
Today in Physical Science Max and I are being noisy and Mr. Heart sends us out. He is out of send-out slips, so he uses the back of a VTO slip. Later, in Tutorial, the teacher brings her dog Marley to class. I play with him and everything is fine until he bites me. The teacher goes to get me a Band-Aid and she calls Maya.

notes
Mom is out of town.

This was the first time I was ever bitten by a dog.

This is the second and last episode where Max and I are sent out together.

I did not get upset about this send-out even though I seem to get the most send-outs of any student. Mr. Heart sends students out quite frequently. This was why he ran out of send-out slips.

This is also my last send-out of this series.

goofs

I was trying to give Marley a chew toy and touched his mouth. That is why he bit me.

Episode 56

title: **PLANS**   air date: **MAY 21, 2003**

---

summary

Matt and I are in PE and we are talking about hanging out outside of school. He gives me his number and e-mail address. I tell him I do not have an e-mail address.

notes

Matt and my first out-of-school hangout was four days later on May 25th.

Matt does not use that e-mail address that he gave me anymore.

trivia

I got my first e-mail address in January 2005.

Episode 57

title: **FALLING APART**   air date: **MAY 23, 2003**

---

summary

Jane and I are doing our usual routine today, but we can't seem to get along at all and it's just one thing after another. Jane tells me not to drink the Powerade drink I brought and I do—this is why we get into a fight. I even have to go to Norm's office three times in the same day. Today is not such a good day.

notes

My freshman year has clearly had enough already.

The good times are not turning out so well anymore: getting bitten by a dog, community service as a present before Mother's Day, fighting with Jane, etc.

trivia

The Powerade was blue.

Episode 58

title: **IF IT WORKS**   air date: **MAY 27, 2003**

summary
Courtney was at my house yesterday. Today she tells me she wants
to do it again, and this time we include Amber in the plan because I
discover that Amber is all bitter about not being included.

quotes
amber: "Hey, Courtney's all going on about the fact that you didn't
invite me to your house."
me: "I'm sorry, all right?"
(Later)
courtney: "When can I come to your house for karaoke again?"
me: "I'll call you and maybe you can come over next Saturday."
courtney: "We'll see."

Episode 59

title: **AWARDS**   air date: **JUNE 10, 2003**

summary
There is an awards ceremony at Fifteenth Street beach tonight. I go talk to
the Headmaster about things. I ask him what date his wedding anniversary
is on and he tells me December 18th. I tell him about what happened on
that day in history. Later I go to the awards ceremony and Amber is there.
We hang out and talk. I get an award for my progress during the year. Amber
then gets an award and later on she disappears. This makes me angry.

quotes
me: "Last year on December 18th, I almost got sent out of class."

Episode 60

title: **WE'RE TOGETHER ALL IN ONE PIECE**   air date: **JUNE 11, 2003**

summary
At school I find Amber and ask for an explanation as to why she

disappeared. She says she went home. Later she hangs with another boy, John S. I have a problem with this. I tell her not to and John gets all defensive about it.

notes

My freshman year is on its last cycle, and it's sad that this good school year has to come to an end.

quotes

me: "Hey, where'd you go last night?"
amber: "We went home early."
me: "Stop hanging out with other guys."
john: "Hey, what the fuck, man?"
(I walk away without saying anything)

soundtrack listing

"You and the Mona Lisa" by Shawn Colvin (*A Few Small Repairs* 1996)
This song plays because everything is temporarily back to normal once more before it's time to say bye-bye to freshman year.

Episode 61

title: **INTO THAT GOOD SUMMER AFTERNOON**　　air date: **JUNE 12, 2003**

summary

There is another field trip—to Fifteenth Street beach. We get on the bus and it takes a while to leave the school. We go and it is a lot of fun, but there is no swimming allowed in the ocean. I do get my pants wet while playing on the beach. I go look at the Powerhouse Park but it is closed for cleaning. There will also be soda after the big beach party. We go back to the school on a long bus. I walk around the school for the last few minutes of the series. I feel fine, ready to move on.

notes

This was a fun field trip.

I learned a lot during my freshman year. I miss it a lot.

This is the heartbreaking, hard-to-accept series finale of my freshman year.

I had been looking forward to my sophomore year somewhat until it actually arrived.

quotes

(On the bus to the beach)
me: "Why do I have to listen to you?"
coach: "I'll have you do pushups on the beach."

trivia

Here is a story I wrote after my freshman year ended, which talked about how I felt about the changes in my life.

The Big Time

When you wake up you feel time is a big fire drill coming on.

Your TV program makes you think it's been hit with a fire drill.

Time grows bigger and bigger. Soon time just gets too big.

Don't you like it? Because you have lots of things to think about.

You would not believe your eyes.

You think you're waking up so stupid, you don't know what to do.

Time is the key to being more powerful.

When a woman is a mother, it's more fun for a father.

You may think something is wrong with your TV.

It's something that will change your life forever.

soundtrack listing

"I Can't Wait" by Hilary Duff (*Lizzie McGuire Soundtrack* 2002)
This song plays because I am now moving to the next level.

Post-Season

Special

title: **FLASHBACK**   air date: **MARCH 1, 2007**

summary

I am in my college film class watching *The Graduate*, and I have a flashback of all the good times of my freshman year.

notes

This flashback was brought on during the part in *The Graduate* where Benjamin has a fight with Mrs. Robinson and is swimming in the pool, dreaming about her. For some reason, this made me think of my freshman year.

soundtrack listing

"I Wanna Be" by Emma Roberts (*Unfabulous and More* 2005)
This song plays because of the way I feel about my freshman year being over and not having a girlfriend nowadays.

"Clean Heart" by Sade (*Stronger Than Pride* 1988)
This song plays because of how I feel in the flashback.

thanksgiving special 2003

title: **THE SUPER VIDEO**   air date: **NOVEMBER 27, 2003**

cast:

blaze ginsberg: himself
mom: herself
maya: aunt
lavander: aunt
déja: aunt
(bodine) bo: uncle
nana: grandmother
papa: grandfather

guest star:

davy: cousin

summary

We're back at Nana and Papa's house for Thanksgiving. I start filming
it early on in the day. Lavander, however, does not feel like being
filmed and we have a brief dispute about it. Later Bo interviews me

with the camera, but it keeps getting messed up. One time it gets messed up by Lavander screeching at Papa (who is talking about farts) and I try to get everyone to imitate Lavander's screeching. Nana's nephew, Davy, comes to visit early in the day but does not stay for dinner. He is visiting from South Africa.

I film the dinner. My filming has improved since the '90s. Déja has brought several six packs of Blue Sky Cola. That puts a grand smile on my face. Later on the family game is Outburst once again. I play with everybody else. This part does not get filmed.

quotes
lavander (screaming): "Daddy, stop it!"
(Later on when Papa and I are under the illusion that we won Outburst)
me and papa (jumping up and down): "We won!" (repeated line)

notes
I use the video camera I got for my sixteenth birthday.

Major Events in 2003
Courtney leaves Surrey and our relationship concludes because she moved and I never called her.

Got my first video camera. The first thing I filmed was Maya interviewing me about how I felt about turning sixteen. After that, I filmed random stuff, like acting out plays that I had written (especially with Matt).

Got some bad grades back in the spring.

Amber betrayed me on the second day of school.

We moved into a new house on November 1st.

goofs
Maya forgot something and had to drive back to our house and get it.

soundtrack listing
"Try It Baby" by Marvin Gaye (1964)

blaze, matt, and
danny I (2003)

series: **2003–2005**

genre: **FRIENDSHIP**

release date: **DECEMBER 7, 2003**

status: **IN SYNDICATION**

cast:

blaze ginsberg: himself

mom: herself

maya: aunt

matt: friend
Matt is a buddy of mine. The first role he played in my life was in 2002 in <u>My Freshman Year</u>. We played basketball together during PE in that series. Because he was vegan and had some OCD issues, he didn't want to touch leather, so he didn't play softball with everyone else. I was afraid of being hit by the softball so the two of us got paired up and made friends with each other. Matt speaks Spanish. He is also Jewish.

daniel (danny): friend
Danny is a really close friend of mine. We met in December 2003 during my sophomore year, and we became friends pretty quickly. He is a very understanding, willing-to-make-things-work kind of guy. Also he is pretty sensitive. He stood up for me once when a student, David M, was picking on me. He took certain medications for his Tourette Syndrome that dehydrated him, so he had to drink a lot of liquids to stay hydrated.

patricia: daniel's mom

lillian: matt's mom

mel: daniel's father

chapter six

ron: matt's father
gabe: mom's boyfriend

series summary

In 2002, when I was in ninth grade, I met Matt in my PE class. We became friends very quickly. He was the same age as me but a grade ahead. I would talk about things that happened to me in my life and he would counter with stuff that happened to him. One afternoon in PE he asked me if I wanted to hang out outside of school with him. I said yes and after that we had had occasional hang-outs outside of school.

One day in tenth grade Danny sat down with us. I had not been very nice to him and told him to "get out of here" and then he walked away unhappy. After I was being rude, a staff member pulled me off campus and had a pep talk with me. My attitude turned around instantly and ever since that day we all three—Matt, Danny and I—became great friends. It occurred to me at a certain point that we were a trio of friends and I liked that idea because three is a good number for a group of friends. I didn't think much about the idea of a trio when I was friends with Courtney and Amber because I was still getting used to interacting with other people who weren't family members. But once I was friends with Matt and Danny, the trio idea became important. By then, I was getting used to the whole interacting-with-other-people deal.

Episode List

Episode 1   Season 1

title: **THE FIRST HANGOUT**   air date: **DECEMBER 7, 2003**

summary

Matt and Danny come over to my house and we hang out for a little while. We are going to the movies to see *Elf*. A little while before we leave, we play some basketball in my backyard. Then it is time to go to the movies. We have an astonishingly good time. After the movies Maya picks us up. When we get back from the movies we have some tea and I say that I will buy them lunch at the Surrey Corner (the school café) the following day. Danny puts ice cubes in his tea to cool it down so that he can drink it.

notes

This was the premiere of our friendship.

This is one of a few episodes where we all ride in Maya's car.

goofs

Danny got in the car early, while Matt and I were still playing basketball.

soundtrack listing

"The Sign" by Ace of Base (*Happy Nation* 1993)

Episode 2

---

title: **ALL TOGETHER AGAIN**   air date: **JANUARY 4, 2004**

---

summary

I go to Matt's house and Danny is unexpectedly there. We hug. Later on Lillian (Matt's mom) takes us out. We try to go bowling, but it doesn't work out because first Lillian can't find the right size bowling shoes for me to wear and then we all decide we don't want to be there. Then we go back to Matt's house. We play some Sorry! and after that Matt's dad takes us on a hike to Torrey Farms. I get into a disagreement with Matt; I want to go down a certain path on the trail I walked on when I was three years old. But he won't let me and then I end up skinning my knee.

notes

This episode aired the day before we went back to school after winter break.

goofs

I hugged Danny twice. Once would have been enough because he's a dude and Mom told me not to hug other guys too much. I wasn't so clear about this at this time.

Episode 3

---

title: **THE BIG MOVIE**   air date: **JANUARY 19, 2004**

---

summary

Matt and Danny and I go to see *Cheaper by the Dozen* and it is pretty good, but just as we are ready to get picked up, Matt leaves his glasses in the theater. We go back and look for them and find them on the seat.

notes

This is the first screen appearance of Hilary Duff. My crush on Hilary Duff took off a few months later, so she became a visual part of our friendship.

quotes

Patricia (Daniel's mom): "Imagine if you had twelve brothers and sisters."

goofs

Patricia dropped us off in the loading dock.

Episode 4

title: **WELCOME TO DANNY'S HOUSE**   air date: **JANUARY 24, 2004**

summary

It's my first visit to Danny's house. We have a good time there. It starts out as just me and him because Matt is still doing Shabbes (see trivia). Later we pick him up, then we go back to Danny's house and play some Sorry! There are cookies and soda and lots of sweets at Danny's house. I knock myself out. Later Danny gets tired and does not come along for the ride to take me home.

notes

This was the first time I rode with Danny's mom, Patricia, alone. We got to really know each other on this night.

goofs

Patricia's car sounds like my school bus on the freeway.

trivia

Shabbes is the Jewish Sabbath. Patricia told us that on Shabbes, you aren't supposed to go out until the third star appears in the sky—that is when Shabbes is officially over.

title: **THE TRIO AND A BIG DINNER**   air date: **FEBRUARY 7, 2004**

summary

Matt and Danny come over to my house and we have a good time.
Maya and Mom cook dinner. They made rice pasta for Matt because
he doesn't eat wheat. I have pasta without sauce and Danny has pasta
with sauce. We play Sorry! with Maya and read a fictional story I wrote
called "The Prophecy." Matt and Danny both like it.

quotes

danny (bumping maya back to start): "I'm sorry."
me: "You're going to make her cry."

trivia

The Prophecy
by Blaze Ginsberg

This is the story of a twelve-year-old girl named Russiana. One day,
Russiana went to the Orange County Fair. At the fair, there was a
fortuneteller in a booth with curtains in a yellow tent. Russiana saw
that it cost four and a half tickets to get her fortune told, so she took
her last five tickets and went into the booth.

The fortuneteller was a very little old woman with white hair, sitting
on a stool. Russiana sat down across from her.

"I am Madam Future," the fortuneteller said and looked into a crystal ball.
"Thou will see unpleasant sights, but thou will ride a school bus with
seventeen children and be dropped off third and when thou gets
home, thou will have ten brothers and sisters."

"When will this happen?" Russiana asked. She had no brothers or sisters.

"It will be twelve days from now," Madam Future said.

"What unpleasant thing will I see?" Russiana asked.

"Thou will see the movie *All Quiet on the Western Front*. Thou will
see the man who inhales the poison gas and the face he makes when
he screams."

"Why?" Russiana asked.

"It is a requirement," the fortuneteller said.

That day Russiana could not stop thinking about the prophecy. That night, she only got four hours of sleep. She fell asleep from 11 p.m. to 3 a.m. She decided she was going to miss the bus and that she would run far away to avoid the prophecy. She didn't want to see unpleasant things. That day she fell asleep in class and had to go see the principal.

Then, finally, it was twelve days later. She ran from the bus and to the West Valley and to the Southern Frontier. Unfortunately, the bus followed her. She faced the music. And she discovered it was not too bad.

When she got home, it was a different story. The house was very quiet. There was a long silence. Nobody knew she was home.

"Surprise!" everybody said.

"But it's not my birthday," Russiana said.

"We just wanted to surprise you for fun," Russiana's mother said.

Ten brothers and sisters appeared before Russiana.

"We adopted all these children from Fullerton," Russiana's mother said. The prophecy had come true! Russiana was very happy. Her brothers and sisters all got to know each other. Then, after a while, they went on a Family Reunion trip to Northern Europe.

Russiana never went back to the fair and never saw the fortune-teller again.

Episode 6

title: **THE VISIT TO LA JOLLA AMC THEATER**   air date: **MARCH 7, 2004**

summary
Danny and I go to the La Jolla AMC Theater after we meet at his house and discuss what we are going to do. Danny offers to go to the mall, but I decide we should see a movie. I go to a drive-through car wash with Patricia and Danny. After the car wash, Danny starts obsessing about something. Danny often obsesses about things like going to stores and buying things. He can't help it, but it sometimes makes me feel uncomfortable because I worry that he might scream or throw a fit. We go see *Starsky & Hutch* and it's all right. They bring me home and come in for tea.

notes

Matt did not appear in this episode due to sickness. This is one of many episode he did not appear in. This is the first appearance of the La Jolla AMC Theater.

quotes

patricia (to danny obsessing): "When you're ready to come back, let me know."

goofs

Patricia drove right past the car wash.

Episode 7

title: **HAPPY BIRTHDAY, MATT**　　　　air date: **MARCH 14, 2004**

---

summary

It's the day after Matt's birthday. We have a celebration for it. We play Sorry!, which I gave him for his birthday. Mom and Maya come over to his house with me for dinner. His sisters and grandmother are there. We leave late at night.

soundtrack listing

"Forever Young" by Alphaville (*Forever Young* 1984)

Episode 8

title: **GOOD TIMES AND BAD TIMES**　　　　air date: **MAY 8, 2004**

---

summary

Danny and I pick Matt up and go to Danny's house. I am not having as good a time as on my first visit to Danny's house because I am in a bit of a bad mood. Patricia offers to drive me home many times, but I persevere through it. We play some cards and hang out in Danny's room.

notes

This episode aired the day before Mother's Day.

quotes

patricia (talking about an issue Danny had with the school bus when he was little): "Daniel worried about taking the bus."

Episode 9

title: **OFF TO SEE SHREK 2**   air date: **MAY 23, 2004**

summary

Matt, Danny, and I go to see *Shrek 2* at La Jolla Village Square after Matt gets done with Shabbes. Danny pays for me.

notes

Danny usually pays for me because he is a good friend and I have budget issues.

This is the last episode broadcast during my sophomore year because summer break starts after this.

goofs

The screen in the movie theater is a little smaller than usual.

Episode 10

title: **OFF TO THE FAIR**   air date: **JUNE 21, 2004**

summary

We go to the Del Mar fair for the first time together. Patricia and Mom go off together and hang out while me, Danny, and Matt all go on the rides. Mom says I can't go on the Ferris wheel because she is scared for me to be up there alone and she doesn't trust the rides at the fair. Danny gets dehydrated and he has to sit down. I go on the Crazy Mouse more than once. I end up going on eleven rides.

notes

This is the first time I go to the fair without parental supervision.

goofs

Patricia has a hard time parking in the fair lot.

I feel very smushed in the car ride to the fair.

trivia
Daniel needs a handicapped pass because of his Tourette syndrome.

Patricia's handicap pass (for Daniel) expires in 2005.

Episode 11

title: **WE'RE ON THE ROAD**   air date: **JUNE 26, 2004**

---

summary
Danny and I go to Birch Aquarium and talk about buses on the way there. We look at all the fish and talk. I have a very good time that night. We hang out at his house and play Sorry!

notes
This is another episode Matt did not appear in. He does not return until August because he is at a cabin in Yosemite with his family. This is one of my all-time favorite episodes because I had the most fun and it was an extremely happy day all around.

quotes
danny (explaining the bus system): "There's the Metropolitan Transit System, San Diego Transit, and North County Transit District."

goofs
Patricia misses the freeway entrance.

soundtrack listing
"Queen in the Black" by Stevie Wonder (*Jungle Fever* 1991)

Episode 12

title: **ROUTE 66 MUSICAL**   air date: **JULY 24, 2004**

---

summary
It's the day after my birthday and Danny and I go see *Route 66* at the La Jolla Playhouse. It is a good musical. He gives me a present: a big striped towel in a canvas bag that he drew a crossword puzzle on. I like the gift. I ride with his dad for the first time and Danny starts with his OCD, just between him and his father. Whenever Danny goes into an

OCD attack (like obsessing about returning something to a store and having to go to the mall), he and his mother, or in this case his father, argue about what he is obsessing over. His father is firm with him. All day, I have been thinking about the recycling truck at our old house when I was five and how I used to follow it.

quotes
danny: "Happy birthday."
(Later)
danny's father: "Daniel, pull it together."

goofs
Maya thought Patricia was me for a minute.

soundtrack listing
"Little Voice" by Hilary Duff (*Metamorphosis* 2003)

"The Last Resort (Live)" by The Eagles (*Hell Freezes Over* 1994)
This song plays because it is sort of a tense song and there were moments in this episode when I was feeling rather tense.

Episode 13

title: **WELCOME BACK TO TOWN, MATT**   air date: **AUGUST 16, 2004**

summary
Matt is back from the cabin and we go to the beach with Mom, her boyfriend Gabe, and Gabe's friends from out of town. We take a long walk all the way to Cardiff. In the ocean, I talk about parking garages with Gabe's friend's son, who is swimming with me and Matt. I ask him if he thinks parking garages suck and he agrees that they do suck. The water is a little cold, but I stay in as long as possible. Matt has a boogie board for me and we ride the waves in.

notes
Danny does not appear in this episode. He doesn't like the beach.

Gabe and Mom and Gabe's friends from out of town go swimming separately.

quotes
me: "Have you ever been doing something and then suddenly it's nighttime?"
matt: "Yeah."

goofs
Matt and I had to wait in the car for a really long time while Mom and Gabe bought sandwiches at Subway.

soundtrack listing
"Rebel Rebel" by David Bowie (*Diamond Dogs* 1974)
This song plays because Matt and I rebelled by walking all the way to Cardiff.

Episode 14

title: **THE TRIO'S ROCKIN' DAYS ON THE ROAD**   air date: **SEPTEMBER 4, 2004**

summary
The trio has not been together for a while. Matt has been at the cabin, and Danny has been busy. We go to the La Jolla AMC Theater, then we go back to Matt's house for a while and hang out. We cruise around for a while in Patricia's car looking at stuff. She doesn't mind driving us around.

quotes
danny: "Next week is my grandma's funeral."
me: "I'm sorry."

Episode 15

title: **BLAZE AND MATT DOING IT UP**   air date: **SEPTEMBER 12, 2004**

summary
Danny is out of town at his grandmother's funeral, so Matt and I hang out and go to Torrey Pines State Reserve. We hike around and look at the view. This time Matt lets me go down the path I took when I was three. We agree I will take five steps and then turn around. It looks different than when I was three. In my memory the path is red but now it is the color of sand. After this, we take Matt's dad to the airport and look around at some of the planes. Then Matt's mom, Lillian, takes me home.

notes

This is the second of only two episodes that Danny did not appear in.

This is the last appearance of Lillian.

soundtrack listing

"Trip on Love and Herald the Day" by Des'ree (*I Ain't Movin'* 1994)
Des'ree's music and my junior year of high school were a major
association, and I also kind of associated "Herald the Day" with friends.

"Michelle's Smiling" by John Stamos (from *Full House Season 2*,
"Baby Love" 1989)
This song plays at sunset when I get to go down the path I like. The
song is a ballad about the character Michelle's happiness, so it goes
with the mood.

Episode 16

title: **BRINGING US DOWN**   air date: **OCTOBER 16, 2004**

summary

Matt and Danny come over for dinner but my performance is very
unsatisfactory. I act out and am somewhat rude. In the moment where
things are okay, I show them a Play CD that Mom got for me. We hang
out in my room briefly. Matt's dad picks them up. After they leave,
Mom threatens that this won't ever happen again if my performance
doesn't turn around. After that, I just eat bread and do my own thing.

notes

This is the last episode taped at our old house. And this was the last
appearance of Matt's dad.

goofs

Matt and Danny were late coming over.

We were planning to take Matt and Danny home, but Matt's dad came
to pick them up, not knowing the plan.

trivia

Play is a self-titled CD released in 2002 by a band called Play (four
Swedish girls named Anais, Faye, Rosie, and Anna). They are all my
age except for Anna.

Episode 17

title: **THE INCREDIBLES**   air date: **OCTOBER 30, 2004**

summary
There is a big long line for *The Incredibles* and Danny gets us past it.
He tells the usher he has Tourette syndrome (which he does) and he
can't stand still in line, and then the usher lets us in. The show starts
really late and I go to the front desk to complain about it. They tell
me it's starting late because there's a long line. I start thinking about
Auntie, Nana's sister, who passed away two years before. A while back
I had a funny dream about her and I started thinking about it again.
When it finally starts, the movie is good. Patricia picks us up and we
hang out at my house for a little bit.

quotes
matt: "Don't tell anyone you have Tourette's, Danny; everyone will want it."

notes
This is the last episode to air at Del Mar Highlands Theater because
the movies we wanted to see were never there after this.

Episode 18

title: **THE DOCUMENTARY OF CHALLENGE**   air date: **NOVEMBER 2004**

summary
Danny, Matt, and I go to see a documentary about high tidal waves
and how people were killed. There are a lot of dates in this movie and
I am fascinated by it. I decide to make my own documentary about
things on my mind, like girls losing their mothers and girls throwing fits.

notes
This is the season finale of Season 1.

trivia
I had been thinking about girls throwing fits and losing their mothers
because I had been seeing a lot of these kinds of stories on the Disney
channel. The girls throwing fits was partially from Amber because she
threw fits a lot in real life. I didn't tell Matt or Danny about these thoughts.

games I (2004)

series: **2004–2006**

genre: **ADVENTURE**

release date: **APRIL 23, 2004**

status: **IN SYNDICATION**

cast:

blaze ginsberg: himself

coach brian (coach): pe coach
Coach Brian was my PE coach at school. He is a very down-to-business guy and is pretty serious with his students. If they are in no mood to participate in the events of PE, then they will just walk laps. I was closer to Coach than the other students were even though there were a lot of times when I did not feel like participating in class.

nick t: friend
Nick T is another buddy of mine. I will never forget the way we met in 2003 when Amber started spending more time with him.* In October 2003, he said if I gave him twenty bucks he would give Amber back. Nick appeared in a few episode of 2007's *My Crush on Sara Paxton*. He graduated Surrey in 2005 and went to Vermont. He came back to California in 2007, and we reunited that summer. In September 2007 we started a short-lived trio *Blaze, Nick, and Dina*. On that same day he got me past a Grand Theft Auto mission that I had been stuck on for exactly one year. Nick has a lot of girlfriends.

clark: friend
I met Clark in the fall of 2003 at Surrey. At the start things were not too good between us. He would always do things to annoy me, like push my desk with his feet in History and if I was stamping my hand with an American flag stamp from the classroom (that I wasn't supposed to be using), he would always say, "Blaze, you're not supposed to be using that." I even hit Clark on his elbow in January 2004. But Clark and I became friends in the fall of 2005, and we started calling each other.

craig: friend

*ON THE SECOND DAY OF MY SOPHOMORE YEAR, AMBER STARTED TO SPEND MORE TIME WITH NICK, IGNORING ME. THIS UPSET ME TERRIBLY AND WAS THE MAIN REASON MY SOPHOMORE YEAR WAS SO BAD. THAT IS WHAT GOT THE "I HATE AMBER" CLUB IN SESSION.

long: bus driver
german: bus driver
althea: bus driver
jesus: bus driver
tammy: bus driver
osborne: bus driver
assorted class members: themselves

---

series summary

This series started when I was sixteen and in the tenth grade. My sophomore year was such a train wreck, and I hated it because on the second day Amber made herself unavailable, even as a friend. I had been having issues with Mr. S, my biology teacher, because he sent me out a lot and I got into a lot of trouble. I had issues with girls hanging out with other boys, and Courtney was not around anymore. On November 20, 2003, I stole candy from Ms. Kennedy's office while she was not around. The substitute speech therapist caught me and yelled at me, and I got into a lot of trouble for that. On that same day, I started a teacher strike against Mr. S and Wendy because I hated them (at that moment). I made picket signs on paper (like the grocery store workers do when they go on strike) and walked around saying, "Strike against Mr. S and Wendy." I got busted for that—the Dean put his foot down hard on that one. I also had issues with Ms. D, the tutorial teacher, so I made a threat toward her, using the word *rape*. I was goaded into saying this by a student, David M. This is a problem of mine: doing things that people goad me into without knowing what I'm doing. Unfortunately, at the time, I didn't even know what the word meant. When I found out what it meant, I was really upset and vowed never to say it again.

One afternoon in PE, I asked Coach Brian to let me start going to the games. He was going to talk to my teachers about my class performance and if it was good enough I would get to go. I wanted to go to the softball games really badly. The team took a school bus to wherever the games were. I wasn't on the team but I wanted to go along for the ride. I had a job where I would go to the storage room and carry up some balls to the field. I got paid for this weekly by my school boss, Ms. J.

The games were important to me because I liked the idea of a field trip every week. I especially liked the idea that this was like a tour group where you go do whatever and the bus driver will wait for you to come back, and I also liked the variety of buses that were used and the routine where I go to games and then go eat lunch. Additional things I liked were hanging with the homies and traveling with a big group. It wasn't really much about the games themselves for me—I sometimes didn't pay that much attention to the games.

I continued going to the games all the way through my senior year.

Episode List

Episode 1	Season 1

title: **THIS IS GOING TO BE A GREAT ADVENTURE**   air date: **APRIL 23, 2004**

summary

In the morning, before school, I ask Mom and Maya to cross their fingers for luck for me, and it works. I get to go to the game. This game was at Stein School. I think this is a school for autistic kids. The bus driver's name is Long and he's driving bus number 4221.

I have a good time chatting with my friends at the game. We sit on the dirt for a while and then we move to a bench. I am preoccupied with watching whatever is around me and I don't watch the game. Afterward we go to McDonald's for lunch. I sit next to an eighth-grader, Michael M, on the bus on the way to lunch. At McDonald's, I talk to my friend Craig about how I feel about the school year. I tell Craig that I miss last year a lot because I have been having a lot of problems this year, like being betrayed by Amber on the second day of school and my best friend and maybe-would-have-been-girlfriend Courtney leaving for another school. I tell Craig this is a bad year for me. Craig listens to me but he doesn't seem that sympathetic. We get back to the school around 2 p.m.

notes

This is the only episode in which Long, the driver, drove bus number 4221.

Number 4221 is a 1984 Blue Bird bus and was retired in the summer of 2004.

This is the only appearance of my friend Michael M, who transferred out of the school in the summer of 2004.

goofs
The bus that Michael M used to get from home to school went to Stein instead.

soundtrack listing
"Rocket Love" by Stevie Wonder (*Hotter Than July* 1980)

Episode 2

title: **WHAT I CAN'T GIVE**   air date: **APRIL 30, 2004**

summary
We go to a field local to the school in Carmel Valley. Ashley and Chelsea (a sophomore and a senior who are friends and hang out together) wander off, and that's where things get out of hand because I keep running after them, monitoring them like I am their father. I don't like people to wander off because I just want people to be around where I can see them. I can't give people the right to do what they want. I go on the field where I'm not allowed to be, and after I do this a couple of times, Coach tells me I have to go sit on the grass. I end up getting my pants wet where I sit on the grass and that is uncomfortable.

notes
At this point I am still learning how to communicate with people. It's been hard for me to do this because all I've been able to talk about is how much I hate Amber for the past six months and that's not such a great topic of conversation.

This is the only appearance of bus number 1930 and the only episode filmed at the Sorrento Valley Field.

trivia
The reason I don't like people to wander off: In the spring of 2003 I was obsessing about how the ostriches in *Fantasia* ran away and whenever people wandered off, I associated it with that one scene.

quotes
coach (after I kept going onto the field where I am not supposed to be): "Ugh, you're killing me."
me (to ashley and chelsea): "What are you doing this weekend?"
ashley: "Hanging out with Amber."

me: "Why? I can't stand it that all my friends are hanging out with Amber."

ashley: "It's a different Amber."

soundtrack listing

"Sound and Vision" by David Bowie (*Low* 1977)

Episode 3

title: **THE END, THE END, WHERE ARE YOU, MY FRIEND?**
air date: **MAY 14, 2004**

summary

We go to a field in Point Loma and the game unexpectedly runs longer than its usual length because it is the championship game. I am still new to this and I think it is going to be the usual length. After a while, I start to get restless and I really want to get out of there. David R. starts teasing me, telling me that we are going to be there for a really long time. I bring my AlphaSmart out to the bleachers and start looking at it to calm myself down.

notes

This is only the third episode and it's already the season finale. The series will continue on through 2006, but this season is over.

quotes

david r.: "We have another four hours left."

goofs

On the way to lunch, the light stayed red for five minutes.

my crush on
hilary duff 1 (2004)

series: 2004–2006   release date: **MAY 1, 2004**

genre: ROMANCE   status: **ENDED**

cast:

blaze ginsberg: himself

hilary duff: herself

haylie duff: hilary's sister

mom: herself

maya: aunt

déja: aunt

bo: uncle

lavander: aunt

gabe: mom's boyfriend

ryan: déja's boyfriend (now ex)

series summary

On December 13, 2003, I saw *Lizzie McGuire* for the first time when I was watching ABC Kids instead of baby kid shows on PBS. On

December 20, 2003, I saw what later became my favorite episode of
Lizzie for the first time, "Inner Beauty." And on January 19, 2004, I saw
Hilary in *Cheaper by the Dozen*. Maya bought me *Cheaper by the Dozen*
in April 2004 and I have watched her in that movie often since then.

How I fell in love:

Part 1

Late at night around ten-ish on April 30, 2004, my sophomore year was
bothering me worse than ever. I watched *Cheaper by the Dozen* and
saw how Lorraine was struggling like me, and I lay on my bed with my
eyes closed and my head down (not asleep) having a little fantasy.

Part 2

On my seventeenth birthday I received a poster of Hilary and hung it
on my door.

Episode List

Episode 1   Season 1

title: **PILOT**   air date: **MAY 1, 2004**

summary

I wake up in the morning and watch *Lizzie McGuire* on ABC Kids
and decide I'm going to be a fan of Hilary Duff. The game I'm playing
on PlayStation that month is Monsters, Inc. and I'm dedicating it to
Hilary Duff. This is like Mom when she was writing her book in 1993
and listening to Madonna a lot for inspiration. I go for a swim at Nana
and Papa's pool. I am, however, thinking about Hilary a lot.

soundtrack listing

"Too Shy to Say" by Stevie Wonder (*Fulfillingness' First Finale* 1974)

Episode 2

title: **THE NEXT DAY**   air date: **MAY 2, 2004**

summary

I go out with Déja to the mall and bring up Hilary Duff. We go for
a drive to the La Jolla AMC parking garage, and later on when I am

having a problem (I want to see a classical music concert but Mom won't buy tickets for just any concert), I pretend there is a paper on my sleeve that says "I love Hilary Duff."

notes

Throughout this month, I watch *Lizzie McGuire* and support my fanhood of Hilary. On Nana's birthday, May 15, 2004, I see *Metamorphosis*, her first album for the first time at Tower Records in La Jolla. I tell people at school that I'm a fan and I get some reactions. Amber tells me Lizzie McGuire is her cousin. Preston calls and pretends to be Hilary on the phone and convinces me it's her. David M tells me he watches the show too. They are teasing me into a riot.

This is the first appearance of Déja.

quotes

me: "If Hilary Duff hated *The Nutcracker* I'd pay her eighteen dollars."
déja: "You'd pay her eighteen dollars?"

trivia

I did not like *The Nutcracker* at the time of this episode.

soundtrack listing

"The Last Resort" by The Eagles (*Hotel California* 1976)

Episode 3

---

title: **FIRST BIG MOVIE**   air date: **JULY 16, 2004**

---

summary

I go to see *A Cinderella Story* with Maya. I enjoy Hilary's performance. She plays a girl who cries when people tease her. It's my first movie as a fan of hers.

notes

This is Maya's first appearance in the series. This is the only Hilary Duff movie I saw at the Mira Mesa Theater.

This is the first time we saw Hilary Duff cry in the series, even though the first time I saw her cry ever at all was back two months ago one night when I was watching *Lizzie*.

quotes

maya: "The movie was okay, but I don't think she's a very good actress."

soundtrack listing

"The Heart of the Matter" by Don Henley (*The End of the Innocence* 1989)
This song plays because the theme of the movie is very sad and it is
kind of similar to this song.

This song doesn't play in the movie and is not included on the movie
soundtrack either.

Episode 4

title: **NOW THERE'S A HOTTIE YOU DON'T SEE EVERY DAY**
air date: **JULY 23, 2004**

---

summary

It's my birthday; number seventeen. I wake up in the morning and the
day is rather nice. I will be going for a massage with Debby, a present
from Maya. My first present is a Dana (see trivia) from Mom. There
is some slight commotion for a while before I leave. Then I leave for
my massage at Debby's house. We get there and my half hour massage
is relaxing. When that's over we leave Debby's house and Maya drops
me off with Déja to take me present shopping. We have to go to
Target. I am very reluctant to go to Target on my birthday because
I hate Target. But we go. I get a chess set, *Dude, Where's My Car?*,
and Monopoly. Then Déja takes me home. I wait for Gabe to arrive.
I'm very anxious for him to arrive because I am expecting Hilary's
album *Metamorphosis* as a present from him. He finally does. I open
one of his two gifts; it's *The Sandlot*. Then the second gift; the grand
prize, *Metamorphosis*. We get ready to go to the beach, but before we
leave my uncle Bo arrives—with a poster of *her*. This day is where my
fanhood of Hilary Duff is really getting serious. Then we leave for the
beach and I put *Metamorphosis* on in the car. We hang at the beach,
then we go home to Lavander who is on the couch. Her gifts are *The
Cheetah Girls* and *The Matrix Reloaded*.

notes

There was a cake with white frosting, which is my favorite. This is the only
appearance of Debby, who is no longer our family massage therapist.

trivia
A Dana is an advanced version of the AlphaSmart. It's like a laptop.

quotes
maya: "You should drink a lot of water after a massage
(Later)
papa: "I need to talk to him now that he's seventeen."

soundtrack listing
"Send Me On My Way" by Rusted Root (*When I Woke* 1994)

Episode 5

title: **OH HILARY**   air date: **JULY 24, 2004**

summary
The next day: Who, what, when, why, where, how—my mind is set
from sunrise to sunset, from the minute I get up to the minute I go
down. Hilary Duff, that's right. I don't obsess about anything else; not
the mysterious Motown song I've been desperately trying to find for
years. Not the hot-air-balloon-sandwich deal that has been going the
past three years, not even how Amber stabbed me in the back on the
second day of school. None of that matters on July 24, 2004, because
Hilary Duff has me. If I could, I'd give my life to her. I go home and
watch *Dude Where's My Car?* Déja picks me up for Dylan's and Alex's
birthday celebrations, and then I go with Danny to see a musical called
Route 66. (See *Blaze, Matt, and Danny* Season 1) Then I go home for
the night.

notes
Dylan and Alex are the sons of Déja's friend, Bessie. This is their only
appearance.

soundtrack listing
"Supernatural" by Raven (*That's So Raven Soundtrack* 2004)

"Queen in the Black" and "Fun Day" by Stevie Wonder (*Jungle Fever*
1991)
This song plays because the singer says to the person he is singing to
that he'd never let her go and basically tells her in the song that he is
crazy about her. That is the same way I am with Hilary right now. Also,

Jungle Fever (the album) and my crush on Hilary Duff were a major association at this point.

Episode 6

title: **WHAT A DREAM**   air date: **JULY 28, 2004**

summary
I have a dream that Hilary Duff is in my school. Later in the dream I am cuddling with her.

In school I continue to obsess about it.

notes
In the dream Hilary is back to being ten years old when *Casper Meets Wendy* (her first ever movie) was filmed.

This is the only appearance of the Surrey school even though it was only a dream.

This is also the only dream episode in this series.

soundtrack listing
"Clocks" by Coldplay (*A Rush of Blood to the Head* 2002)

"Living in the City" by Stevie Wonder (*Innervisions* 1973)

Episode 7

title: **THERE YOU ARE, GIRL**   air date: **AUGUST 15, 2004**

summary
Mom comes home with a calendar of Hilary Duff for me. Fifteen months of Hilary. I go lie down on my bed while I wait for Bo to pick me up and go out. I cuddle with a pillow and pretend it's her.

notes
From today until the end of 2005, Hilary was going to be on my wall.

quotes
mom (shouting): "Hilary Duff!!!!!!!!!!!!!!!!!!!!!!!!"

goofs
Bo was late to come pick me up because he had miscalculated the end of the Del Mar races.

soundtrack listing
"Just My Imagination" by The Temptations (*Sky's the Limit* 1971)

Episode 8

---

title: **GOING TO HIL**   air date: **OCTOBER 23, 2004**

---

summary
I go see my second movie as a fan: *Raise Your Voice* with Maya. Maya is the one who goes to all these movies with me because she loves me and I love Hilary Duff. The movie stars Hilary Duff as Terri Fletcher and the son of the late John Ritter, Jason Ritter, as Paul Fletcher, who was killed in a car accident. Hilary is crying quite a bit.

notes
Hilary Duff with Rita Wilson was very cool. I nominated her as the best mother of any of Hilary Duff's characters.

I had the most fun time seeing *Raise Your Voice* in the movies and wanted to reincarnate the experience by finding a movie exactly like this one and seeing it the same way.

quotes
mom: "How was the movie?"
me: "I love it because it starred my girlfriend."
maya: "Hilary is not your girlfriend."
maya: "I liked *A Cinderella Story* better."

trivia
I like to reincarnate good experiences a lot.

Lavander called Hilary Duff my girlfriend once.

soundtrack listing
"Say Goodbye to Jr. High" by Emma Roberts (*Unfabulous and More 2005*)
Even though this song was released in 2005 and this episode is from

2004, it plays during the car ride home because I now associate it with the conversation.

"Hide Away and Fly" by Hilary Duff (*Hilary Duff* 2004)

Episode 9

title: **EVERYWHERE YOU LOOK, HILARY WILL BE**   air date: **OCTOBER 31, 2004**

---

summary
It's Halloween and I am out furniture shopping with Mom, Maya, Nana, and Déja. We are shopping for a new dining room table and chairs. We find one at Jerome's. I sit on the couches and lie on all the beds in the store. Before we leave, I run into a magazine with Hilary Duff on the cover. I take the magazine because it's free.

notes
This is the first groove where Mom, Maya, Nana, Déja, and I all go out together in the series.

This groove does not take place on a Saturday.

soundtrack listing
"Walk Slow" by Chris Isaak (*Speak of the Devil* 1998)

Episode 10

title: **HILARY IS WORTH SOMETHING**   air date: **NOVEMBER 28, 2004**

---

summary
I am out with Bo and he stops at Circuit City and is in there for a long while. I wait in his truck. When he comes out, he's bought me *The Girl Can Rock* CD. Hilary again.

quotes
bo: "I'm the best uncle."

soundtrack Listing
"Sugar Pie Honey Bunch" by The Four Tops (*The Four Tops Second Album* 1965)

Episode 11

title: **IT'S HERE**   air date: **DECEMBER 2, 2004**

summary
My crush is real hot. I receive Hilary Duff's second album titled, *Hilary Duff*. I listen to it a lot, and in the morning I listen to it when I don't want to hear Mom yelling my name to get up.

Episode 12

title: **IN MY MIND**   air date: **DECEMBER 11, 2004**

summary
I go on my first visit to Déja's apartment in Pasadena, where she has moved with her boyfriend (now ex) Ryan. I talk about Hilary Duff. I play my first-ever game of Grand Theft Auto. In bed that night, I listen to a couple of tracks of her album.

notes
This is Ryan's first appearance in the series. He joked around and said, "Hilary Duff's my girlfriend" a lot off set.

quotes
me: "I imagine Hilary Duff singing the fourth track on her album at sunset."
ryan: "Four times?" (Ryan misheard me. He thought I said she was singing the song four times.)

Episode 13

title: **THE TROUBLE WITH HILARY'S SINGING STYLE**
air date: **DECEMBER 12, 2004**

summary
I am having a slight problem with Hilary's singing style and get worried I will end up like Tia on that one episode of *Sister, Sister*, where she and her boyfriend broke up. But I manage to bear with it.

notes
I almost cried like Tia did in that episode of *Sister, Sister.*

quotes
me: "I am having a slight problem with Hilary Duff's singing style. She sings one part of the song over and over again."
mom: "Is it like that Bill Withers song; I know, I know, I know, I know?"
me: "No."

trivia
I am very sensitive to the way other people talk or sing or yell.

soundtrack listing
"Why Can't He Be You?" by Patsy Cline (1962)

Episode 14

title: **HILARY TIMES HILARY**   air date: **DECEMBER 25, 2004**

---

summary
It's my first Christmas with me being crushed over Hilary Duff. I receive two gifts related to her. One is a picture collage that Ryan made for me. When I see one of the pictures that has what looks like a guy in it, I presume it's her boyfriend in real life. False alarm. For a minute my crush on Hilary Duff was just inches away from getting axed because I had felt like ripping those pictures to bits. But it survives that near brush with death. My second gift is A *Cinderella Story* on DVD.

notes
I taped today with the camera I got for my sixteenth birthday.

soundtrack listing
"Clean Heart" by Sade (*Stronger Than Pride* 1988)

Episode 15

title: **I'LL SEE HER TONIGHT**   air date: **JANUARY 28, 2005**

---

summary
Tonight Hilary is appearing on *Joan of Arcadia* as Dillon Samuels. The show is about how Dillon starts out as a bully to Joan (Amber Tamblyn) and then she almost gets run over and Joan saves her life. Then they become friends. I had watched *Joan of Arcadia* once before and liked it because I liked the idea that she could talk to God.

notes
This is the first time I saw Hilary on TV since *Lizzie McGuire*.

soundtrack listing
"Speed of Sound" by Coldplay (*XY* 2005)

Episode 16

title: **HILARY IS NOT HARD TO FIND**   air date: **FEBRUARY 21, 2005**

---

summary
Hilary is on *Oprah*. This is the first appearance of her sister Haylie in my crush. On the show, Hilary talks about her life and her mother comes on. I learn about the rules of her house and how she was punished once for not calling her mother to tell her the schedule for the evening.

notes
Hilary got a tear in her eye in reality when it was time for her to leave *Oprah*. This is the only time Hilary has cried for real in the series.

trivia
Hilary is two months younger than I am.

Episode 17

title: **GO, HAYLIE**   air date: **FEBRUARY 25, 2005**

---

summary
A fluke occurs: Haylie Duff is crying on *Joan of Arcadia* as Stevie Marks. This is very unusual. In the past nine months, I have only been crushed over Hilary. Now I have to think about her sister.

notes

Hilary Duff does not appear in this episode. This is the second consecutive episode in which she does not appear. There is no explanation for her absence.

trivia

Soon after this episode I vowed never to let Hilary go.

soundtrack listing

"Soul Inspiration" by Anita Baker (*Compositions* 1990)
This song plays because the singer is singing about how she hasn't really been treating the one she loves that well and that it would kill her to lose him. Now it would really kill me to lose Hilary. This song plays for that reason, because I really love Hilary too much to let her go.

Episode 18

title: **RAISE YOUR VOICE IS MINE**   air date: **MARCH 5, 2005**

---

summary

Maya buys me *Raise Your Voice* (Hilary's movie) on DVD while we are out on our Saturday groove. I go home and watch the movie and see it differently than I did the first time.

notes

After this episode, I started getting ideas for storylines similar to those in *Raise Your Voice* to put in my stories.

This is the only time a groove is on a Saturday (which it usually is) in this series.

soundtrack listing

"Haters" by Hilary Duff (*Hilary Duff* 2004)

"Why's It So Hard" by Madonna (*Erotica* 1992)

Episode 19

title: **OFF MY GIRL**   air date: **MARCH 20, 2005**

---

summary

I am out with Lavander at Red Robin, and we are having a nice time until she says this: "Guess what, Hilary Duff has a boyfriend." She continues, "Guess how old he is? Twenty-seven." I am not happy to hear this news but she even agrees with me that they need to break up. Later, I go for my second visit to Déja's apartment in Pasadena.

notes

This is the second and last appearance of Déja's apartment in Pasadena.

quotes

ryan: "I know about her boyfriend."

thanksgiving special 2004

title: THANKS(HANG YOURSELF)GIVING   air date: **NOVEMBER 25, 2004**

cast:
blaze ginsberg: himself

mom: herself

maya: aunt

lavander: aunt

déja: aunt

bodine (bo): uncle

nana: grandmother

papa: grandfather

guest stars:
ryan: déja's boyfriend (now ex)

bessie: déja's friend

alex: bessie's son

summary
We are back at Lavander's house for Thanksgiving this year. Déja's friend Bessie and her one-year-old son Alex are attending this year.

It starts off fine. I film for a little bit. Then Bessie and Alex arrive. That too starts off fine. Alex is in a happy mood even when we play a DVD trivia game titled Scene It?. Alex looks at the TV screen and is interested in it. But later he starts crying, and it carries on throughout the rest of the day. Nobody can figure out why he won't stop crying. It is a traumatizing sound. He watches *Arthur* and that calms him down temporarily. Then it is back on again. The crying does not stop until they leave. He even cries when Bessie is on the phone with a friend. At dinner it begins to get serious. Alex has some bread and soup and he wants to feed himself, but he can't. He even tries to hit Bessie. He mellows down but only for a little while. At the end of the evening he is still crying. He finally stops when he and Bessie leave. I think he misses his older brother, who is visiting their father in Florida.

quotes
me: "I'm thankful that my sophomore year is over."
papa: "Oh, please." (meaning I should stop complaining).
(Later on)
mom (fake crying like alex): "What's the matter now?" (talking normally) "Did you drop your binky?"
(Later on when Alex wants to go down the stairs)
bessie: "Not now Alex!"
(Later on at dinner)
bessie: "Alex, you're too little to do it yourself."
(When he tries to hit her)
bessie: "Alex, no!"
me: "This is Thanksgiving 2004. Food is all gone, fun is all had. Alex is still crying."
bessie (laughs): "Alex is still crying."

notes
As with Thanksgiving 1997, this was not such a good Thanksgiving.

This is the last Thanksgiving celebrated at Lavander's house.

This is the last episode with Bessie and Alex. I never see them again after this.

major events in 2004
I really fell in love for the first time (with Hilary Duff) and experienced what it is like.

I became a fan of the Disney Channel and Disney Channel stars and shows.

I partially made up with Amber.

I began going to the races at the Del Mar Fairgrounds with Papa and Bo in the summer.

I got my first job (working at the Surrey Corner at lunchtime serving hot lunches).

I was able to start going to the school games.

I began hanging out with Matt and Danny regularly.

trivia
Outside-of-school weekend events during 2004 (my junior year):
Going to Chevy's
Watching *Full House* on Nick at Night (irregular)
Watching *The Fresh Prince of Bel-Air* on Nick at Night
Watching *Joan of Arcadia*
Watching *Nanny 911*
Going grocery shopping (irregular)
Taking coffee to Bo and Papa
Déja coming to visit from Pasadena
My diet dilemma*
The Saturday groove
Writing e-mails
Pretending Hilary Duff is my girlfriend
Going to Elijah's
Going to the mall a lot
Rolling down the window to listen to buses
Watching *World's Wildest Police Videos*
The poetry project**
The mints dilemma†
Watching *Inner Beauty*
Talking about college
Burning CDs

soundtrack listing
"Can't Do A Thing to Stop Me" by Chris Isaak (*San Francisco Days* 1993)

*MY DIET DILEMMA IS THAT I WOULD ALWAYS WANT TO HAVE A CUP OF TEA WITH FOUR SUGARS AND A MUFFIN WHEN I GOT HOME FROM SCHOOL INSTEAD OF LUNCH. MOM INSISTED THAT I EAT LUNCH AND SO IT BECAME A DILEMMA AND A REPEATING PATTERN.

**IN ENGLISH, MY TEACHER ASSIGNED US A HUGE POETRY PROJECT TO COMPLETE BY THE END OF THE YEAR. IT HAD TO BE A WHOLE BOOK FULL OF VARIOUS POEMS, LIKE SONNETS, CONCRETE POEMS, HAIKU, ETC. I HATED THE POETRY PROJECT.

†THE MINTS DILEMMA INVOLVED MY WANTING MINTS A LOT AND MOM NEVER WANTING TO BUY THEM FOR ME BECAUSE I WOULD ALWAYS EAT THE WHOLE ROLL OR BOX AT ONE TIME.

blaze, matt, and danny 2 (2004)

cast
See Cast, *Blaze, Matt,* and *Danny* Season 1

Episode 19   Season 2

title: **TO THE CONCERT WITH A FRIEND**   air date: **DECEMBER 19, 2004**

---

summary
Danny and I go to Maya's Christmas concert with Patricia and Mom. Danny falls asleep in the middle from the medication that he takes. The orchestra plays holiday music. There is an intermission. I enjoy all of Maya's concerts—that's what makes me want to go to another classical music concert. I have been going to see her in her concerts since 1991.

quotes
patricia: "Daniel, wake up. I'm not going to carry you out there."

notes
Matt does not appear in the premiere of Season 2.
This is the only live performance we go to.

trivia
Maya plays the violin. She has been playing since she was nine years old.

soundtrack listing
"Where Did I Go Right?" by Hilary Duff (*Metamorphosis* 2003)

"Glamour Profession" by Steely Dan (*Gaucho* 1980)

Episode 20

title: **A COMPLETE WASTE OF TIME**   air date: **JANUARY 29, 2005**

---

summary
I go over to Danny's house and we watch *Napoleon Dynamite*. Matt is
there. I do not have such a good time. I get yelled at by Danny's dad
twice. The first time because I am playing with Danny's dad's drill and
the second time because I am playing with the light switch, which
I think controls the lights in the room we are in. But it controls the
lights in the room his dad is in. After that we play Card Gazetteer, the
game I made up on Thanksgiving 1996. We make up our own rules.

quotes
danny's dad: "Hey, hey, stop doing that!"
me: "Ugh, sorry!"

soundtrack listing
"Wasted Time" by The Eagles (*Hotel California* 1976)

Episode 21

title: **ROLLING WITH DANNY**   air date: **MARCH 13, 2005**

---

summary
Danny and I go see a movie at La Jolla AMC and I lose my ChapStick.
We go to Sav-On (now CVS) to replace it and then go briefly to see
Matt and hang out for a little bit.

notes

This episode aired on Matt's eighteenth birthday. This is the last appearance of Matt's house in the series.

quotes

danny: "Blaze lost his Birdie Bees" (meaning Burt's Bees—my lip stuff).

Episode 22

title: **A CRUSHING FILM**   air date: **MARCH 27, 2005**

summary

Danny and I go to see *Millions*, a sad story about two boys whose mother died. Today something happens that has never happened before; Danny cries because it is so sad.

notes

Millions is an English film.

This is the only episode in this series where someone cries.

Danny was crying because the film reminded him of his grandmother who died last year.

quotes

me: "Danny, let's go."
danny: "Just a minute."
me: "What's wrong, buddy?"
danny: "Nothing."

Episode 23

title: **OUR SECOND VISIT TO THE FAIR**   air date: **JUNE 22, 2005**

summary

It's our second visit to the Del Mar fair together. When we first enter, there is a ride Matt wants to go on but I don't, so then we negotiate and go on another ride. We pretend the rides are different kinds of cars. The ride I didn't want to go on is a Honda Civic. One of the tilting rides is a Volvo S40. Matt and I go on one ride three times. We have a great time.

chapter ten

notes

This is our last fair visit.

Matt and Danny will be going away to college at the end of August.

quotes

matt: "I will still call you when I go to college."
(Later)
me (recalling a memory of something that never happened):
"Remember when we hung out with that girl in 1959?"

goofs

Patricia was late picking me and Matt up because there was traffic in La Jolla.

Episode 24

title: **OUR LAST LATE NIGHT OUT**   air date: **JUNE 25, 2005**

---

summary

Danny, Matt, and I go to catch a late movie at the La Jolla AMC theaters. On the ride there I am restless when one light takes a while to turn green.

notes

After this episode, Patricia always took us home before or exactly when it got dark outside. Danny got tired and had to get ready to go away to school, so we couldn't have any more late nights.

Episode 25

title: **THE PREMIERE OF A BIG MOVIE**   air date: **JULY 15, 2005**

---

summary

I go to the premiere of the new *Willy Wonka and the Chocolate Factory* with Danny. I do not like the scene where Dr. Wonka burns his son's Halloween candy. Johnny Depp is good. However I am mostly thinking about a girl from school, Danielle, whom I have developed a crush on, so it gets hard to focus on the movie. I learn the next day that Danielle is too young for me.

notes

This was our last movie theater episode because we never really looked at what was playing. And I wanted to spend time doing other things with Matt and Danny.

quotes

me: "Where's Willy Wonka's mother?"
danny: "I don't know."
(The next day)
mom: "Danielle is only thirteen. That's too young to date."
me: "I didn't know that."
mom: "You can talk to Gabe about it. He can explain it."

Episode 26

title: **THE RECYCLING AND DANNY'S ALARM CLOCK**
air date: **AUGUST 2, 2005**

---

summary

Danny comes over to my house. We play Grand Theft Auto and then suddenly the recycling comes. I come running out of my room like a bullet from a shotgun. Danny comes upstairs with me to watch it.

notes

This was a very brief visit.

This is the second and last episode where recycling trucks are a focus.

quotes

patricia: "Daniel's alarm clock sounds like that."
me: "Like the recycling truck's beeper?"
patricia: "Yes."
danny: "It goes beep, beep, beeeep."

goofs

The recycling truck backs in differently than it usually does.

trivia

Matt is absent from both of the episodes involving recycling trucks. I now talk to him endlessly about them on the phone.

Episode 27

title: **TO ELIJAH'S WITH FRIENDS**   air date: **AUGUST 5, 2005**

summary
I hang out with Danny and we go to the San Diego Bay and see the view and then Elijah's, my favorite restaurant (now ex-favorite because they were out of English Breakfast tea one time when I went in with Lavander). Patricia sits with us. I call Mom to tell her that we're going out for dinner. I have french fries and a soda. Danny buys dinner.

quotes
daniel's mom (when I am not very happy): "Hey Blaze, what's wrong?"
me: "I'm fine."

soundtrack listing
"You Learn" by Alanis Morissette (*Jagged Little Pill* 1995)

Episode 28

title: **DANNY'S LAST DINNER**   air date: **AUGUST 19, 2005**

summary
Patricia and Danny come over for dinner. We have pasta with breadcrumbs and roasted peppers. I eat french fries before they get here due to me not liking pasta. We have dessert. We talk about Danny going away to college. He's excited.

quotes
mom: "You are a nice friend, Daniel."
danny: "Thank you."

soundtrack listing
"Beautiful Disaster (Live)" by Kelly Clarkson (*Breakaway* 2004)

Episode 29

title: **THE TRIO'S LAST REUNION**   air date: **AUGUST 12, 2005**

summary
It's not long before Matt and Danny are going away to college. We pick Matt up and then go to Danny's house, hang out, play Sorry! We hug and tell each other we will stay in touch. It's a crushing day.

notes
Danny has only visited me twice since he left for college, but I speak to him on the phone and in e-mails.

This is the series finale.

quotes
danny: "This is the trio's last hug."

goofs
This episode is out of chronological order because it is the last time all three of us are together before they leave town, even though Danny's Last Dinner happened a week later.

soundtrack listing
"Jericho" by Hilary Duff (*Hilary Duff* 2004)

"These Three Words" by Stevie Wonder (*Jungle Fever* 1991)
"These Three Words" is a song saying that you should love the people such as your family and that they can be gone in an instant. In this case, Matt, Danny, and I were thankful to have each other for the time that we did and we were now being separated.

games 2 (2005)

cast

See Cast, Games 1

guest star

lindsey: friend
Lindsey and I met in September 2004 when she was petting Mrs. L-D's dog, Molly, and she was giving me lessons on how to touch the dog. Our friendship got serious on November 4, 2004, when I witnessed her crying case. She was crying because something really sad happened to her, and I was there for her every minute. Lindsey was not a terribly serious person because she would always joke around and she even burped during lunchtime.

lindsey trivia:
Lindsey cried countless times, even after the day she hit me in the Dean's office, which happened on March 10, 2005 (see episode 8).

She left Surrey after my junior year ended, which was her first and last year at Surrey.

She had tons of boyfriends.

Episode 4   Season 2

title: AWAY WE GO   **air date: JANUARY 14, 2005**

summary

It's the beginning of the 2005 basketball season and the premiere of

Season 2, and we go to the Tierra Santa gym. There is a minor problem—it's indoors and there is a buzzer. The buzzer is very loud and this is one of my problems, worrying about loud noises. But other than that, things are okay. I hang out with Ryan's mom (Ryan is a senior) and she claims that he doesn't like loud noises either. She says that when he was four, she had to cover his ears when there were fireworks.

notes
This was the first of three indoor events for this season.

quotes
coach: "Remember, it's indoors and these people just want to play the game."

Episode 5

title: **BOO, STEIN**   air date: **JANUARY 21, 2005**

---

summary
We go to Stein and it's a long drive there. I do get upset about that and say bad things about the school, that it's a horrible school. Shaun asks me how I would feel if people said they hated my school, Surrey. Lindsey tries to calm me down by telling me it's okay. I do wind up enjoying the game less because of how long it took to get there. I temporarily blacklist Stein.

notes
This is the first appearance of Lindsey at the game.

quotes
me: "Don't you just hate Stein?"

Episode 6

title: **SECRETS**   air date: **JANUARY 28, 2005**

---

summary
We go to Tierra Santa gym and I ask this guy Chris why our former classmate Travis left the school. I learn he was caught with beer. The

Dean of Students found him drinking beer at school. The Dean tried to give Travis a second chance, but Travis didn't want to come back.

notes
This was the second of two games where there was no lunch.

quotes
me (stunned): "Travis was caught with *beer*?"
chris: "Shh, yes."

goofs
Chris was filming the game while we were talking about the Travis incident, so it got caught on camera.

Episode 7

---

title: UNBELIEVABLE   **air date: FEBRUARY 4, 2005**

---

summary
We go to Sierra Mesa gym outdoors. When Long has to repark the bus because he's next to someone's house, he backs up over and over again. I'm stunned. I can't stop talking about it. The only vehicles I've seen backing up so many times are tractors and garbage trucks. Over by the bleachers, I talk to another senior, Kathy, in obsession about the bus. She tries to change the topic but she tells me I see things very well.

notes
This was the first time Long ever backed up four times. He also had to back up leaving Burger King and McDonald's (which he does every Friday), which would make a total of five times the bus backed up in one day.

This is also the only obsession episode of this series.

This is the first appearance of Kathy in the series.

quotes
me (repeated line): "Did you see the bus backing up over and over again?"
kathy (trying to distract me): "You're sexy."

soundtrack listing
"Hide Away" by Hilary Duff (*Hilary Duff* 2004)

"Golden Years" by David Bowie (1975)

"You're a Wonderful One" by Marvin Gaye (1964)

Episode 8

title: **I'M BACK IN TOWN, BABY**   air date: **MARCH 11, 2005**

summary

It's been a while since I've been to a game. Lindsey is not here due to her being suspended from the game. We go to Tierra Santa gym for the championship basketball game. There is a kid there from Tierra Santa who is just wandering around, touching things, and acting up and making a lot of noise. It is embarrassing for me.

notes

Lindsey had hit me the day before this episode. This came on when we were messing around and it began to get out of hand. Lindsey wanted me to come closer to her, and I didn't want to but then my friend Caitlin forced me into it. Then Lindsey hit me in the face. I had to go speak to the Dean about this, and Lindsey was ineligible to go to the game.

Lindsey and I made up the following Monday.

Episode 9

title: **THINGS ARE DIFFERENT TODAY**   air date: **APRIL 1, 2005**

summary

Today is the first softball game of 2005. When I see a different bus, number 4174, I'm somewhat reluctant to ride it but I bend to it. Long is absent. The driver, German, takes us to Stein. On the way there I sit with Lindsey and she is crying. We get there and I see Jessica holding Michael in her lap. I don't like this because I still don't believe in girlfriends and boyfriends. (I'm not ready to date, so I don't think anyone else should either.) After the game, German comes with another, bigger bus, number 1926, because the one we took there was not big enough.

notes

This was the only appearance of German. After this episode I started complaining a lot about Jessica.

These are also the only appearances of buses number 4174 and 1926.

quotes
lindsey: "I saw a vision of my friend stabbing himself."
me: "Hey, Coach—"
lindsey: "No, it's okay, don't worry about it."

goofs
German ate lunch with us.

trivia
Things that set off my alarm:
1. Jessica holding Michael in her lap
2. Elijah's
3. Places that take too long to get to
4. Poetry
5. Jessica Simpson
6. Graphing solutions on number lines
7. Whirring sounds
8. Tea by itself (without sugar)
9. The torture that happens at school
10. The garbage company EDCO*
11. Uncle Vernon and Aunt Petunia from Harry Potter being married instead of brother and sister**
12. Pasta
13. The year 2003
14. People throwing things at me
15. Daphne's Greek Café
16. Russell's dad from *The Kid*
17. Ren Stevens from *Even Stevens*
18. Boys being the youngest and girls being the eldest†
19. Taking ten minutes to get ready to go (which is too long)
20. Bus number 59

Bonus:
1. Butter
2. Ralph's in La Jolla

---

*WHEN I WAS LITTLE, THIS GARBAGE COMPANY ALWAYS CAME LATE TO PICK UP OUR TRASH AND RECYCLING, AND THIS IS WHY I DON'T LIKE IT.

**I REALLY WOULD HAVE PREFERRED IT IF THESE CHARACTERS WERE BROTHER AND SISTER INSTEAD OF MARRIED.

†IN MY MIND, BOYS SHOULD BE THE ELDEST AND GIRLS SHOULD BE THE YOUNGEST. I DON'T KNOW WHY THAT IS.

Episode 10

title: THE RETURN TO THE ONCE HATED　air date: APRIL 15, 2005

summary

We go to the field where the championship was last year. (This was another field I had blacklisted because the game took a long time to end.) Long drops us off. I sing some songs on the ride back—made up songs dedicated to Courtney as practice for the talent show, which is coming up in May.

notes

The bus driver Long has returned.

Even though sometimes the games take a long time to end, I still enjoy going to them.

This was the first time in the almost two years it has been since Courtney has been gone from Surrey that I've made a dedication to her.

This is the only musical episode of this series.

quotes

coach: "It's going to get too loud for Long. Keep it down."

goofs

There is a dirt-drying machine that says "Honda" on it, but it's not a car.

Episode 11

title: HIGH FENCES AND HIGH TARGETS　air date: MAY 13, 2005

summary

We go to a field that is inside high fences. It is a very cloudy day. I do enjoy the game mostly because it was originally scheduled to be canceled, so it was an unexpected outing. I see some trash trucks.

notes

Unexpectedly this is the season finale of Season 2 for me due to my not being eligible for this game (because of a problem with a teacher) and going anyway, which meant I had to make it up the following week, and then I was ineligible again the week after that—on championship day.

my crush on
hilary duff 2 (2005)

cast

See Cast, *My Crush on Hilary Duff 1.*

Episode 20   Season 2

title: **A YEAR AGO TODAY**   air date: **MAY 1, 2005**

---

summary

It's been one year since the start of my crush. I talk about it a lot. We
go on a Sunday groove this time to the mall. After that, we stop at
Chevy's and eat. On my Dana, I make a list of things that make me
ecstatic.

notes

Hilary does not appear in this episode. This is the third consecutive
episode in which she does not appear because of lack of material
belonging to her.

This is the last groove of the series.

trivia

Things that make me ecstatic:

1. Hilary Duff
2. The garbage company Waste Management
3. The Haylie Duff song "One in This World"
4. Firefighters
5. Boys being the eldest and girls being the youngest
6. Red Robin
7. TGI Friday's
8. *The Fresh Prince of Bel-Air*
9. My aunts and uncle being brother and sisters
10. Haylie Duff
11. My sympathy for Lindsey
12. Picking up Nana on Saturdays
13. Maple syrup
14. Soup
15. The nickname "Sissy"
16. Only taking 5 minutes to get ready
17. *Joan of Arcadia*
18. Peet's Coffee in Rancho Penasquitos
19. The softball games

Bonus:

1. The bus we take to the softball games
2. Summer from *Napoleon Dynamite*

Episode 21

title: **THE MOVIE IN THE HOUSE**   air date: **JUNE 17, 2005**

summary

Maya takes me to see *The Perfect Man* starring Hilary Duff and Heather Locklear. I don't get a whole lot out of it like I did with *Raise Your Voice*. Maya hates the movie. Other than that, it is pretty uneventful.

quotes

maya: "That movie sucked; bad acting, bad plot, bad writing."
me: "I didn't like it that much either."

Episode 22

title: **HOST HILARY**   air date: **AUGUST 2005**

summary

Hilary hosts or is a guest on a variety of TV shows. She hosts the *Teen Choice Awards* and talks about people who got killed in car accidents because she is trying to raise awareness about teens getting drunk and driving. She says that the people who got killed in the car accident would have been there at the *Teen Choice Awards* that night if they were still alive. On another day, she is on *Regis and Kelly* with her sister Haylie.

Episode 23

title: **SEVERE CRUSH DAMAGE**   air date: **SEPTEMBER 11, 2005**
(Reliving December 2004 But In A Negative Way)

summary

I'm out walking with Mom and we run into *OK!* magazine with an article about Hilary Duff and her home life. I don't want to get it, but Mom buys it for me. I read about Hilary and her boyfriend Joel Madden and I am disgusted. Only this time I let it ruin my day. I obsess about it like Danny with his OCD. The possibility of my crush getting axed is great today, more than ever before.

notes

Two years ago, Courtney left my school and I feel the same way I did then.

Hilary and Joel apparently started dating in 2004, but it was not explicit till 2005.

Joel Madden is eight years older than Hilary and me.

quotes

mom: "I want you to focus more on Kelly Clarkson."
me: "She's five years older than me."
mom: "So? I'm sick of hearing about Hilary Duff."

soundtrack listing

"Dummy" by Emma Roberts (*Unfabulous and More* 2005)
This song plays because the singer is saying that she is being taken

advantage of. In this case I was becoming Hilary's dummy because I was clinging to her all this time while she was with Joel Madden.

Episode 24

title: HILARY'S LATEST AND GREATEST CD   air date: NOVEMBER 10, 2005

summary

I'm waiting for my bus at the end of school. I feel bad for my friend Tina C in Lower School because her dog got eaten by a coyote. Then I see Tina (my friend Ryan's sister) and that goes away instantly. I get Tina's e-mail address and my crush on Hilary goes on hiatus again while I am crushed over Tina. But this hiatus lasts very briefly when I get an e-mail from Tina telling me she has a boyfriend. Later on, Déja buys Hilary Duff's album *Most Wanted* for me.

notes

This is the second and last hiatus of my crush on Hilary Duff.

Deja bought me *Most Wanted* on November 28, 2005.

trivia

Small pets often get eaten by coyotes in this part of town, where there are canyons and the coyotes come out at night.

Episode 25

title: HIL, I'M VERY FOND OF YOU   air date: DECEMBER 21, 2005

summary

A year ago this month, my crush was real up but now it's just regular. We do however go see *Cheaper by the Dozen 2*. Hil is pretty good. Ryan asks if I am going to marry her, as if I am going to be having a reality relationship with her. Which I thought I might.

notes

This was Ryan's last appearance in the series because of the breakup between him and Déja in February 2006.

soundtrack listing
"Is It Love?" by Play (*Play* 2002)

Episode 26

title: **ABOUT HILARY**   air date: **DECEMBER 30, 2005**

summary
I am in the Ralph's Coffee Shop. I see a magazine about the true life story of Hilary Duff and read a little about Joel Madden. This time I am able to read it without getting disgusted. I even learn about Joel Madden. He has a twin brother, an older brother, and a younger sister.

notes
This was Joel Madden's second and last appearance in the series.

Episode 27

title: **THE SAME OLD, PART 1**   air date: **DECEMBER 31, 2005**

summary
I watch Hilary on TV. Her voice sounds really different than it has in the past year. It's New Year's Eve and it's been almost two years that I have been crushed over her. Unfortunately, Green Day interrupts the session with Hilary and I'm really irritated.

notes
My hatred of Green Day was brought on when my annoying old friend from elementary school told me to like them instead of Hilary Duff.

I now like Green Day.

trivia
I don't really like to be roped into things. Whenever I am, I begin to blacklist the things I'm being roped into.

Episode 28

title: **THE SAME OLD, PART 2**   air date: **JANUARY 1, 2006**

summary
It's now the New Year and Hilary Duff is hosting *New Year's Eve Live*. She sings "Beat of My Heart." I lie in bed and watch her. I also watch *Napolean Dynamite*, which her sister Haylie stars in as well.

quotes
mom: "She just keeps singing the same thing over and over; 'beat of my heart, beat of my heart, beat of my heart.'"
me: "Mo-om, for crying out loud!"

Episode 29

title: LET'S GET THIS MOVIE ON THE ROAD   air date: **MARCH 5, 2006**

summary
Bo buys me *The Perfect Man* on DVD. My collection is now as follows: the *Lizzie McGuire* movie; the poster, which is no longer hung on my door; the collage; *Cheaper by the Dozen*; *A Cinderella Story*; *Raise Your Voice*; and last but not least, *The Perfect Man*. I don't really know how I feel about *The Perfect Man*.

notes
I have not watched *The Perfect Man* since this day.

Episode 30

title: I LIVE IT AGAIN   air date: **APRIL 1, 2006**

summary
It's been twenty-three months since I became a fan of Hilary Duff. It's a Saturday. I go for a driving lesson with Gabe and then go out to the 99-cent store in Encinitas with Mom and Nana. Then I go out with Bo. We go to the hot tub, sauna, and pool (the "Jewish Triathlon").

notes
On this day I become a fan of Andrea Barber who plays Kimmy Gibbler on *Full House*. I've been watching this show in syndication for a while, but I become a fan of hers for only one day.

Hilary Duff does not appear in this episode. This is the fourth consecutive episode in which she does not appear. Cause: Focus on another girl.

Episode 31

title: **THINGS THAT COME**   air date: **MAY 27, 2006**

---

summary

When a Saturday groove plan doesn't work out, I get really upset. But aside from that, in addition to being a fan of Madonna (not a crush, just fanhood) I have developed a crush on Tatyana Ali (Ashley Banks on *The Fresh Prince of Bel-Air*). I go out and get a haircut with Lavander that day. The next day my thing with Tatyana Ali is getting warmed up. In the afternoon I go out with Gabe and Mom to look for a suit and tie for graduation. Then I go out with Bo. He buys me Grand Theft Auto, San Andreas.

notes

This is the last appearance of Gabe in the series.

Hilary Duff does not appear in this episode—the fifth consecutive episode where she does not appear. Reason: Focus on another girl.

This is also the last time I am seen shopping in the series.

Episode 32

title: **CODE HILARY**   air date: **JULY 14, 2006**

---

summary

My crush happens to be back to normal. I wake up in the morning from having a dream of being in an elevator with a chick and being romantic. It was an unidentified chick, so I decided it was Hannah Montana from the *Hannah Montana* show. I decide to be crushed over her for the day and pretend to run away from my problems with her. I then think about her from the minute I get up to the minute I go down, just like I had done with Hilary Duff. When a swimming plan doesn't work out and I get into a fight with Déja, I pretend Hannah Montana is sitting next to me on the couch and we are talking. But this crush ceases after only one day.

Episode 33

title: **THAT MOVIE ROCKS (Wrapping The Crush) Part 1**
air date: **AUGUST 18, 2006**

summary

Material Girls opens and I go to see it with Maya. In the movie Hilary and Haylie Duff play two sisters who go broke. Today it seems like everything related to Hilary has happened before, except for two new things:

Happened Before:
1. Hilary and Haylie being in the same movie or show together
2. Haylie Duff crying
3. Hilary Duff crying constantly like in *Raise Your Voice*
4. Haylie having a spell on me
5. Another star of *Lizzie McGuire* starring in the movie with Hil
6. Hilary Duff singing

New Events:
1. Hilary Duff performing a song by another artist; "Material Girl" by Madonna

2. Hilary Duff going to jail in the movie

Episode 34

title: **THAT MOVIE ROCKS (Wrapping The Crush) Part 2**
air date: **AUGUST 18, 2006**

summary

I enjoy the movie as today is the last day of my crush on Hilary Duff. It is as if the spirits know that today is going to be the day when my crush ends. I've been listening to Jimi Hendrix singing "Red House." The last lyric says, "If my baby don't love me no more, I know her sister will." I consider doing this with Haylie and potentially being crushed over Haylie maybe in a couple of years. Later on when the movie ends, right there is where my crush on Hilary Duff ends for good. I decided to end it because she has not had much work this year and I have been interested in other girls. Matt has a very hard time believing this when I tell him. I kind of knew ahead of time that this was going to be the last event of my crush on Hilary Duff. But then it was uncertain for a while what was going to happen to the crush. But then, official decision: Today it ends.

notes

This episode was split into two parts because I had to go to the bathroom in the middle of *Material Girls*.

In 2002 production on *Lizzie McGuire* was wrapped when Hilary wanted to move higher with her career and they did not want to replace her. Four years later I land in the exact same bubble and wrap production on my crush on Hilary Duff for the same reason. However, I gave no indication that this would be the series' last episode.

This is like *Full House* on the last episode of the series, which was titled "Michelle Rides Again." In this series finale, Joey, Uncle Jesse, and Danny try to reboot Michelle's memory after she falls off her horse. All the regulars who had ever starred on the show appeared in the last few minutes of the series. Today, everything I've experienced during my crush happens on the same day, the last episode of my crush on Hilary Duff. It ends the same way *Full House* did, but eleven years later.

quotes

maya: "I think Haylie's a better actress than Hilary."
me (last line of the series): "Jimi Hendrix is in the house."
(Maya doesn't really listen to this comment or care much about it)

Special	Post-Season
title: **MY LIFE AFTER HILARY**	air date: **AUGUST 21, 2006**

summary

I start college and meet a girl, Lexa, in Yoga. I have developed a friendly relationship and plan to start off as just friends. And we are off to a good start. Down at Jimbo's Market, a Goth girl named Tiana has been checking me out a lot and scanning my items. At college, I also meet Tara A, who I help get her soda when it is stuck in the machine. She's a potential girlfriend for about 30 seconds. At work, I meet a girl, Anna, who claims to be "my number 1 fan." I ask her out on a date but she says she is focusing on school and is not dating. But I did ask her. Matt comes into town to visit and we exchange words about how my crush on Hilary Duff ended.

notes

My crush on Hilary Duff was a legend. From 2004 to 2006 it was the line of entertainment for the Ginsberg family. It exists now only in memory after dying of natural causes.

In memory of my crush on Hilary Duff, 2004–2006.

senior year I (2005)

(A.K.A. PRE-ADULT WORLD LIFE DAYS I)

series: **2005–2006**

release date: **SEPTEMBER 6, 2005**

genre: **SENIORITIS**

status: **ENDED**

main cast:

See *My Freshman Year of High School 1* and *Games 1*

additional cast:

ian: counselor
Ian was my third counselor at the Surrey school and my second male counselor. He officially became my counselor in the summer of 2004, and he is a very nice, cool person. His personality was similar to Dr. R's except he has a longer joking span where Dr. R had a more serious span. Ian has a daughter who is younger than I am by eleven years. Ian is a good counselor because he listens really well and has good advice about how to deal with problems.

brian s: ta (teacher's assistant)

clark: friend

mr. c: math teacher

tina c: friend/cyber buddy
Did not go to Surrey. I met her when she picked up her brother Ryan from school (Ryan went to Surrey). Is very hyperactive and talks very fast. Shakes people's hands really hard. Was crushed over her in 2005.

cliff: friend
Was kind of a friend of mine during senior year. Had a lot of issues, like anger management problems. Had Group with him and Clark. Once said he wanted to blow up Green Day.

trivia

Outside-of-school weekend events during 2005/my senior year:

Going to Pizza Nova (a.k.a. "Ass Bread," see Episode 21)
Going to Chevy's
The Saturday groove
Watching the recycling truck
Writing e-mails to Tina C
Hoping Tina C will be my girlfriend
Looking forward to graduation
Balloons popping
Going grocery shopping
Going for a walk to the liquor-deli with Papa
Watching the garbage truck
The softball and basketball games and all field trips

series summary

My senior year was the final school year I would be spending at
Surrey. It was talked about how I would be missed a lot. I got really
close to everyone. My classes were Government and Economics with
Ms. C first period, English with Mrs. L-D second period, third period
Tutorial with Norm, fourth through sixth Math with Mr. C, and
seventh period PE (a.k.a. Physical Education), then "Home, James."
It was somewhat of a rough year because my friends Matt and Danny
were not around. But I tried to put my best effort forth to make it
a good year. I really wanted a new trio of friends (and a girlfriend),
which was why it was somewhat bad. After Matt and Danny left
and went away to college, I thought my not having a trio was only
temporary because when Courtney, Amber, and I stopped being
friends it was temporary. But no such thing happened.

Episode List

Episode 1   Season 1

title: **THE FIRST DAY (a.k.a. Pilot)**   air date: **SEPTEMBER 6, 2005**

summary

It's the first day of my senior year. I get my class schedule and for the first time, PE is my last class of the day. I go to government class with Ms. C and she has us name something we want to learn. I want to learn how a bill becomes a law. Next, it is off to English with Mrs. L-D where she discusses the material we will go over this year. Unfortunately, it's poetry but it's fine; it won't be as hard as the poetry project Ms. C gave us last year. Then it's break time. That goes well.

In Math fourth period, I report to my seat. I am in front of Tate and Eric. I hope to start a new trio with them. We even pick on student Prem, a freshman, when he butts into our conversation about hating Nick Lachey. Then it's lunch. I have Math again after lunch, and it is just as smooth as last period. And to finish the day, there is PE. Coach B gives his speech about how his class works. When a bus passes by I think more about that than him talking.

trivia

Prem was an acquaintance of mine at Surrey. After I graduated, I didn't see him for two years. Then he started working with me at Vons in 2008. I invited him over to my house one day, and he managed to take control of my computer and put new software on, which made the computer harder to manage. He also asked for pizza and gave me the numbers of some girls from Surrey.

notes

This was the first time I picked on a student instead of picking on a teacher. I was doing it to get a new trio together, but it didn't end up working.

soundtrack listing

"Who Am I?" by Tiffany Evans (*Tarzan II Soundtrack* 2005)
This song plays because the singer sings about learning who she really is and that sometimes she doesn't always have things her way. I am kind of in the same bubble as she is.

Episode 2

title: **THE BUS DESTRUCTION**   air date: **SEPTEMBER 7, 2005**

summary

I wake up in the morning and I need a ride to school because all the Special Ed buses have been vandalized. Mom and Maya give me a ride. Later on the garbage truck blocks our path. I don't make the situation any better because I am complaining constantly. Finally it moves. I have to bring my cell phone to school to find out who my ride home will be. Normally, I do not bring my phone because we are not allowed to speak on our cell phones in class.

notes

My bus driver took me home in a Nissan SUV.

This was the only time I brought my phone to the Surrey school.

quotes

mom: "Put your phone in your pocket."
me (referring to the truck): "Go around it."
mom: "Come on, Blaze."

Episode 3

title: **THE FIRST GROUP SESSION**   air date: **SEPTEMBER 12, 2005**

summary

Group is a time for us to get together with a counselor and talk about life and how it is affecting us. I have been dying to know who the new group members are going to be. Last year it was me, Matt, Danny, and Clark in Group. This year in Group it's me, Cliff, and Clark. We talk about our lives. I talk about Hilary Duff. Cliff talks about his mother who died in 2002. But Group goes wonderfully.

notes

This is the first mention of Hilary Duff in Group.

At this point Clark and I become friends and I get his home phone number and start to call him. We had not been very close the other two school years before this.

quotes

me: "Have you ever heard of Lizzie McGuire? As some of you know, I have a crush on Hilary Duff."

cliff: "That's nice."
clark: "Oh yeah, I know about that."
(Later)
cliff: "My mother died from multiple sclerosis."

soundtrack listing
"When I Come of Age" by Michael Jackson (1986)

Episode 4

title: **THE RECYCLING GOAT**   air date: **SEPTEMBER 13, 2005**

summary
I am in OT (Occupational Therapy) with Jane and I keep hearing the recycling on the street outside Surrey. So I run out a lot to catch it. Jane revises our plan so that I ask before I run out of the room.

notes
This is the first episode where I obsess over recycling trucks (a recurring theme).

This is the first OT session of the series and the first appearance of Jane.

quotes
jane: "If you need to get up for whatever reason, you need to ask me first."
me: "Okay, sorry, I just really wanted to see that recycling truck."

Episode 5

title: **THE BIG ASSIGNMENT**   air date: **SEPTEMBER 28, 2005**

summary
Wendy is subbing for Mrs. L-D in English. We read *The Lion, the Witch, and the Wardrobe* and then it's assignment time. We have to compare and contrast real life with Narnia. It is somewhat difficult but I am allowed to dictate my assignment to Wendy, then I have to take it to Tutorial to finish it.

quotes
wendy: "Now you've got to back that up and put that into sentences."

notes

The assignment Wendy gives us reminds me of a Saturday groove that happened not long before this episode. There is something about the way Wendy is talking to me (telling me to support my points and put them in sentences) that makes my brain get jumbled up. In my mind there is a collage of scones, eating at Chevy's, and fawns (from *The Lion, the Witch, and the Wardrobe*) all put together.

soundtrack listing

"Love's in Need of Love Today" by Stevie Wonder (*Songs in the Key of Life* 1976)

Episode 6

title: **MY JOB**   air date: **OCTOBER 5, 2005**

---

summary

After my IEP meeting Mom and Papa discuss how I need a job. A few days later I am hired at the Surrey Corner, the café at school that is open during lunch. My boss Becca goes over the rules of how it will work. The first day is fine. My position is running the lunch order numbers to the other student workers Tim, Ben, and Quentin. A senior, Justin, steals licorice and I encourage him. That's one strike against me.

notes

I encourage Justin to take the licorice because we're buddies and supposed to back each other up even if it's a stupid thing.

All grilled cheese sandwiches go to Tim. The rest go to Ben or Quentin.

trivia

The Surrey Corner serves grilled cheese sandwiches, Hot Pockets, chimichangas, chicken and beef taquitos, pizza (cheese and pepperoni), licorice, and Dino Buddies (later discontinued).

Episode 7

title: **MY LOVE**   air date: **OCTOBER 14, 2005**

---

summary
There is a field trip to Fifteenth Street beach for a fun day of events. It starts off with the three-legged race, then bicycle racing. Later on, after the events, I continue playing with the bikes till Wendy kicks me off. I think of what Bo would do in this situation because he is always on my side. Later on I am thinking about Danielle, a girl I like who is too young for me to date. I imagine us riding horses. Then we go back to the school. Coach and I talk about the so-called remains of Surrey once I leave.

quotes
wendy: "Okay, Blazer, that's it—off the bike, you've lost your privileges."
me: "Why?"
wendy: "Because you were out of bounds."
(Later)
coach: "When you leave, the whole school is shutting down."

trivia
Back in the summer before the school year started, I was madly in love with Danielle and thinking about her constantly even when times were bad, like when I was shopping in the hated Fashion Valley Mall. I talked to Mom about her, and Mom said that Danielle was only thirteen and too young for me to date, but later Danielle told me that she had a boyfriend.

Episode 8

---
title: **YOU DEFROST IT, YOU PAY FOR IT**   air date: **OCTOBER 11, 2005**

---

summary
I report in to work one day and we discover the food has been defrosted because of me. I left it out the previous day instead of putting it back in the freezer. I didn't think I was supposed to put it away. I end up getting suspended for it. I then go to Ms. K and we talk about it. I'm worried I will be punished when I go home but I don't get punished. I even get to watch the recycling.

notes
This is the second time I've been suspended from work since my sophomore year.

quotes

ms. k: "If someone left my food out, I'd make them pay for it."

Episode 9

---

title: **PLEASE TELL ME THAT WON'T HAPPEN**   air date: **OCTOBER 2005**

---

summary

I have been doing some research on Tammi Terrell (see notes). In PE I think about her death and get worried that the same will happen to me. When I am out sick one day, I still continue thinking about it and hoping it won't happen to me.

quotes

me: "How do you get a brain tumor?"

maya: "We think diet has something to do with it. You're not going to get a brain tumor."

mom: "Let it go. Tammi Terrell had something wrong with her brain."

notes

Tammi Terrell, Marvin Gaye's singing partner, was only twenty-four years old when she died. She collapsed into Marvin Gaye's arms on stage in 1967.

This is the only episode where I am out sick in this series.

I was worried I was going to lose my life at a young age, and this is also a reason for my senior year not being so hot, because I worried about this on and off throughout the year.

trivia

This episode takes place over a few days.

I have always been interested in Marvin Gaye and a fan of his and have done research on him, especially how he was killed by his father. This is what led me to do research on Tammi Terrell.

Episode 10

---

title: **THE GROOVE AND THINKING ABOUT DANIELLE**
air date: **OCTOBER 15, 2005**

---

summary

Groove Day. Nana, Maya, and I go out on our weekly Saturday groove. It's a short one. We go to the mall, Elijah's, Peet's, and then I go home with Nana. I start thinking about Danielle later on and thinking romantic things directed toward her. I write a song dedicated to her and then have some soup.

notes

This is another episode focusing on Danielle. On the last day of the summer session she took a picture of me on her camera phone.

trivia

Danielle went to summer school at Surrey, which is how I met her. I found out she was an only child like me. On the first day I met her I looked at her as a possible girlfriend because I really liked her personality and was practicing the whole romance deal.

soundtrack listing

"My Song to Danielle" by Blaze Ginsberg (2005)

Episode 11

title: **MY GRAND OBSESSION**   air date: **OCTOBER 2005**

summary

When I go to Mrs. L-D's class I begin obsessing over the year 1994 and make up some dates that have that year involved. This is already something I do in Mr. C's math class. Later on at home I write a play where a character died in 1994.

notes

This is the first episode where I am obsessed with 1994.

trivia

There is something about the numbers in the year 1994 that draws me to them. In a way, they are hollow like a parking garage and they have a sound that appeals to me. Certain numbers and years are like that for me. For example, I also like the year 2001 because it is white and very bright.

play synopsis

Levi Sullivan was a mean man whose wife died in childbirth. He hit his son and his son went on drugs, happily getting himself kicked out of his father's house. Levi Sullivan passed away on October 7, 1994, at the age 84.

In memory of Levi Sullivan (1910–1994)

Episode 12

title: **CLIFF, MR. GRUMPY**   air date: **OCTOBER 2005**

summary

In PE one day Daniel R. and I start calling Cliff "Phyllis." It goes on the entire period long. Later it begins to get out of hand. Cliff yells at me when I try to back him up (saying the same thing he's saying at the same time). He yells at Daniel too, but nobody even talks to him about yelling. I get rather mad at him for this.

quotes

cliff: "Daniel, shut the fuck up now!"
daniel (to me): "Spell Phyllis."
me: "P-H-I-L-L-Y-S."
cliff: "That is the most incorrect spelling of that name ever."

trivia

You do not want to piss Cliff off.

Episode 13

title: **TALENT SHOW PLANS**   air date: **OCTOBER 18, 2005**

summary

In PE one day I talk with Coach. I ask him how old he is. We sing "Since You've Been Gone" by Kelly Clarkson and we discuss what we (Coach and I) will sing at the talent show. Later that night I buy a remixed version of Kelly Clarkson's song on iTunes. The whole album was different remixes of that one song.

trivia

Coach is twelve years older than I am. He was born in May 1975.

Jason Nevins was the main remix person of Kelly Clarkson's 2004 hit "Since You've Been Gone" on her album *Breakaway*.

I end up performing "I Won't Back Down" by Tom Petty at the talent show. Coach doesn't sing anything.

Episode 14

title: **THE EVIL RELAX WEEK**   air date: **OCTOBER 28, 2005**

---

summary

Maya wants to take a weekend to relax instead of going on a groove. I don't like that one bit. But I watch *The Fresh Prince of Bel-Air* in my bed, and the relax day is not so bad.

notes

I am not against relaxing in general, but I did not want to take time off from the groove to relax. This is similar to how I am not against buses in general, but there are certain buses that I don't like.

Episode 15

title: **WHAT A SHAME**   air date: **NOVEMBER 10, 2005**

---

summary

One day at break I see Sarah P in tears because her dog got killed.* I let that really affect me. I feel bad for her for the rest of the day. Later, at the end of the day, I am ready to cry I feel so bad. But then I see Tina C and that feeling goes away instantly. I get her e-mail address.

notes

Nicole, another student, was worried about her dog as well.

trivia

Sarah P is in Lower School and she is younger than me by six years.

Ryan C is a couple of grades behind me. He is Tina C's younger brother by two years.

*SEE *MY CRUSH ON HILARY DUFF 2*, EPISODE 24.

Tina C is only seven days younger than I am. She picks Ryan up from school and drives a black 1999 C220 Mercedes Benz.

quotes
a student: "Your dog's going to be fine, Nicole."
another student (to me): "It's okay to cry when you feel bad about someone."
tina c: "How are you doing, buddy?"
me: "Can I get your e-mail address?"
tina c (to another student): "Sweetie, can I borrow your pen?"

Episode 16

title: **THE BALLAD OF THE FIELD TRIP BUS**   air date: **NOVEMBER 18, 2005**

---

summary
I am worried that Long will replace his bus with a short bus. I don't like the dark interior of the short bus. I ask Mr. S about it. Then later I ask Long and he did in fact end up replacing it.

notes
Long's previous bus (number 1917) was a 1993 model according to him. At the beginning of last year he was driving number 65 (which is the same kind of bus he is driving now, number 17), but then switched over to number 1917.

Bus number 17 is a 1997 Crown International bus. But Long did not know that at the time.

Crown is a bus/motor coach company that went out of business in 1991. But according to another First Student bus driver, they still make the kind of Crown that Long was driving.

quotes
me: "Did Long replace his bus?"
mr. s: "Last time I saw him he had the short bus."
(Later)
me: "Is this your new bus?"
long: "Yes."
me: "How old is this bus?"
long: "Five years old."

Episode 17

title: **THE TRUTH ABOUT TINA C**   air date: **NOVEMBER 21, 2005**

summary

After learning that Tina C has a boyfriend, which she tells me in an e-mail, I go ask Ryan, her brother, about him. I get really heartbroken that she has a boyfriend and scared half to death because I really am not expecting this. I thought she might be my girlfriend and now I feel burned.

notes

Tina's boyfriend's name is Adam.

Episode 18

title: **I WON'T ALLOW THE NEW WAY TO MEET FOR GROUP**
air date: **NOVEMBER 2005**

summary

When it's time for Group today there are no offices available where we can meet, so we have to meet outside. I get very upset about this and end up making Group get canceled. I let that bother me and continue complaining about it for the rest of the day.

notes

It bothered me that we could not meet indoors for Group like we usually did, and I could not adjust to the change. One main reason my senior year was so bad was because of change. Matt and Danny were gone and everything felt new and different. I have problems with change and when things are different than the way they usually are.

Episode 19

title: **WILL ANY ROUTINE OF THE TRUCKS**   air date: **NOVEMBER 8, 2005**
BE THE SAME AGAIN?(Get Ready for the Truth)

summary

It's a Wednesday. Trash pickup is getting pushed back one day due to a holiday. I'm however under the impression that everything is going to be the same as when we first moved into our house, as in I would be able to watch the recycling truck when I get home. But two things are against my having a peaceful day: (1) The recycling truck is leaving as I get home and (2) I now have to pass the evil California High School Exit Exam due to Governor Schwarzenegger vetoing the bill that says Special Ed students don't have to pass it to get a high school diploma.

Episode 20

title: **THE TRIP PLANS**   air date: **NOVEMBER 2005**

summary
I talk with Mrs. L-D about the trip to see *The Chronicles of Narnia*. I find out that we will need a lot of buses for this. I hope there will be no city buses involved.

notes
The trip did not end up happening, but I spent many days worrying about the buses.

I did not want there to be city buses involved because there were a total of three buses from NCTD (North County Transit District) that I did not like because of my own *mishegoss.* *

Episode 21

title: **THE RECYCLING AND GARBAGE MARATHON** air date: **NOVEMBER 22, 2005**

summary
I go for a walk with my counselor Ian to Fifteenth Street beach. On the way we see a recycling truck. I get worried that the hydraulics will screech as I walk past them. They don't, but it *is* unusual for me to be standing right next to the truck. Later I go back to the school and watch the garbage truck on the street. Also later that night I go to Pizza Nova for dinner with Déja, Lavander, and Maya. The bread arrives at the table and it is shaped like somebody's ass. This becomes the first Ass Bread Night. I am still thinking about that sight I saw with the recycling truck.

*SEE EPISODE 30 OF *MY FRESHMAN YEAR OF HIGH SCHOOL 2.*

notes

The garbage man and recycling man were standing talking to each other during the job.

Episode 22

title: **NEW STUDENT ON OUR HANDS**   air date: **NOVEMBER 2005**

summary

Nolan, a sophomore, and I have been expecting a new student on our afternoon bus ride home. His name is Alex. I talk to him and find out he has an older sister who is a little older than I am. But she already has a flipping boyfriend, darn it.

notes

This is another episode to feature me in want of a girlfriend.

quotes

me: "Do you have any brothers or sisters?"
alex: "Sister."
me: "How old is she?"
alex: "Eighteen."
me: "Does she have a boyfriend?"
alex: "Yes she does."

Episode 23

title: **CLIFF'S AND CLARK'S BIG BLOWUP**   air date: **NOVEMBER 2005**

summary

Cliff and Clark are at each other's throats. I do not know what the problem is. Clark keeps yelling, "Oh my God!" Ian's assistant goes to talk to them about it and that settles them down.

notes

It doesn't bother me that Cliff and Clark are fighting. I find it interesting.

Episode 24

title: FLIPPING OFF THE BUS   air date: **DECEMBER 8, 2005**

summary

I am in PE. Since the first day of school I have been watching buses on the road above the field. When one that I don't like passes through, I flip it off. I don't like it because that bus, number 1103, passes by at the same time every day and I don't like the pattern. I get paranoid that someone saw me flip off the bus and that they're going to kill me.

notes

Ever since David M threatened to kill me last year, I've been worried that other people will too.

quotes

me: "What's paranoia?"
mom: "When you think other people are out to get you."
me: "I'm worried that someone's going to kill me because I flipped off the bus."
mom: "Why did you flip off a bus?"

soundtrack listing

"High Fidelity" by Elvis Costello and the Attractions (*Get Happy* 1980)

Episode 25

title: WE HATE CHELSEA   air date: **DECEMBER 2005**

summary

Three other guys I know at school and I start a "We Hate Chelsea" club. Chelsea is also a senior but I have never had any classes with her. She is more of an acquaintance than a friend. The guys and I talk about our New Year's Eve plans and how to celebrate. We are going to celebrate against Chelsea. We all have our own problems with Chelsea. However, Coach threatens that I will go to *no* games if this continues.

notes

Mom is really upset with the "We Hate Chelsea" club and she too tells me to stop doing it and so I do. Later, one of the guys got mad at me for dropping the club entirely.

quotes

mom: "It's cruel to start a hate club against that poor girl."

trivia

The real reason I hated Chelsea is because I liked her a lot and she had a boyfriend, causing her to be unavailable as a potential girlfriend.

Episode 26

---

title: **CONSTANT WANTS**   air date: **DECEMBER 2005**

---

summary

I will be receiving Grand Theft Auto Vice City for Christmas. I keep thinking about certain stuff in it, like hotwiring cars. I can barely wait.

notes

This episode features high anxiety because I am waiting for the game to arrive. Grand Theft Auto on PlayStation 1 is from a bird's eye view, while Grand Theft Auto on PlayStation 2 is from a regular point of view.

quotes

daniel (explaining how to hotwire a car in real life): "You tell your friend to put your ear on the car and then it starts up."
coach (joking, as the ball rolls toward his car): "That ball is going to hotwire my car."

Episode 27

---

title: **MY LATEST ENEMY**   air date: **DECEMBER 2005**

---

summary

It's lunchtime and I have gotten off from work. I go hang out with Clay, a seventh grader, in the quad at school and I ask for some of his sunflower seeds. He pretends to give me some. I get ticked off by that. When I ask him to really give me some he still continues to fake give me some. We go talk to Mr. P, the Headmaster, about it. Clay and I are not buddies anymore after this day.

notes
Clay is five years younger than I am.

quotes
mr. p: "Clay, don't do it again."

Episode 28

title: **OUR PLANS FOR THE END**   air date: **DECEMBER 2005**

summary
The year is drawing to an end. I'm inviting a bunch of guys from school over to my house to celebrate. We are going to count down how much time is left of the year.

notes
I was going to have a party for New Year's Eve but it ended up not happening due to my never arranging it.

Episode 29

title: **THE FUNNIEST MOVIE YET**   air date: **DECEMBER 16, 2005**

summary
In Ms. C's class we watch *Monty Python and the Holy Grail*. It runs throughout second period. Later, I am still laughing at the king cutting off all the knight's limbs.

trivia
Reasons why 2005 was a bad year:
1. Changes
2. Issues
3. Hurricane Katrina and what happened in New Orleans
4. Danny and Matt going away to college

5. Hilary Duff having Joel Madden as her boyfriend
6. Moving to a new house
7. Being ineligible to go to the championship softball game
8. Changing routines
9. A bad dream about Ian being run over and killed by a Blue Bird bus.
10. Issues with the ground saw on the street next to the school making a lot of noise.

thanksgiving special (2005)

title: WHAT IT IS ALL ABOUT   *air date:* **NOVEMBER 24, 2005**

cast:

blaze ginsberg: himself
mom: herself
maya: aunt
lavander: aunt
déja: aunt
bodine (bo): uncle
nana: grandmother
papa: grandfather

guest stars 2005

ryan: déja's boyfriend (now ex)
juan: family friend

summary

We go to Nana and Papa's house. I have written a toast speech about how we are special, and I read it at the table. Everyone is touched by it.

Before Thanksgiving I had a crush on Tina C and hoped she would be my girlfriend, but I found out that she has a boyfriend already. This dilemma gets worked into my speech. I've also been hearing "Eleanor Rigby" in my head a lot lately. I go for a walk to the Ocean Room with Juan and Papa. The Ocean Room is a short walk from Nana and Papa's house. It's really a lounge where you sit and people drink beer and play poker and look at the ocean out the window. I've been going there with Papa and other people since 1991 because it's a quiet place to talk. Later on at dinner I have my homemade soup that Mom made me. For the first time ever, I get to carve the lasagna. I have been dying to do so for a very long time. This goes well. Déja promises to buy me Hilary Duff's *Most Wanted* CD. Later we play Scene It?. That goes on for a while. Bo and I get rather anxious for it to be over because we are both over it and I want to go home. At the end of the day I have a little accident with lemonade. I spill it on the carpet and Déja yells at me to clean it up. But then I get to take out the recycling bottles, which makes me feel better.

quotes
me: "Is 'Eleanor Rigby' a Beatles song?"
juan: "Yes, it is."
(Later on)
papa: "That box goes in the garbage."

notes
This is the first Thanksgiving that features the Ocean Room.

Major Events in 2005
Matt and Danny leave for college.

We move into a new house on June 1.

I begin seriously wanting a girlfriend and a new trio of friends.

I turn eighteen—old enough to bet, buy a lottery ticket, join the army, join clubs (for eighteen or older), vote.

I develop a five-day crush on Tina C.

I learn I cannot date girls any younger than seventeen.

trivia
I kind of knew that "Eleanor Rigby" was a Beatles song, but sometimes I like to check things I know just to make sure.

My Thanksgiving Speech
We are thankful to be together. We may look for the right person
to be boyfriend and girlfriend with. And even though they are
already together with someone else, they don't have what we have:
togetherness. God has blessed us with this family, and we may not find
the right person but we will always be blessed with what we have. We
shall cherish these days that we have with each other.

games 3 (2006)

cast:

See Cast, *Games Season 1*

guest stars

diva: friend
jenny: good friend
I met Jenny at Surrey in March 2005, but she was originally my neighbor when we were kids. Jenny is younger than I am by four years, and I think she is very cute. Early on after we got reunited at Surrey, her attitude toward me was similar to Courtney's (calling my name a lot and wanting me to give her a hug), but not nearly as wild. One day in 2006 when she was having a crying case, she wanted me to talk to her about it. She claims we had an incident when she was very small at the pool where she splashed me and she was just joking around; I told her baby-sitter that she was being mean and her baby-sitter made her sit in time out for a very long time.

jenny trivia:
Dyed her hair blonde, then a whitish color, then red, now back to blonde.

She is adopted.

She has a lot of friends.

She dated Andrew at Surrey until early 2006.

She also liked that I liked trash trucks and in 2006 she started liking them with me.

Episode List
Episode 12 .... Season 3

title: **THE GREAT BUST**   air date: **JANUARY 13, 2006**

summary
It's the premiere of Season 3 (the third and final season). Diva, another senior, has started attending the games as well. Diva and I have had a complicated friendship. I've known her since summer 2002. She used to butt into my affairs with Courtney even though we (Courtney and I) weren't dating. Later we became friendly and now we talk.

The bus that Long replaced his previous one with (that I had not wanted to ride on) unfortunately I now have to ride on, but it's not that bad. We go to the Carmel Valley Rec Center. Osborne, the driver, is extremely late to pick us up due to a time confusion that messes up the day completely. Everything is out of order. That causes me to be grouchy, and I start ruining other students' good moods by yelling at them.

notes
This is some way for the final season of *Games* to kick off.

This was the only appearance of Osborne.

quotes
diva (tired of standing around and waiting for the bus): "Let's start walking."

Episode 13

title: **TAKE 2**   air date: **JANUARY 17, 2006**

summary
We go to Carmel Valley Rec Center again. However, this time things are way better than they were the last time around. Long is back and he doesn't even leave while we are at the game.

quotes
me (pretending to sub for coach): "Coach couldn't make it because his nephew is sick. Stay in your seat while the bus is moving and don't leave any trash on the floor. We're ready to go, Long."
long (laughs and starts bus): "Ha, ha."

goofs
On the way to McDonald's, there was a forklift driving backward on the road.

Episode 14

title: **IT'S ON**   air date: **JANUARY 27, 2006**

---

summary
There was a bye (see trivia) originally scheduled for today but the game happened anyway. There is a new driver for the games, Tammy, who I've known since freshman year. She's nice and not strict.

I have to borrow money from Coach when we go to lunch due to my thinking that the game was off. I borrow six dollars and I buy french fries and a soda.

notes
This is the first appearance of driver Tammy.

trivia
A bye is when you have a day off from a game because there is nobody to play against.

goofs
Tammy accidentally locked herself out of the bus.

soundtrack listing
"Jump Around" by House of Pain (*House of Pain* 1992)

Episode 15

title: **THE STEIN BOYS**   air date: **FEBRUARY 3, 2006**

---

summary
We go to Stein and on the ride there I sit next to Laura who is Ben B's (also known as "Ben Squared" because he was the second Ben to come to economics class) younger sister. When we're at Stein I go swing with some girls on the swing set. Later on into the day an autistic kid throws a fit the size of the Empire State Building. Tammy is the driver and

she is a little late to pick us up, and I get a bit angry and yell at Joseph, another schoolmate, while we are waiting.

quotes
coach: "Hey, she's only a couple of minutes late."

Episode 16

title: **MORE DISAPPOINTMENT**   air date: **FEBRUARY 10, 2006**

summary
Today we go to a gym next to where Shawn Nelson, a crazy guy, stole a tank in 1995 and drove it all around until the police shot and killed him. Long is back to drive us; he hasn't done so in a while. He backs up over and over again as expected by me. I expect this because of the small size of the parking space he is trying to get into. On the way to the bathrooms, I have a conversation with Diva about her mother. We lose again; it's the fifth time in a row. On the bright side, we get to see Long back up four times.

notes
I learned about Shawn Nelson by watching *World's Wildest Police Videos*, which was one of my favorite shows for a while.

quotes
me: "Is your mom mean?"
diva: "No, she just gets unreasonable."

goofs
Diva walked all over the field looking for a bathroom.

soundtrack listing
"As If You Read My Mind" by Stevie Wonder (*Hotter Than July* 1980)

Episode 17

title: **IT'S TODAY**   air date: **FEBRUARY 23, 2006**

summary
The game is today and I have to borrow money from Coach because it is again unexpected and I thought it was supposed to be on Friday. At the game, I talk to my friend Nolan about Grand Theft Auto and PlayStation 1.

notes
Long is driving bus number 17, which he has been driving since episode 13 of Season 3.

quotes
me: "Don't you just hate Grand Theft Auto and PS1?"
nolan: "Yes."
me: "Why?"
nolan: "The graphics are no good."

Episode 18

title: **THE SO-CALLED GAME**   air date: **MARCH 10, 2006**

summary
We try to go to a game and we get to the school where it is supposed to be, but there is nobody there due to the school not bothering to tell Coach that they moved. Chris tries to get me to think of a place to go instead of the game but I can't. I let this really ruin my day and don't stop moaning on about it.

notes
This was my last ride on bus number 17, the bus Long used to replace his previous one.

quotes
chris (chanting): "Think Blaze, think Blaze, think Blaze."
diva (chanting): "Shut up Chris, shut up Chris, shut up Chris."

goofs
The whole day was a goof. We didn't even get off the bus at the school.

Episode 19

---

title: **WE PLAY THEM**   air date: **MARCH 24, 2006**

---

summary

It's the first softball game of the season. We go to Stein but once again, same as last year on this day, the bus we take (number 33) is too small to fit us all, so we have to switch buses (transferring to number 1932). This is the day when Clark starts saying, "I don't want poison" all the time. I don't know what he means by this, but I get a kick out of it and laugh every time he says it.

notes

This was the only appearance of driver Jesus.

This was the last episode filmed at Stein.

quotes

coach (talking to jesus): "Are you sure about this?"
jesus: "This is the bus they told me to bring."

Episode 20

---

title: **THE GREAT SURREY MELTING POT**   air date: **MARCH 31, 2006**

---

summary

Almost the entire school goes to the game at the Carmel Valley Rec Center, except for Lower School (sixth through eighth grades). It takes only two buses to get everyone there. Long and Tammy are the drivers. I am on number 1933, Tammy's bus. It starts to rain during the game and we have to use a cover over the bleachers. I am not particularly comfortable in the rain.

notes

This is driver Tammy's final appearance. It was also the only time we take two buses.

quotes

me: "Can First Student buses go into Carmel Valley to chauffer kids to school?"
tammy: "No."

trivia

First Student is a private school bus company.

I have always had fantasies of having a private chauffeur.

Episode 21

title: **TRUE FEELINGS**   air date: **APRIL 7, 2006**

---

summary

We go to the Point Loma Field and before we leave I talk with Long and learn something about him. Later on, when we are there, I talk with Jenny about how I don't like outings on cloudy days. Aside from this, the team that we are supposed to play against doesn't show up. We play against ourselves. We win. We also lose.

notes

Ryan C stood up for me when two other kids were picking on me.

quotes

me: "Is your father still alive?"
long: "No."
me: "When did he die?"
long: "Fifteen years ago."
me: "I never met my father."

Episode 22

title: **SO WE MEET**   air date: **APRIL 21, 2006**

---

summary

We go to the Carmel Valley Rec Center and a while into our stay I say some bad things about a teacher to another student who then also says some things. My friend Greg threatens to rat on me when he overhears. But he is just kidding. We make up. A little while after that I hear a trash truck, and when I see it I notice it belongs to the company Pacific. It makes funny squeaking noises, like a bird, and I think about that for the rest of the day.

notes
This is Long's final appearance in the series.

quotes
me (crying on jenny's shoulder): "I hate Greg."
jenny (hugging me): "It's okay, best friend."

trivia
Jenny calls me "best friend" a lot.

goofs
The bus did not start when we were trying to leave McDonald's and made a loud grinding noise.

soundtrack listing
"Rebel Rebel" by David Bowie (*Diamond Dogs* 1974)

Episode 23

title: **WHAT'S WRONG WITH THE GAME, MAMA? PEOPLE ACTING LIKE THEY DON'T KNOW HOW IT RUNS, MAMA**   air date: **APRIL 28, 2006**

summary
There is a new bus driver, Althea. She goes through the emergency procedures with us before we leave. It's a cloudy day. We go to a field downtown. I see some trash trucks because it is trash day on the street outside the field. I have been thinking endlessly about *Sleeping Beauty*, especially the crying scenes, because I had watched it the night before after taking it out of a packed box in the garage. I see Allison (my imaginary future college girlfriend) acting out those scenes. I think about fairy tales to write and jot down some plot lines I have in my head. One storyline I have is that a princess has to go live with three fairies because it's not safe in her real home when Germany calls for war against her father the king. Another idea is that a princess cries when her plan gets ruined. Even though Sleeping Beauty is an animated character, I am virtually crushed over her. But I keep this to myself because I don't want people to tease me about watching a cartoon movie, especially a girl's cartoon movie.

notes

This is the first appearance of bus driver Althea. This is the last time trash trucks are seen in this series.

The umpire messes up the timing, causing the game to be longer than it was supposed to be.

quotes

me: "Hey Coach, is this game going to be over soon?"
coach: "I don't know when it's going to be over!"

goofs

One trash truck, number 815182, has an engine that screeches whenever it moves from house to house.

trivia

The title of this episode is taken from The Black Eyed Peas song, "What's Wrong with the World, Mama? People Acting Like They Ain't Got No Mama."

Biography for Princess Aurora
by Blaze Ginsberg

date of birth: june 16, 1977, manchester, england, uk
birth name: aurora
nickname: sleeping beauty

Mini Biography

Princess Aurora (Briar Rose) was born to her father King Stefan and her mother Queen Stephani. Maleficent the wicked witch put a spell on her when she was one day old. The three good fairies were sworn to protect her. Before all that she was engaged to Prince Phillip. When she was ten she once fell into a well and fell asleep for two hours. This reminded the fairies that this was only a penalty shot. In six years, she will fall under the real spell. When she was twelve, her favorite pet rabbit she got when she was nine passed away. She did not know how to deal with death. She was taught when something dies it never returns. She was heartbroken by this news.

In 1993 on her sixteenth birthday she would be leaving them forever. Fairy Fauna wanted to bake her cake for her. On that day she met the young man she was engaged to since the day she was born, not knowing it was him. When she told the fairies about this she was banned from seeing him again. She broke down crying about it. This was the second time in four years the fairies had seen Rose cry. When it was time for her to return to the kingdom, she broke down crying a second time. This put the fairies in a very unique position. She has been engaged to Prince Phillip since she was five minutes old and now she has met someone else. Only nine out of sixteen years that she has been alive has she has been talking. And in her sixteen years, she has only cried three times. Then she fell under her deep sleep. Prince Phillip came to her rescue. They were married a week later. They lived happily ever after for twelve years. In 2005, they got a nasty divorce when Aurora started taking Henry VIII as an example for ruling a country. She had an affair with a sixteen-year-old boy. As of then to now she lives as a single queen.

spouse: prince phillip
trademark: sleeping and singing opera
personal quotes: "i was glad i experienced love on first sight with phillip; had i not been attracted to him lord only knows what could have happened to me."

soundtrack listing

"What's Wrong with the World, Mama?" by The Black Eyed Peas (*Monkey Business* 2005)

"Speed of Sound" by Coldplay (*XY* 2005)

"Young Americans" by David Bowie (*Young Americans* 1975)

Episode 24

title: NOT THE BEST DAY   air date: **MAY 5, 2006**

summary
We go to Carmel Valley Rec Center. I don't have a killer time. I am a bit out of it, as in a somewhat off mood. Chemicals did not align with me and this day.

notes
This was my last game visit to Carmel Valley Rec Center.

goofs
Althea drove through the entire parking lot instead of just backing up and turning around.

Episode 25

title: WHEN THIS BUS MEETS WORLD   air date: MAY 12, 2006

summary
We go downtown to a field, and before we leave I bring up the show *Full House* to my friend Taylor. A little while into the day Ryan C meditates by sitting under a tree with his legs crossed and his fingers in circles. I do the same for about fifteen minutes on a bench. Then some of my friends hang out with different people from somewhere, not our school.

quotes
taylor: *"Full House* is the best show ever."
lenny: "Candace Cameron's hair got all short."

goofs
We got locked out of the bus and Althea had to go to the emergency exit to let us in.

Episode 26

title: PARTING IS SUCH SWEET SORROW   air date: MAY 26, 2006

summary
We go to Point Loma, and it's the championship game and the series finale. I will be graduating next month and won't be coming anymore. I do enjoy it a little less for that reason, but I talk with Althea while we are there and ask her what happened to Long. She explains that he was transferred to San Diego Unified School District.

notes
This was the last episode of the series to be made. I will miss it much.

Coach interviews me later on at the school.

I had not wanted this to be the last game I would go to. I had wanted there to be one more, but it didn't work out. This was the most fun event to ever be had during my days at Surrey because it had two things I really loved: taking the bus and having someone waiting for me (the bus driver) while I'm doing my thing.

quotes

coach: "You've changed; you're not all anxious asking 'Where's the bus?'" (Points a pen to my mouth like a microphone)

me (talking into microphone, a.k.a. pen): "I'm glad I got to do this for two years. I'm going to miss this even though given time I'm going to forget about it. My bus is here. Have a great three-day weekend. It's in syndication."

(Later)

coach: "That's a good word—'in syndication.'"

althea: "My daughter's a week younger than you."

me: "She is?"

althea: "Yes, but she already has a boyfriend."

senior year 2 (2006)

(a.k.a. Pre-Adult World Life Days 2)

cast

See Cast, *Senior Year 1*

Episode List

Episode 30   Season 2

title: CRAZINESS   air date: **JANUARY 3, 2006**

summary

It's the beginning of Season 2. I get on the morning bus to school.
Jenny is with me. I see what I think is the trash truck as we are passing
by. But then when we arrive at school it turns out it was recycling. The
trucks look exactly alike. I report into class and everything is running
on a smooth basis. There is a new female TA named Alex. Later on
when I am in the bathroom I hear the recycling truck. I see it briefly.
This is an okay day until I get home and the driver slows down to a
crawl because the recycling is blocking where she usually pulls in. I get
out and alert the guy that she is behind him. Later I go out with Déja.

notes
The recycling truck was established early on as a theme of this series.

goofs
I got weirded out by having to see the Dumpster empty from right next to the truck.

soundtrack listing
"The Gift" by Annie Lennox (*Diva* 1992)
Annie Lennox and her album *Diva* and my senior year are an association in my mind.

Episode 31

title: **THE SECOND TUESDAY**   air date: **JANUARY 10, 2006**

summary
It's the second Tuesday of school in Season 2. I go to school and I see a different recycling truck on the street picking up the recyclables. When I see it I also hear it screeching. Then much later at home the garbage has not come yet. I do my homework, then it comes. I pause to watch it.

notes
This is the first and only time the garbage was late.

trivia
When the garbage and recycling trucks come, I pull up a chair and sit by the window to watch. Mom calls this my *"Cat in the Hat* pose" after the kids in the book who sat in their chairs watching the rainy day before the Cat in the Hat showed up.

quotes
me: "The garbage hasn't come yet."
mom: "That's not good. It better come or else the garbage is going to overflow."
(Later)
me: "The garbage is here."
mom: "Fine, but after it leaves you have to get back on the homework."

Episode 32

title: **LOOKING FORWARD TO THE GAMES**   air date: **JANUARY 12, 2006**

summary

It is the day before the school basketball game field trips begin. I am very exited. Also, today is the first day I start working with Brian S, a new TA, in math class. He is a very cool guy. We play hangman and do math as we go.

notes

Brian was born in 1981. He is six years older than I am. He always quotes *Napoleon Dynamite:* "Uugh friggen idiot gosh."

Episode 33

title: **THE HIGH SCHOOL EXIT EXAM**   air date: **FEBRUARY 7, 2006**

summary

It's the first day of testing for the California High School Exit Exam. I have to pass this exam in order to graduate and get my diploma. I've taken it twice and have not passed either time. This is my second-to-last chance to pass. I'm with the backup speech therapist who fills in when Ms. Kennedy is not around. When I get to the description essay part I try to describe something I saw on *Full House*. But I end up replacing that with an essay I call "Welcome to San Francisco" about San Francisco. In PE I see the type of bus I've been wanting to see since the first day of school: a Flxible bus number 918.

notes

There was originally a confusion over which section of the exam I was supposed to be taking.

trivia

In my essay, I write that there is a sign on the Golden Gate Bridge that guides you into San Francisco.

I've looked up Flxible buses on the Internet and have learned that they are pronounced *Flexible* but are not spelled that way. The company that made these buses was around from 1915 to 1996. The 900 series buses are 1992 models.

quotes

jane: "We're supposed to be doing math today."
me: "No, we're doing English."
me (about my description essay): "This exhibit will be coming in 1993."
backup speech therapist: "But 1993 is over. You can say it will be coming in 2006."

Episode 34

title: **THE NEXT TEST**   air date: **FEBRUARY 8, 2006**

summary

Now it's onto the math portion of the High School Exit exam. Ms. Kennedy and her assistant switch off as we go. The math section goes nicely. I do enjoy working with the ladies.

notes

I passed both sections of the High School Exit Exam.

trivia

On April 21, Mr. Kent came into my first period class and announced, "Blaze has passed the High School Exit Exam!" Ms. Kennedy hugged me and people in the class cheered, "All right, Blaze!" That was a pretty happy moment.

As a reward for passing the exam I got a CD player.

Episode 35

title: **ALEX COMES TO GROUP**   air date: **FEBRUARY 2006**

summary

A classmate named Alex is being added to Group because we need to have more group members to talk about stuff. However, early on in the session it is a little chaotic when an argument occurs with a lot of yelling. Mostly it's between Cliff and Clark, but I throw a few words in. Alex helps it out by yelling at us to be quiet, ending the commotion. We talk about stuff that has gone on in our lives.

notes
From this day on I sit with Alex at lunch every day after I get off work.

quotes
ian: "Boys, stop it."
alex: "I have an older sister and a younger brother. My little brother is incredibly annoying."
me: "I'm an only child. I always wanted a sister five years younger than I am."

Episode 36

title: **VALENTINE'S BLUES**   air date: **FEBRUARY 14, 2006**

---

summary
On the morning bus, Jenny, Patrick, and I all talk about who our valentines are. They still think that Tina C is my valentine. Tina, unfortunately, cannot be my valentine due to her already having a boyfriend. Jenny and Patrick do not have valentines either.

notes
Jenny did not know that Tina C had a boyfriend.

Episode 37

title: **THE WORST DAY EVER (MY SENIOR YEAR IS A CURSE)**
air date: **FEBRUARY 21, 2006**

---

summary
My day starts off fine. I get onto my morning bus and talk with Jenny. I learn that her younger brother tried to eat a poisonous plant on a camping trip back when she was ten. Apparently she took it from him and he started hating her. I see the recycling truck has already picked up the recyclables on the street by Surrey. I have a hard time with the algebra problems in math class. In PE I am not able to see any trash or recycling trucks and the bus I flipped off, number 1103, passes through again. When I go home it only gets worse. The recycling and garbage trucks have both come already. I am, however, looking forward to Ass Bread Night. When my afternoon bus driver

drops me off, Maya is pulling out of the garage and tells me it might get canceled. To my utter dismay, it does get canceled because Déja has broken up with her boyfriend for the second time in two years and is too upset to go out. I feel my day is going as badly as Kurt Cobain's life. Déja is going to bring Nana to the house to hang out as a replacement plan, but I am an asshole about this and it doesn't happen. I go in my room and cry about the stuff around me and not being able to handle things.

notes
This episode features me really having a negative attitude toward my senior year.

Changing of plans is very difficult for me to accept.

soundtrack listing
"Smells Like Teen Spirit" by Nirvana (*Nevermind* 1991)

"Mary Jane" by Alanis Morissette (*Jagged Little Pill* 1995)

Episode 38

title: **THE FIRST FUN DAY EVENTS**   air date: **FEBRUARY 26, 2006**

summary
Yesterday I had my first real driving lesson with Gabe. We drove around the lot of Torrey Pines High School. It was a little bit nerve-racking but fun. Today's a Sunday—a big fun day at school on the field. I am going with Mom and Gabe. It's sunny. However it is very hot. The theme is "Save Surrey" because the land the school is on is for sale and we are trying to raise money to keep the school where it is. There are barbeques and iced teas, but I decide to buy myself a soda. Later, Ryan C meets Mom and Gabe. I do see Jenny later, as expected, and as hoped, Tina C arrives. She gives me a huge hug and digs her nails into my back while she does it. But nonetheless I am still happy to see her. She meets Mom and Gabe as well and then Ryan performs with the school band.

notes
This was the first time I had seen Tina C since Season 1.

quotes
(during driving lesson)
gabe (repeated line): "Start straightening up, start straightening up!"
me (repeated line): "I'm trying, I'm trying!"

Episode 39

title: **THE VANISHING TRASH TRUCK**   air date: **FEBRUARY 28, 2006**

summary

It's Tuesday again, but this week everything is different from the way it was last Tuesday. A week later, everything is different. I get to see the trash truck on the street outside Surrey a while after I get to school. Jenny alerts me that it is present. Later, when I am alone it backs into one street and vanishes. That causes me to be looking all over for it. I start thinking that the police will be here shortly to investigate. Finally, after about twenty minutes, it reappears. I watch it as it makes its rounds over the three streets surrounding Surrey. This period I have Tutorial and am supposed to be in the auditorium, but today is a day when I can pretty much get away with murder because there is a substitute supervising Tutorial and she is a soft pillow. Today is also Maya's birthday, so obviously there will be no Ass Bread Night because she wants to celebrate her birthday at home. I am prepared for the change of routine this week, so I'm not thrown off. Plus, there will be cake for Maya's birthday.

To my great surprise the recycling has not come yet when I get home. I feel like I may have made this happen with the power of my mind because of wanting it so badly. I sit around all day waiting for it to arrive. It doesn't arrive at all. Perhaps my powers are too strong. Then at Maya's birthday party, Lavander brings balloons. This is a problem because I am having a big issue with balloons lately because of the fact that they pop loudly. Balloons can pop for no reason and can pop unexpectedly, and I am now constantly worried that the same kind of unspecified popping can happen again. Maya takes the balloons to her room. Papa and I go take a walk to the liquor-deli for chocolate. It's about seven or eight and the recycling still has not come yet. Papa and I talk about it. Later everyone goes home and the recycling truck never shows up. It is a mystery.

notes

The recycling did not show up till the next morning.

Episode 40

title: **A SATIRICAL DIFFERENCE**   air date: **MARCH 2006**

summary

Ms. C has been filling in for Mrs. L-D, who has been out due to a lot of personal problems occurring at home. We are reading material by Jonathan Swift. Today it is "A Modest Proposal." This satire that Ms. C reads to us takes place around the time Jonathan Swift himself was around. In the satire, Swift suggests that parents eat their one-year-old babies for food if they're too poor. Ms. C starts joking around by saying she should do this to her baby, Casey, and I get somewhat restless. Our assignment is to write our own modest proposal. I get started but my writing does not exactly meet demand. I think this is because I don't fully understand what satire means. I work on it with Maya over the weekend while Nana hangs around our house.

notes

This is the first episode where Ms. C's jokes affect me.

Mom is in New York for book business, so I work with Maya on my homework.

trivia

My satire was basically about air pollution and that you should go to jail because of sunburn.

Episode 41

title: **THE CONSEQUENCES**   air date: **MARCH 2006**

summary

At the end of break one day Justin is playing with a Ping-Pong ball. It hits me. I squash it flat. Ms. K hears about this and tells me that I have to replace it. Now, in addition to my homework, this is something else I have to worry about over the weekend unless I can talk Ian into going with me to buy a new one today. (I can usually talk Ian into anything.)

We get into Ian's C280 1995 Mercedes Benz. First we stop at Long's Drugs: no luck. Then off to Big Five. Here we're in luck. We buy a box of Ping-Pong balls. Ian pays but I will have to give him the money back. We then go back to school. Later, Brian S (the TA), not knowing that it has already been replaced, gives me another Ping-Pong ball. I explain that I have already replaced it.

notes

On the way to Long's Drugs there is a Bobcat tractor that beeps when it backs up. All the new Bobcats have beepers.

trivia

Bobcats are small white tractors. The old models had a picture of a bobcat as its logo next to the word *BOBCAT*. When I was about five years old, I would see Bobcats often. One day one was following me from behind when I took a walk with Mom. In 1997 a construction worker at school allowed me to sit in a Bobcat and play with the controls (while it was off). In 1998 Mom took me to the Bobcat garage on Miramar Road and I got a scale model of a Bobcat model number 753.

Episode 42

title: **FIELD DAY (Cleaning Up The School)**	air date: **MARCH 2006**

summary

It is Field Day. I go around helping people do certain stuff, like carrying dirt. I go back and forth on the field quite a bit with the dirt. There is a minor confusion when I am told to meet with Jane, but then it turns out I am not supposed to just go by myself. I am supposed to wait for her. Later it's time for math class. Prem brings up an inappropriate issue about something that happened before the school year started, something to do with a sexual something. He gets sent out of class. After, he tries to renegotiate it and he manages to escape punishment. However, he did have to discuss the issue with the Dean. Later on its time for work and that goes smoothly.

notes

I have gotten in trouble once for saying inappropriate things (during my sophomore year). This is the only time during high school where this has happened.

quotes
math teacher: "I'm sorry Prem, but I have to send you out."
prem: "No, please don't."

Episode 43

title: **BOO ON JANE** air date: **MARCH 2006**

---

summary
English is in the auditorium today. I see the trash truck arriving. I figure out the mystery of its vanishing (see notes). Later on a bad fight occurs between me and Jane. We are in the teacher's lounge and I look at a piece of paper on the table, which is personal (meaning I'm not supposed to look at it). It's about an MS Walk to raise money because Cliff's mother died from MS. Jane pulls me away from the note; then I fire back at her and turn into an asshole and OT gets canceled. I go watch the trash truck.

notes
The disappearance of the trash truck was that it pulled over to the far side of the road and I could not see it from where I was sitting in Tutorial.

quotes
jane: "I'm sorry for pulling you."
me (furiously): "Apology not accepted."

Episode 44

title: **THE GROUND SAW'S REAPPEARANCE** air date: **MARCH 2006**

---

summary
I am working on math with Brian S. We are having a good conversation until I hear what I think is the ground saw. I rush up to go see it. I have connected the appearance of the ground saw with last year being bad because I feel very uncomfortable with that whirring sound. I hope this won't affect how good the year will be.

notes
On March 14, 2005, I saw the ground saw for the first time. Exactly a year later I see it again.

Episode 45

title: **DÉJA'S BIG PLAY IN VISTA, THE DEPRESSION DUMP HOLE**
air date: **MAY 2006**

summary

Déja is in a play in Vista today. The schedule is as follows: We are going to pick up our family friend Juan, who lives not far from the theater, and then we are going to head to the play. Early in the morning Mom calls Gabe, who does not answer his phone. Later we find out that Gabe didn't answer because he had to talk to the police about a problem with his neighbor, who beats up his wife and kids and mother. Later on, we leave and I am still thinking about Gabe's neighbor. When we arrive in Vista there are a lot of buses. Even one short bus from the 2100 series, which I do not like very much. We then arrive at Juan's house and pick him up, after which we stop at Panera for cake and coffee. I get in and out of the car to look at the buses until Juan decides to show me the transit station, which is very close by. Finally, it's off to Déja's play, *The Women*. It's fine, but not the best play I've seen her in. It's not really my thing.

quotes

juan (explaining how the buses work): "They have a schedule to follow."
me (when I think the driver of one of the parked buses is going to restart it): "You're going to want to cover your ears; she's going to start it."
juan (to the driver): "Good evening Ma'am." (She doesn't answer; just gets her coat out of the driver's seat).
juan: "I try to catch the 10 o'clock bus in the morning. If I don't make it, I have to catch one of these [the 2100 series], and they can only fit twenty-six passengers."
(The parked bus we were just looking at starts up)

notes

Vista was incredibly depressing. (My brain was kind of muddled thinking about Gabe's violent neighbor, so perhaps that was why I found Vista depressing.)

I hoped to see a Flxible bus because there were so many buses there. This episode is not like any of the others because it is the only episode to take place in Vista.

trivia
Vista is about 35 miles northeast of where we live.

Episode 46

title: **MATT AND DANNY'S VISIT**   air date: **MARCH 27, 2006**

---

summary
Matt and Danny are coming today for a visit. Both of them are on the East Coast for college and are now on spring break. I take a VTO from math class when I see Danny and Matt. We get briefly reunited. I even introduce Prem to them. Later I report to work, then after that I sit down and have lunch with them. Clark gets reunited with them as well. Then I have a running competition with Matt to see who can run down the field ramp fastest. Then it's back to class with me. I do however get sent out. I then talk to Jenny about my anger at Matt and Danny for leaving. Later, Matt and Danny come over to my house.

notes
On this day Matt starts to agree with me that fiscal policy is the cause of us not being together anymore. *Fiscal policy* means something about what people can spend and what jobs they have to do and where they work, and my theory is that this is the reason Matt and Danny have to end up on the other side of the country. I call this the fiscal draft. This is the first time we have been together since they left for college. We play some Grand Theft Auto, have tea, and then they leave.

quotes
me: "I am mad at them for leaving."
jenny: "Are they your brothers?"
me: "No."

Episode 47

title: **HOW I FEEL**   air date: **APRIL 2006**

---

summary
I have been having a very bad day. At work I talk to Quentin about how badly I want friends, but he's no help. He tells me that it's a bad

idea to make friends right before you graduate because then you leave them behind right away. It gets no better in Group. Clark wants to take a walk and I don't. A commotion occurs between the two of us and I get mad. I start hating my senior year a lot. Ian talks with me about it. Later on, when it's time for me to go to work, I'm still miserable about not finding a new trio of friends. When I get the food ready for lunch, Mr. K sees me and wants to know why I am in such a bad mood.

notes
This episode really showed me missing Matt and Danny and hating my senior year.

quotes
quentin: "If you meet new friends before you graduate you're a loser."
mr. k: "Everything was so good, Blaze. Now it's bad. What happened?"

Episode 48

title: **COLLEGE HUNTING**   air date: **APRIL 2006**

summary
On the morning bus I get into a little standoff with Patrick. He keeps telling me to shut up and I keep saying no. Later I take a ride with Ian to the Vista View campus. When we arrive there we talk about all the courses I can take. We walk around the campus and stop in at the bookstore. I buy a pack of bubble gum with my twenty. We then move to the lounge and talk about how I want to meet a girlfriend. We decide her birthday should be December 1987 and call that our password. We continue our hunt around the campus and pop into a classroom. We go to the library and look in the lab. I get scared of fire drills happening. After we leave that campus we go to Carl's Jr. and get lunch. I talk about how I will be when I am twenty-three. I plan to be pimpin' (like the average male). We return to the school. I chat with my schoolmates about how I am leaving in two months.

notes
Eleven months later, our password takes effect. Ashley in my film class was born in December 1987. And it seems as if she likes me because she calls me "sweetie" and "babe."

quotes

ian: "You can take all kinds of courses."
me: "Will they have fire drills?"
ian: "I honestly don't know, man."

soundtrack listing

"Love Just Is" by Hilary Duff (*Metamorphosis* 2003)

"Fragile" by Sting (*Nothing Like the Sun* 1987)

Episode 49

title: **THE REPLACEMENT RECYCLING TRUCK** air date: **APRIL 2006**

---

summary

One morning I am hanging around with Jenny and her friends when I hear a different recycling truck pick up the recyclables in the neighborhood outside the school.

notes

This episode airs because the recycling truck is an ongoing theme for the series.

Episode 50

title: **LARRY G TO THE GROUP** air date: **APRIL 2006**

---

summary

We add another member to Group, my friend Larry G. We talk about our lives and get to know him. I do not remember what I learned about him.

quotes

ian: "Let's welcome Larry to Group.
me: "I've been going to the games with Larry. It's nice to have you here, Larry."

Episode 51

title: **I CAN'T WAIT**   air date: **APRIL 2006**

summary
During a homework-gone-bad night I get really upset with my senior year and get really anxious for it to be over. It's Ass Bread Night, but I am still somewhat miserable about my senior year when we go.

notes
This was the last Ass Bread Night of the series. My senior year is taking forever to end.

quotes
me: "Why is my senior year not over? I hate it."
maya: "Oh, please."

soundtrack listing
"Learn to Be Still" by The Eagles (*Hell Freezes Over* 1994)

Episode 52

title: **THE DEVIL IS BACK**   air date: **MAY 2006**

summary
At lunch, I sit down with Natalie, a sensitive girl in my math class, and her friend Preston. I talk with him. When I hear the ground saw I rush over to see it. There are two guys operating it. I hear it in my head for the rest of the day.

notes
This is the second appearance of the ground saw in the series.

trivia
Preston, Natalie's friend, is a year older than she is.

goofs
The ground saw spits out some liquid.

Episode 53

title: **MY AUNT IS MY TREAT TO THE SCHOOL**   air date: **MAY 2006**

summary
Maya and her piano quartet are coming to play at the school. Before they arrive I watch the garbage truck in the neighborhood outside the school. It's a different truck than it usually is. Later, after that is done, I go sit down and watch the performance, which is good. Later on at work a major commotion erupts when a lot of customers order taquitos. I throw a tantrum about it. I get out of work early today.

notes
I missed my junior year a lot in this episode because it seemed like my junior year was a lot easier and everyone was a lot cooler.

trivia
I have a problem when a lot of customers order the same thing. The pattern really bothers me and I can't deal with it.

soundtrack listing
"Shower the People" by James Taylor (*In the Pocket* 1976)
This song plays because the customers were showering me with the same order over and over.

"Holy, Holy" by Marvin Gaye (*What's Going On* 1971)
This song plays because Marvin Gaye often sings about the hard times of his life, and I kind of feel like my senior year had some pretty hard times in it.

Episode 54

title: **MRS. L-D IS BACK FINALLY**   air date: **MAY 1, 2006**

summary
Mrs. L-D has been out for quite some time. She gives us a really fun project. We have to listen to a song and analyze what it is about. Then later she announces that Grad Night is coming up. I get very excited about it and don't stop thinking about it for the rest of the day. When I get home, I talk to Mom about it and we decide Grad Night is on, but not the prom. So I end up not going to the prom with Jenny like I was originally planning to.

notes

Mrs. L-D's mother died of a heart attack.

Mrs. L-D said that her mom felt like a freight train hit her in the heart.

Mrs. L-D's daughter was the only one around when it occurred and she called for an ambulance.

I was glad Mrs. L-D was back because Ms. C was subbing, and I didn't like having her for two periods. I felt very bad for Mrs. L-D.

soundtrack listing

"We Didn't Start the Fire" by Billy Joel (1989)

"American Pie" by Don Mclean (1971)

Episode 55

title: **THE FUN-FILLED DAY**	air date: **MAY 20, 2006**

summary

It's a carnival of fun-filled events at Surrey. There is cotton candy, a teacher dunk, and of course I will be performing "I Won't Back Down." Ms. C's room is turned into a coffee house. Mom really wants me to see Jenny. Susan C (Tina's and Ryan's mom) and my mom talk about their pregnancies with us. Tina C and I were born seven days apart. Later on the show does happen. Mom and Gabe like my performance very much. Later on it's dunk time. I get to free-dunk Mr. C as payback for sending my friend Natalie out the day before. Later on Tina C arrives. It startles me to see her, even though my crush on her is long over. We talk about my graduation. She has an eye appointment and leaves shortly after that. We leave as well. It's off to Déja's friend's house to celebrate the friend's birthday. There are balloons there. I struggle with it.

notes

Back in mid–Season 1 during a Saturday groove, my balloon phobia debuted. Ever since then I've been afraid of balloons. The balloon phobia was brought on when I was having a conversation with Maya and Nana and suddenly a balloon popped. It was very loud because we were in a small space. I didn't know why the balloon popped.

quotes

déja: "The only reason a balloon pops is because something sharp touches it.

me: "Or it gets melted."

déja: "Right. They [the balloons] have been here for four hours."

soundtrack listing

"Giving You the Best That I Got" by Anita Baker (*Giving You the Best That I Got* 1988)

"Fun, Fun, Fun," by The Beach Boys (*Shut Down, Vol. 2*, 1964)

Episode 56

title: **TALENT SHOW DAY**   air date: **MAY 22, 2006**

summary

On talent show day, I just end up singing "I Won't Back Down" by Tom Petty and the Heartbreakers again. I did not plan in advance at all and it goes well.

notes

This was the second time I sang this particular song at school.

Episode 57

title: **THE WORST FIELD TRIP**   air date: **JUNE 9, 2006**

summary

Mr. C has invited me on his field trip to the Museum of Making Music with his music class. But on the bus ride to school I get into a fight with Patrick and start hating him. Later on, when we go to the museum, Althea (the bus driver) brings the bus I don't like, number 8778. I get really upset about this. At the same time, I'm still mad at Patrick and start acting like Danny Tanner from *Full House*. The field trip is okay. We go into the museum. At first I dislike our tour guide because I'm not crazy about her attitude, but then for a little bit she becomes somewhat hot. We then go to In-N-Out for lunch. I am still a bit mad at Althea for driving number 8778. When we are leaving In-N-Out, Clark and I get the "I don't want poison" gag going. Larry doesn't want to hear it after a while, but Clark and I keep it going until it goes in reverse when Larry wants to do it and Clark doesn't.

notes
I do not like bus number 8778 for these two reasons:
1. It is dark and has a somewhat growly engine.
2. It reminds me of when I read about Hilary Duff and Joel Madden and how he was her boyfriend and not me. I don't know why it reminds me of this.

Number 8778 is a 2004 Thomas Freightliner bus.

I do not see Patrick till after this series is over. He has forgotten about this incident and is nice to me.

The "I don't want poison" gag consists of me and Clark saying, "I don't want poison" over and over again endlessly for no apparent reason.*

quotes
me: "I'm going to have Patrick in jail."
jenny: "Are you mad at Patrick? It's okay."
mr. c: "Hey Clark, can you keep it down?"
clark: "No, I don't want poison."
me: "I don't want poison."
(Later on)
larry: "Mr. C, help!"

soundtrack listing
"You Can't Take Me with You" by Monsoon (*Monsoon featuring Sheila Chandra*, 1995)

"Young Americans" by David Bowie (*Young Americans* 1975)

"Zeroes" by David Bowie (*Never Let Me Down* 1987)

"You're All I Need to Get By" by Marvin Gaye and Tammi Terrell (*You're All I Need* 1967)

trivia
This episode has a long soundtrack listing because it is a very active/busy day.

*SEE *GAMES 3*, EPISODE 19.

Episode 58

title: **THE LAST GROUP**   air date: **JUNE 5, 2006**

summary
It's the last Group day. Larry is out so it's me, Clark, and Cliff. We go for a walk to Fifteenth Street beach. We talk about how nice it is to be in Group with each other. Then we go back to school.

notes
I brought chocolate chip cookies. There was also soda and ice cream brought by Ian, Cliff, and Clark.

trivia
This is the last episode in this series to have any dialogue about buses.

quotes
ian: "Now say one thing nice about each person."
me: "Cliff, I like you for helping me know about the buses and Clark for making me laugh."
cliff: "Clark, you're funny. Blaze, you're unique."

soundtrack listing
"Connected" by Sara Paxton (2006)

Episode 59

title: **MERCURY RECORDS VS. CIRCULATION**   air date: **JUNE 2006**

summary
We are hoping to have one more softball game trip, but that does not pan out. So we decide to have one more softball game at school instead. There are two teams. I make up the team names. My team's name is Mercury Records. The other team is Circulation. The game goes on for a while. Later on after the game there is a barbeque. That goes smoothly.

notes
My team Mercury Records beat Circulation. I named the other team Circulation because I hate air circulation in my bathroom and am blacklisting it.

Episode 60

title: **LAST MEETING WITH IAN**   air date: **JUNE 12, 2006**

summary

I go with Ian to Carl's Jr. We talk about Madonna on the way up there.
We continue talking about it even when we are there. Then later we
leave and a bus follows us. It gets out of hand because everywhere we
go, it goes too. We finally take the Fifteenth Street beach road back to
the school to avoid the bus.

notes

I miss my sessions with Ian a lot. He is an understanding person and
very easy to talk to.

quotes

me: "Did you know Madonna's mother died when she was five years
old?"
ian: "Yes, I did know that. She had a pretty rough life when she was a
kid. Her father was really strict."
(Later)
me: "That bus is as annoying as Kimmy Gibbler from *Full House*.
ian (laughing): I know, man. It's a Gibblermobile!"

soundtrack listing

"Babylon Sisters" by Steely Dan (*Gaucho* 1980)

Episode 61

title: **A LAST FOR EVERYTHING**   air date: **JUNE 14, 2006**

summary

It's the day of Grad Night. At school I am rather excited about going
to Disneyland. I go to lunch with Ms. Kennedy and we talk about
a lot of stuff. I turn to her because I am worried about the stress to
come in my future. After lunch, she drops me off at my house. Later,
I go pick up Matt for Grad Night. We hang at the house for a while
talking about my crush on Tatyana Ali. I pretend to get married to
her. When it's time for Grad Night, we get on the bus. We arrive
in the park, and first we all go on the Haunted House ride and that

works out well. I want to go on the Alice in Wonderland ride, and we try to decide whether or not to split up. We are walking around deciding what to do, and I have the idea that if we get stranded in the Disneyland area, my friend Lucinda and I will get an apartment together and be stuck with each other for the rest of our lives. It is very late at night by then, but I am not very tired yet and things are still in an orderly form.

Things start to go downhill rapidly when we make an attempt to go on the Space Mountain ride, but there is a very long wait to the line. Then instead of waiting to go on rides, certain people decide that they want to eat (Clark) and other people need to go to the bathroom (Danny). I start to get frustrated because it is difficult to control the whole group and everybody wants something different. I end up in a fight with Clark, then I kick a trash can, and I'm not positive but I might have said something vulgar to the group. In my anger I call Disneyland the worst theme park ever.

Sometime after the second ride on Star Tours, I start feeling very sleepy like I can't keep my eyes open. The night has fallen apart enough that I decide to boycott Disneyland forever. It has become my ex-favorite theme park. Part of what happens when I am so tired is that I start to feel depression around me. Being up so late, wandering around, and arguing with my friends messes up my mind and makes me want to repeat stress and problems that I had in the past, which is crazy because why would anyone want to repeat stress and problems? I am incredibly overwhelmed, a natural reaction to Disneyland at night.

This night messes up all my plans. I thought I was going back to my junior year (which was a good year—everything nice and familiar), but instead I am going farther back than that to the summer of my freshman year when everything was a new experience, unfamiliar and strange. At the end of the night we walk to the bus. It is after five o'clock in the morning and the sun is rising. It is a twenty-minute hike back to the bus, where we wait for almost an hour for everyone else to show up so we can leave. I can't wait to get out of the park. Later on, back on the bus, the stress I had wanted to avoid I want now to re-live. My mind is so screwed up.

notes

I invited Matt to come be my guest at Grad Night. He missed his own Grad Night at Surrey the year before, so he was really excited about it.

Burt was our bus driver. The bus was number 1933

Number 1933 is a 1992 Blue Bird/International bus.

I fell asleep on the bus ride home.

goofs

When we tried to leave and Burt tried to start the bus, it didn't start and sounded exactly like a car blowing up in Grand Theft Auto: San Andreas.

Lucinda fell off her seat when the bus stopped suddenly on the freeway.

Episode 62

title: **GRADUATION**   air date: **JUNE 16, 2006**

summary

It's the last day of school in my senior year, so it's the last day of high school altogether. It's a short day. I pick up a yearbook and all my friends sign it. Later on, my friend and I do a countdown till the end of the school year. My friends will miss me a lot. I ring the bell. In the evening, it's time for the ceremony. I wear my new suit that Mom and Gabe bought for me. Ms. K announces me and is in tears when I go to pick up my diploma. We have a big party at my house afterward. Everyone gives me gifts. I am pretty happy about all of this.

notes

My friend Natalie signed in my yearbook that she thought it was funny the way I always quoted *Napoleon Dynamite*.

There was a big party at home with mini-cupcakes, and Danny appeared there briefly.

quotes

tina c: "How are you doing, nice young man?"
(We hug)
(During the ceremony)
ms. k (in tears): "I'm glad to congratulate Blaze Ginsberg."
(We hug)

(Later)

me: "Want to meet my uncle? This is Tina C."

bo: "Oh, hello, Tina C."

tina c: "Very nice to meet you."

déja: "I was just so proud of you."

soundtrack listing

"Mandolin Rain" by Bruce Hornsby (*The Way It Is*, 1986)

"How Sweet It Is" by James Taylor (*Gorilla*, 1975)

"Changes" by David Bowie (*Hunky Dory*, 1971)

vista view college days 1 (2006)

series: **2006–**

genre: **GROWNUP WORLD LIFE**

release date: **AUGUST 21, 2006**

status: **CONTINUING**

cast:

blaze ginsberg: himself

ms. g: english professor (2006)
Ms. G was maybe one of my worst teachers since kindergarten. From the first day of class, she gave me a hard time and never believed that I was doing my own work. Also, she did not smell so nice.

linda: yoga teacher (2006–2007)
Linda is the family Yoga teacher. Maya, Déja, and Nana have all taken Yoga lessons from her. She teaches Yoga at Vista View, is a very nice woman, and is willing to take her class into anything.

lexa: potential girlfriend (2006–2007)
Was in my Yoga class. Was very nice and friendly. Would make me laugh from time to time, causing me to feel like the two of us were in our own world together. Had a younger sister with autism.

terry: friend (2006–2007)

dava: friend (2006–2007)

lindsey: potential girlfriend (2007)

jerry: the bad counselor (2006)

mom: herself (2006–)

trivia

Outside-of-school weekend events during 2006/my first year at Vista View:

The Saturday Groove

Matt and I talking on the phone and e-mailing

Watching old shows on YouTube that I used to watch on PBS

YouTube not working in my room on my computer and having to use Maya's computer to watch videos on it, which she allowed me to do because she is such a nice auntie.*

Grocery shopping

Taking walks to the various shops around where we live.

Calling Logan on his phone/Logan not answering more often than answering.**

Making countless plans with Logan to do a film shoot that did not end up happening.†

Making plans to involve Clark in the film shoot‡

Calling Jenny§

Working on my book

The Jewish Triathlon

series summary

My start of college was very bumpy. The first day was easy because it was just Yoga. But the second day completely messed up my good summer. And it got worse and worse as it went along.

---

* YOUTUBE DIDN'T WORK IN MY ROOM WHENEVER I TRIED TO PLAY A VIDEO; IT POPPED UP SOME MESSAGE ABOUT THE JAVA SCRIPT PLAYER.

** LOGAN WAS MY BOSS/FRIEND AT THE NATURAL MARKET, A GROCERY STORE I STARTED WORKING AT IN OCTOBER 2006 (SEE THE *"ALL-STORE MEETINGS AT NATURAL MARKET"* SERIES).

† THE FILM SHOOT WAS GOING TO INVOLVE THE NATURAL MARKET ENSEMBLE PLAYING THEMSELVES. WE WERE GOING TO GET A FIRST STUDENT BUS AND HAVE LOGAN'S WIFE PLAY ALTHEA, A FIRST STUDENT BUS DRIVER (SEE *GAMES 3*, EPISODE 23). THE PLOT OF THE FILM SHOOT WAS THAT LOGAN AND I WERE PRETENDING THAT SOMEONE WE DON'T LIKE WAS DEAD. WE WERE GOING TO GO TO A SOFTBALL GAME AND SING MUSIC ABOUT IT. WE PLANNED TO FIND A GIRL TO PLAY THE GIRL I WOULD ROMANCE. THIS DID NOT WORK OUT BECAUSE HALF THE TIMES THAT I TRIED TO CALL LOGAN TO MAKE A PLAN ABOUT IT HE WOULD NOT RESPOND TO HIS PHONE OR CALL ME BACK. ON THE DAY IT WAS SUPPOSED TO HAPPEN HE SENT ME A TEXT MESSAGE SAYING HE WAS SICK AND COULDN'T MAKE IT. MOM THOUGHT HE NEVER PLANNED TO DO IT AT ALL AND WAS JUST LEADING ME ALONG.

‡ I WAS GOING TO HAVE CLARK PLAY A ROLE IN THIS FILM SHOOT AND JUST MOSTLY SAY, "I DON'T WANT POISON." I CALLED CLARK AND TOLD HIM WHAT HE WAS SUPPOSED TO DO BUT, I DIDN'T HAVE A DATE THAT IT WAS SUPPOSED TO HAPPEN AT THAT TIME. THEN WHEN I FINALLY DID HAVE A DATE HE SAID HE COULDN'T MAKE IT.

§ ONE DAY IN AUGUST, MOM RAN INTO JENNY AT THE MARKET AND GAVE HER MY NUMBER. JENNY LATER CALLED ME AND GAVE ME HER NUMBER. JENNY DOESN'T REALLY ANSWER HER PHONE THAT OFTEN, AND THEN SOMETIMES SHE WILL LOSE IT AND IT WILL BE OFF FOR A LONG PERIOD OF TIME. SHE ALSO TENDS TO LEAVE WEIRD MESSAGES ON HER OUTGOING VOICE MAIL.

Episode List

Episode 1   Season 1

title: **PILOT**   air date: **AUGUST 21, 2006**

summary

I check in to Yoga. Linda is my teacher. She explains how the class
will work. I meet a girl in my search for a girlfriend. Her name is
Lexa. We meet and listen to Linda speak, then the day is over.

notes

Yoga was my favorite class.

Lexa is one year older than I am.

In this episode I am trying to reincarnate my junior year because that
was a great year for me.

Lexa is my first potential girlfriend since Courtney (see *My Freshman
Year of High School* and *Blaze, Courtney, and Amber*).

soundtrack listing

"All This Time" by Sting (*Soul Cages* 1991)

Episode 2

title: **REALITY BITES**   air date: **AUGUST 22, 2006**

summary

It's my first real day of college. I meet a friend, Rick, in English 802. We
talk in the empty classroom about stuff. I ask him if he likes *Full House*.
He says yes. We realize we are in the wrong room because nobody else is
coming. Then, after about three minutes, we finally find Ms. G's room.
When we first arrive she is writing on the chalkboard. I get scared and
have to leave the room. I'm scared because I'm worried the fire alarm is
going to malfunction. Then I go back in and then out, a nonstop battle.
I meet two Brazilian girls in English and we talk a little bit. They are
concerned about me because I am a bit panicky. Later on, during the
break between classes I call Matt and Danny to see what's up. Then it
is time for Spanish class. That goes well. I am still trying to rebirth my
junior year and it does seem to be working. I go to Spanish with Professor
H. She is pretty nice. Later on Mom, Maya, and Nana pick me up.

notes

The rebirth of my junior year did not end up working, even though I thought it was at the time.

This was the day where the good of the summer for me was demolished into oblivion, although the good of the year was not destroyed until a short time later.

The Brazilian girls transferred out of English shortly after this episode.

trivia

In October 2000 in middle school the fire alarm malfunctioned; that is what caused this phobia.

soundtrack listing

"Tumi Bhaja Re Mana" by Manish Vyas (*Sattva: The Essence of Being* 2003)
The lyrics to this song are not in English. The rhythm of the song is heavy on drums and chanting, sort of like the up-and-down energy of this episode.

"The Tide Is High" by Atomic Kitten (*Feels So Good* 2002)

"Mad About You" by Sting (*Soul Cages* 1991)

"China Girl" by David Bowie (*Let's Dance* 1983)

Episode 3

title: **THE SECOND YOGA SESSION**   air date: **AUGUST 23, 2006**

summary

It's the second day of Yoga. Linda takes roll to make sure we are all present. Then we get started with Savasana. I don't quite get it but bear with it.

trivia

Savasana is also called "corpse pose" because you lie as still as a dead body. This is my favorite Yoga pose.

Episode 4

title: **STILL TODAY THE STRUGGLE WILL REMAIN** air date: **AUGUST 24, 2006**

summary

The second day of English I go to the computer lab. My fear of the fire alarm malfunctioning remains. It's a stressful day. Today's project is about Malcolm X. I once again begin leaving the room. Ms. G gives me a hard time about getting up and down in the middle of class. After a while I sit down and see one of my middle school homies, Matt. We get reunited. I ask him a lot of questions about the past. On the way to Spanish class I feel a lot of depression because of how college is treating me. A student falls asleep in Spanish. We tease him but then he gets all mad at us. Later, at home, Mom wants me to log on to the online Spanish tutorial but I resist it.

notes

This episode aired on my aunt Lavander's birthday.

This summer I've been thinking a lot about things that bother me and that would drive me to go on drugs if I were Jodie Sweetin (the actress who plays Stephanie on *Full House* and who actually did go on drugs, had to go to rehab, and was interviewed about it).

trivia

Things that would make me go on drugs if I were Jodie Sweetin:

1. Green Day
2. Balloons
3. Planning ahead
4. Howard Ashman (producer of Disney films) dying at age forty
5. There being two guys in a garbage or recycling truck (there is usually only one guy in the truck, and when there are two it messes me up)
6. The bad experience with Grad Night I had at Disneyland
7. Pei Wei (an Asian cafeteria-style restaurant that I don't like very much)
8. Air circulation
9. The bus I took to the Museum of Making Music with my math class
10. The scene in *Pinocchio* where Stromboli locks him in the cage
11. Nana canceling an outing
12. Relaxing weeks (boring)
13. The Nordstrom parking lot
14. New routines

15. Meeting up for lunch
16. Encinitas
17. Politics (except for law enforcement)
18. The word *concentrate*
19. Visits from friends who live far away (because they have to leave again)

Episode 5

---

title: **CURSES, CURSES**   air date: **SEPTEMBER 7, 2006**

---

summary

Today is my meeting with my Disabled Student Services counselor, Jerry. I report to the office. He is with another student. He is taking a while. Then finally after about fifteen minutes he is done. We talk and he starts with "How is it going?" Then we begin to talk about my performance in the class and he talks about how I am doing in my classes. I'm not meeting demand according to him. He has to call Mom. At first I don't want him to but finally I cave and say all right. He uses my phone and talks on it with Mom. He wants me to drop out of English and Spanish. He tells Mom that these college classes are not in the cards for me. He says it's okay to keep Yoga. I end up dropping the Spanish. Later on, when Déja picks me up, she is not happy with Jerry. I try to tell her that I am not meeting demand in my classes.

notes

This is where the problems with Vista View got serious.

Jerry called the house later that night and left a message on the answering machine that I should drop my classes.

Jerry is as bad as Stromboli from *Pinocchio*, the way he locked me in a cage.

trivia
Biography for Pinocchio (2006)
by Blaze Ginsberg
date of birth: may 5, 1881, rome, italy
date of death: september 30, 1975 (heart attack), san diego, california
birth name: pinocchio john sabatora
nickname: pinoc'
height: 3´ 10˝

Mini Biography

A wooden puppet who wanted to become a real boy, Pinocchio had an unusual birth. He was carved. He began his acting career early, the morning after he was brought to life by the Blue Fairy, but all did not go well. Stromboli, his director, locked him in a bird cage. After that he was almost turned into a donkey. When his father Geppetto was swallowed by Monstro, the great huge whale, Pinocchio went to find him. But he too was swallowed, and then he knew that inside the whale was his new home. Pinocchio had a great idea to get them out and to their real home. Then he became a real boy. He grew up with his father. His education was very successful. In college he got a degree in acting. Then he hit the road and tried out for parts in movies. He met his wife, Isabelle, while on the set of *A New World*. They got married and had their first child named Geppetto Jr. He was named after his grandfather. In 1950 he tried out for a part in the TV series *What People Say* and was cast as Sherlock Holmes. But unfortunately it was canceled after only a year. In 1956 he tried out for another part in TV in the hit series, *Families* in the role of Grandpa Fred, which ran for thirteen years. In 1972 he played the hero in his final movie, *Beauty and the Train Robbery*. He retired from acting and moved to a Mission Valley retirement home, where he lived until his death. He died on September 30, 1975, of a heart attack. He was ninety-four years old.

spouse: isabelle sabatora
trademark: pinocchio was famous for his nose, which grew every time he told a lie. later in life, he had plastic surgery to correct this problem.
personal quotes: "I remember all those days I spent with Jiminy Cricket."

soundtrack listing

"Clean Heart" by Sade (*Stronger Than Pride* 1988)

"I Think We're Alone Now" by Tiffany (*Tiffany* 1987)

"Life in the Fast Lane" by The Eagles (*Hotel California* 1976)

Episode 6

title: **DESPERADO**   air date: **SEPTEMBER 10, 2006**

summary

I am hanging out with Lavander and we discuss joining online dating Web sites because we are both looking for love. Then we go to Peet's and I find some girl, but she has a boyfriend already so she is out. Later, at home, I talk with Mom and Bo about online dating.

notes
The girl at Peet's was named Gabby. She has moved away. She is a year younger than myself.

quotes
mom: "Dating websites are not a good idea for someone your age. The best place for you to meet girls is at school. Bo didn't have a girlfriend when he was your age."
bo: "Yeah, don't go on dating Web sites."

soundtrack listing
"Desperado" by The Eagles (*Desperado* 1973)

Episode 7

---

title: GIRLS ALL OVER   air date: **SEPTEMBER 18, 2006**

---

summary
I report to Yoga. I see this girl who I like and introduce myself to her. Her name is Terry. She is very friendly and sounds a lot like Hilary Duff. We get off to a very good start. I ask about her classes and her occupation, and I ask about when she started at Vista View. We do the balance poses together and that goes nicely. Later, at the end of class, I get her number. At home, I call her and she does not answer her phone.

notes
Terry works at Panera. She is older than me by four months.

She answered zero calls that I made to her, so I started calling her "Terry Fairy" because I associated the negative/depressing vibe I got from her never answering my calls with the fairies in Walt Disney's *Sleeping Beauty*.

soundtrack Listing
"Mexico" by James Taylor (*Gorilla* 1975)

"Superwoman (*Where Were You When I Needed You?*)" by Stevie Wonder (*Music of My Mind* 1972)

Episode 8

title: **DR. LOVE WAYS**   air date: **SEPTEMBER 25, 2006**

summary
I am in Yoga today doing the usual routine. I go to work on the poses with a girl named Jessica and that goes wonderfully. Jessica and I talk a little bit and get to know each other. I get a girlfriend vibe from her and I get her number. When I take a break from English, I see another girl, Nikki, and I go introduce myself to her and we get to know each other. I ask for her number and she gives it to me.

notes
Jessica never answered any of my calls and her phone was always off when I called her. I think she might already have had a boyfriend.

Nikki's phone was always off when I called her.

quotes
me: "Hi, I'm Blaze."
jessica: "I'm Jessica."
me: "How old are you?"
jessica: "Nineteen."
me: "I'm nineteen as well. When is your birthday?"
jessica: "May."
me: "Mine is in July."
(Later)
me: "Can I get your phone number?"
boy with jessica: "Just give him the number."
(Later)
me: "Hi, I'm Blaze, what's your name?"
nikki: "I'm Nikki."
me: "How old are you?"
nikki: "I'm eighteen."
me: "I'm nineteen."
me: "Do you have any brothers or sisters?"
nikki: "I have an older sister."
me: "I'm an only child. Can I get your phone number?"
nikki (programs her number into my phone): "Sure."

soundtrack listing

"I'm Going to Love You Just a Little Bit More" by Barry White (*Let the Music Play* 1973)

Episode 9

title: **CRUISING WITH LEXA**   air date: **OCTOBER 4, 2006**

summary

Eleven years ago today I had the most dreadful day, and it falls on the same day of the week as it did eleven years ago. But as bad as it was back then, that is how good it is going to be today. Maya drops me off at Yoga. I start talking to Lexa and we have a good conversation even as Linda is taking roll in Savasana. I imagine us driving away together. We talk some more and she makes a very funny remark. Then later on we are doing a balance pose; I have to hold her by the hips. Then it's the end of Yoga for today.

quotes

me: "Did you have a senior Grad Night?"
lexa: "Yes."
me: "Mine was a complete bust."
lexa: "I have old woman syndrome."
(I laugh)

soundtrack listing

"Is It Love" by Play (*Play* 2002)

"Two Gunslingers" by Tom Petty (*Into the Great Wide Open* 1991)

Episode 10

title: **I DID MY WORK, YOU HEAR ME?**   air date: **OCTOBER 12, 2006**

summary

I go to Ms. G's class one day. It starts off fine until Ms. G pulls me out of the class to talk to me about my work. She doesn't believe me—that I did my own writing. I get really furious about this. I end up not getting any credit for the work I did. I take a break, go to the lounge, and punch a soda machine in my anger.

notes
This is where Ms. G really started to get to me. I got no credit for the assignment, which was to write a narrative essay.

quotes
me (mad at ms. g): "I think I know why Matt (another student) transferred out of this class."
ms. g: "Why?"
me: "I can't say. I'm going to take a break."

soundtrack listing
"How Do You Stop?" by Joni Mitchell (*Turbulent Indigo* 1994)

Episode 11

title: **MOM'S COMING IN AND THERE'S GOING TO BE TROUBLE**
air date: **OCTOBER 19, 2006**

---

summary
Today I have a crush on a new celebrity: Kirsten Storms (who stars as Zenon in *The Zenon Trilogy*). I am thinking about her a lot. At the same time I am in a 1994 mood. I go to class and Ms. G as usual pulls me out to talk about the assignment and as usual no credit. Mom and Maya are outside to pick me up. Mom comes in to talk to Ms. G about the problems I am having in her class and why she doesn't believe I am doing my own work. It takes quite some time. I get worried about Mom (thinking that Ms. G might murder her), but she is okay. We go to the Apple store at the UTC mall to replace my iPod, which had died very recently. There is a Santa Ana wind today (see trivia).

notes
I had gotten into a fight with Mom the night before this episode (because she asked me to do her a favor and I gave her attitude about it after I did it), and I tied it together with everything else that is upsetting me, like college in general.

I bumped into my friend Aaron from Yoga and his girlfriend (now ex)

Amanda.

trivia

UTC stands for University Towne Center, a mall in La Jolla.

A Santa Ana wind blows west from the desert to the ocean. It is very hot and dry and makes you feel all dehydrated and sick. Sometimes it even causes wildfires to rage out of control.

quotes

me (to maya): "Why is it ridiculous to say that I have been mad at Hilary Duff since 1994?"
maya: "Because you haven't been mad at her since 1994."
me (calling aaron): "Hey, where are you?"
aaron: "I'm at UTC."
me: "Me too. Where in UTC are you?"
aaron: "The food court."
me: "I'm at the food court too."

soundtrack listing
"Barbie Girl" by Aqua (*Aquarium* 1997)

Episode 12

---

title: **IS IT TRUE ABOUT LEXA?**   air date: **NOVEMBER 22, 2006**

---

summary
I go to Yoga and hope to see Lexa. We do our meditation exercises. Later on into the day I overhear her talking with some of the other girls and get worried that she has a boyfriend. Linda has us get into groups. I am very depressed about Lexa, worrying about losing her as a potential girlfriend.

soundtrack listing
"Everybody Hurts" by R.E.M. (*Automatic for the People* 1992)

Episode 13

---

title: **IT'S OVER**   air date: **NOVEMBER 29, 2006**

---

summary

I go to Yoga today. I sit next to Lexa and we talk for a little while about her Italian philosophy teacher. Later we get into our day of Yoga. Linda makes a funny remark. I laugh at it, but then Lexa tells me not to laugh. This makes me rather angry. Later she does it again. Then I yell at her and that ends our friendship and her potential as a girlfriend. Déja picks me up for a massage. I talk about it with her.

notes
I was already losing with Lexa as it is. Whenever there was a test in class, it put her in my head in a negative way.

soundtrack listing
"Learn to Be Still" by The Eagles (*Hell Freezes Over* 1994)

"Y.M.C.A." by The Village People (*Cruisin'* 1978)

"Can't Do a Thing to Stop Me" by Chris Isaak (*San Francisco Days* 1993)

Episode 14

title: **MADNESS**   air date: **DECEMBER 8, 2006**

summary
It's Déja's birthday and everything does not go as planned. Bo is trying to show me how to eat an apple correctly, and then Maya gets on him for getting on me and he leaves, shouting, "Fuck you!" This trauma-tizes Déja and makes her cry. I also get a little upset about this incident. Déja then gives me a ride to work at Natural Market.* I am so upset that I kind of want to cry too.

quotes
bo: "No, no. Now I'll show you again."
maya: "Bo, leave him!"
bo: "Don't yell at me; don't yell at me. Fuck you! I'm leaving—good luck, Blaze."

soundtrack listing
"Beautiful Disaster (Live)" by Kelly Clarkson (*Breakaway* 2004)

*SEE ALL-STORE MEETINGS AT NATURAL MARKET SERIES.

"Heaven" by Los Lonely Boys (*Los Lonely Boys* 2004)

Episode 15

title: **PREPARING FOR FINALS**   air date: **DECEMBER 12, 2006**

summary

I report to Ms. G's class. We talk about the final. She gives us the material we will need to study for it. The article is called "Why We Love Bad News."

trivia

The article said that we pay more attention to bad news because our brains are more sensitive to bad news or negative information because we evolved that way to avoid dangerous situations.

Episode 16

title: **YOGA FINALS**   air date: **DECEMBER 13, 2006**

summary

I report to Yoga for the final. It works this way: We start with Savasana, then each member of the class will lead a pose. I lead my poses. Then Lexa even leads some.

notes

I do not remember what my poses were. This is the last appearance of Lexa. I did run into her once the next semester, but we did not talk.

Episode 17

title: **THE LAST OF THE LONG RUN**   air date: **DECEMBER 14, 2006**

summary

Today is the last day of my first semester in college. I report to Ms. G. She tells me to go to the office. I take my test in the office, and I even ask the proctor some questions about Vista View. Then I leave when I am done. This has been a really difficult semester and I feel that everyone in the family has just been trying to push me through without thinking about my feelings. I really don't want to be here anymore.

notes
This is the finale of the rough Season 1.

I do not pass the English final, or the class.

trivia
I learn that the school has been around since 1966.

soundtrack listing
"Ashes to Ashes" by David Bowie (*Scary Monsters* 1980)

"Family Affair" by Sly and the Family Stone (*There's a Riot Going On* 1971)

knowing tara (2006)

series: **2006–2007**

release date: **AUGUST 22, 2006**

genre: **ACQUAINTANCES**

status: **ENDED**

cast:

blaze ginsberg: himself (2006–2007)

tara: potential girlfriend/acquaintance (2006–2007)
Was an acquaintance with whom I had a complicated relationship. Did not respond to the two e-mails I sent her. Was generally nice but her attitude messed up our almost-friendship.

monique: tara's cousin (2006–2007)

boy walking with tara: himself (2007)

series summary

I met Tara on my second day of college in between English 802 and Spanish. I saw her in the lounge and instantly I liked her a lot. She was very pretty and seemed to have a nice personality. We became friends quickly. Tara is five months younger than I am. I originally thought she was a whole year younger than me.

Episode List
Episode 1

title: **PILOT**   air date: **AUGUST 22, 2006**

summary
I'm eating my lunch in the student lounge on campus. It will be time
for Spanish soon. I'm hunting for a girlfriend. Suddenly I see what
could be the greatest chance to get one. There is a girl whose soda is
stuck in the soda machine. I help her get it out. We talk about our lives
and I get to know her. I tell her what classes I'm taking this semester,
and I ask her what she does with her free time. Then she leaves.

quotes
me: "Don't you just hate getting your soda stuck in the machine?"
tara: "Yeah."
me: "Hey, I'm Blaze Ginsberg."
tara: "I'm Tara."
me: "How old are you?"
tara: "Eighteen."
(We shake hands)
me: "I'm taking Yoga, English, Spanish, and the History of Jazz
online."
me: "What do you do with your free time?"
tara: "I go over to my boyfriend's house."
me: "All right."
(Our conversation ends)

soundtrack listing
"Forever More" by Shawn Stockman (from the movie *Seventeen
Again* 2000)

Episode 2

title: **THE REUNION**   air date: **NOVEMBER 2006**

summary
I see Tara but she does not remember me. I remind her how we met,
and then she remembers who I am. We talk about how stuff is going
and it is all great between us.

Episode 3
___

title: **THE TRUTH** air date: **NOVEMBER 15, 2006**
___

summary

I see Tara when I'm picking up a test accommodation form for my
English 802 class. I ask her what siblings she has. She has a younger
brother. I obsess over that for the rest of the day.

notes

Tara tells me her brother is two years younger than she is.

Episode 4
___

title: **THE STUFF I NEVER KNEW** air date: **NOVEMBER 29, 2006**
___

summary

On my way to Yoga, Tara spots me and points me out. I give her a
hug; we talk. I then bring up her brother and ask her how much
younger than she her brother is. She tells me he's seventeen. So I
figure that he is only a year younger than she, but she tells me two
years because she is turning nineteen this Sunday. I obsess over that
for the rest of the day.

notes

I thought Tara was a year younger than I am. It turns out she's only five
months younger.

soundtrack listing

"Pumping Up the Party" by Miley Cyrus (*Hannah Montana
Soundtrack* 2006)

"Say Goodbye to Jr. High" by Emma Roberts (*Unfabulous and More* 2005)

Episode 5
___

title: **LATE GIFT** air date: **DECEMBER 6, 2006**
___

summary

I briefly see Tara. She says hi, we talk, and I wish her a late happy birthday.

Episode 6

title: MY GREAT DEPRESSION   air date: **JANUARY 23, 2007**

summary

It's my first day of semester number 2 at Vista View. I hope to see Tara. My wish comes true. I see her outside between classes. She is with her cousin Monique. I ask Tara what classes she is taking and I tell her mine. I get her e-mail address for further contact with her. Later that night I get all depressed over her because of what she said about e-mailing (see quotes).

notes

I think when I first met Tara I might have gotten depressed after we were done talking, so that would mark this as the second time I have gotten depressed after a conversation with Tara. Also her cousin Monique may have appeared in the pilot without my knowing that she was Tara's cousin.

This is the third and last consecutive episode where I obsess over something about Tara.

I learn her last name in this episode.

quotes

me: "Who's this?"

tara: "This is my cousin Monique."

tara (after I have asked her for her e-mail): "What, are you going to start sending e-mails now?"

soundtrack listing

"Mexican Wrestler" by Emma Roberts (*Unfabulous and More* 2005)

"Baby Love" by Diana Ross and the Supremes (*Where Did Our Love Go* 1964)

Episode 7

title: SURPRISE, SURPRISE   air date: **MARCH 20, 2007**

summary

I'm taking a quick break before class begins when I see Tara. I think that she is Anais Lameche from the all-girl Swedish group Play.* Then I realize that it is Tara. I say hi to her and we shake hands.

notes

Tara has dyed her hair black. That is what provoked me into thinking she was someone else.

This was the first time since the reunion that we did not hug.
In February I had a crush on Anais Lameche.

Episode 8

title: **RIOT TARA**   air date: **MAY 1, 2007**

summary

I see Tara. We talk briefly. She makes a very funny remark. We talk for a little while and I ask her how her boyfriend is. He is good apparently. Then she has to go to the bathroom, which cuts this episode and our conversation short. Later on I see her as she is leaving the school.

notes

In this episode I learn Tara's boyfriend is two years older than she is.

quotes

tara: "I have to pee really badly."
(We both laugh)

Episode 9

title: **OUR FEELINGS**   air date: **MAY 8, 2007**

summary

I see Tara and we talk about stuff when I am on my break from English 802. I ask her what other classes she is taking because I don't remember what she said when I asked her before.

notes

Tara does not like her classes either.

*SEE *BLAZE, MATT, AND DANNY 1*, EPISODE 16, FOR MORE INFORMATION ABOUT PLAY.

chapter eighteen

This is the second episode where we both laugh at the same time.

Later, at the pool, I get briefly depressed for five seconds over her attitude and tone, but not as bad as last time.

quotes
me: "What other classes are you taking?"
tara: "I don't want to talk about it; I hate class."
me: "I've hated it since I was a month old."
(We both laugh)

goofs
I have not seen Tara since this episode.

trivia
I am no longer interested in Tara because I never actually forgave her for her rude comment about e-mailing back in January, which she never apologized for.

all-store meetings at
natural market (2006)

series: **2006–2007**   release date: **DECEMBER 14, 2006**

genre: **BUSINESS**   status: **ENDED**

cast:

blaze ginsberg: himself (2006–2007)

logan: boss/friend (2006–2007)
Logan was like an older brother to me. He was older than me by twelve years. I met him on November 18, 2005, when my two favorite soups were out of stock at Natural Market and we had a long, drawn-out conversation about it. From then on, we were like brothers. In January 2006 he had the idea that he would love to have me on the grocery team. He told Mom that after I graduated from high school, I should come in and they would hire me. Logan liked to agree with me about how I felt about my celebrity crushes. Basically if there was anybody I didn't like he would not like them either. Logan got along very well with Papa and liked my family. Logan didn't really like to deliver bad news, so as a result, he didn't always tell me when things were not working out.

kellie: logan's cute daughter (2006–2007)
Almost three years old at the time of filming. Looked like a little doll. Called me "Bwaze" and liked me a lot. Liked to get wild and run around.

matthew: the boss of grocery

horlix: grocery worker

michelle: store team leader

anna: cashier/my number one fan

kenny: grocery team leader

glenn: grocery team member

other natural market employees: themselves

series summary
Before Natural Market, I had a job at Surrey at The Surrey Corner, which is the lunch café. I worked there my sophomore and senior years (see *Senior Year 1*). That job, however, was nothing like Natural Market.

On a very festive winter holiday evening of November 18, 2005, my favorite soup flavors, Fantastic Foods' Curry and Chickenless Ramen were out of stock. I asked for customer service at Natural Market and a guy named Logan came to help me. We had a conversation about this, and he went to check in the back to see if they had any more. Nay. Logan and I became friends shortly after that turn of events. In January 2006 Logan gave me a beanie that had Natural Market's name embroidered on it and said, "We'd love to have you on the team."

After graduating from high school, I went in to apply for the job. I was supposed to be hired there on September 1, 2006, but due to labor issues it did not work that way. I was finally hired on October 29, 2006. My first day was not so great. I was having issues with being anxious to leave before it was time. Another problem that was an issue from early on until the end of my days at Natural Market was the "afternoon face," where everybody in grocery goes through the aisles and brings the product forward on the shelf and facing outward with the tag showing. I was never properly trained on how to do that. Also, the only reason I really went to work at Natural Market was to spend more time with Logan. I was Logan's project and everything was more about him than the work itself. In February 2007 I was cut down to one day a week because of that and the problems with the face, although that is not what they told me. Also, Logan and Matthew, the other grocery team leader, did not get along and that caused problems. Finally, I was supposed to have gotten voted onto the team (meaning a permanent grocery team member), but was lied to about being voted onto the grocery team because later Matt told me I was not meeting demand and had not been voted on after all. I was never given any more hours than five per week after February.

Episode List
Episode 1

title: **ALL-STORE MEETINGS**   air date: **DECEMBER 13, 2006**

summary
I am making up the first day of my Natural Market orientation because of the government card issues I had at the beginning and having to go back and forth to the DMV to get my ID. Steve, the in-store trainer, announces there is a meeting tomorrow at six o'clock in the morning and it is mandatory that the whole store attend.

Episode 2

title: **THE STORE IS BARELY HANGING ON**   air date: **DECEMBER 14, 2006**

summary
It's an early start for me. I have to go to Natural Market for the 6 a.m. meeting. I fill the Peet's travel mug with tea and Maya takes me there. I clock in and go up to the conference room. The meeting starts off with the teams going into rooms and talking about how they are doing. Matthew makes a list of things that needed to get discussed. When that is over, we all go downstairs to listen to Michelle, the store team leader, talk.

Matthew talks about issues occurring in grocery. Logan's daughter, Kellie is unexpectedly there and that makes my day very early on because she is agonizingly cute. Then Logan tells us that also scheduled for today is a fire drill. I am a little concerned about the fire drill, but it's nothing serious. There is no alarm sound for the Natural Market fire drill, which eliminates a lot of my anxiety. We will be called on the intercom when it is time to go out. When that is over we go inside and watch a video. One of our shifties (see trivia) is leaving in January. The video is dedicated to him, with everybody saying things like "Good-bye, we'll miss you" and that kind of thing. When that's over, they mush a pie in his face.

notes
Annie, Logan's wife, goes to work. That is why Kellie attends the all-store meetings.

This was the only fire drill at Natural Market.

trivia
A "shifty" is a shift leader.

quotes
matthew: "We're going to discontinue any product that isn't selling right?"
kellie: "Da-da."
logan: "What is it, sweetie? Can't get your juice open?" (helps her)
matthew (repeated line for whole series): "Facing and stocking standards have to improve. You can't leave things unattended in the back room." (Later on)
kellie (after logan comes on the "Good-bye Shifty" video—as loud as a 1993 New Flyer D60 bus): "That's you, Da-da!"

soundtrack listing
"Behind the Hazel Eyes" by Kelly Clarkson (*Breakaway* 2004)

"Breakaway" by Kelly Clarkson (*Breakaway* 2004)

"Mr. Vain" by Culture Beat (1993)

Episode 3

title: **BE TRUE TO YOUR TEAM MEMBER**   air date: **FEBRUARY 15, 2007**

---

summary
It's the meeting and team member voting. We talk about grocery issues. I am nervous about not getting voted on. Then it's voting time. Erin, who is also a new employee, is waiting to see if she gets voted on. We both make it.

quotes
glenn (yelling): "Ay, Blaze. How is it going!!!!!"
kenny (nudges him to keep it down): "Ay."
(Later on, after the meeting)
kellie: I have to go to 'cool [meaning *school*].

Episode 4

title: **KELLIE'S MONKEY (a.k.a. Grocery Needs to Improve)**
air date: **MARCH 22, 2007**

summary

Today at the all-store meeting we have a new member, Ben. There will be more voting today, but in the meantime we do what we have to do. Kellie, on the other hand, starts sinking Logan down when she wants to play with the daughter of a Natural Market cashier and she becomes restless. Business is fine. We talk about expired product and what to do with it and how it is very bad. Then it is time to go downstairs.

notes

Kellie was cuter than ever. I hugged and kissed her at the end of this episode.

quotes

nate: "There is nothing worse than out-of-code product."
kellie: "Let's go, Da-da."
logan: "Not yet, Kellie. You just really want to play with your friend."
matthew: "We're stocking the cold box and it's not getting done right. There's stuff missing and we have to improve."
horlix: "I do the cold box. I'm sixty-two years old."
(At the end of the meeting)
logan (when kellie has taken medicine from the shelf): "Go put that back, Kellie."

soundtrack listing

"Golden Lady" by Stevie Wonder (*Innervisions* 1973)

Episode 5

title: **ROCK N' ROLL**   air date: **MAY 10, 2007**

summary

It's an all-store meeting day. I go there and there is a minor problem— Matthew forgot to print the list of things we're supposed to be talking about. Then it comes out; we talk about facing and stocking and how standards must improve. Later, Michelle brings up a problem she had with a customer. Today is a rather fun day. Kellie is not as wild as she was last time. Toward the end of the grocery meeting she gets ready to play with Rebecca; then we go downstairs. I have fun with Ben and Logan. We talk about stuff when the meeting is over. Rebecca does not want Kellie to leave and cries.

notes

There was a customer making sexually inappropriate comments about women, and Michelle said she was glad he was gone from the store permanently.

quotes

logan: "You're ready to play with your friend."

kellie: "He forgot the milk, Daddy."

me: "Kellie is talking to you."

logan: "What's that, baby?"

(Later on when meeting is over)

logan (to kellie): "Remember when you went to Blaze's house and you hit your head and you cried a little bit?"

michelle: "There was a guy who came in here and kept making sexually inappropriate comments about women and was finally kicked out not long ago."

michelle: "We lost one of our ex-Seafood members. He died in a car accident."

soundtrack listing

"Do the Rubber Duck" from *Sesame Street*

"A Mind with a Heart of Its Own" by Tom Petty and the Heartbreakers (*Full Moon Fever* 1989)

Episode 6

---

title: **CHANGING HEARTS**   air date: **JUNE 21, 2007**

---

summary

I go to Natural Market for a meeting. Today things are not as bad as they usually are. (Things have been going downhill. I have been cut down to one day a week and have not been given any more hours. Matthew keeps telling me it is because there is a labor deficit.) I make a comment about the chip aisle and how chips get misplaced. So it starts off good. We are upstairs for longer than usual. Later on, when we go downstairs, there are a couple of unfortunate events. Michelle has accepted a position at another store and is leaving. And Logan is moving to Texas tomorrow. He says he can't handle his problems with Matthew anymore and he's finished with California. Michelle breaks down in bitter tears. Later I walk Logan out to his truck.

notes

Logan and Kenny, one of the other grocery assistant managers, were like brothers. Like me and Logan.

This is obviously Logan's last appearance.

Kellie did not appear in this episode. She could not ride in the moving truck, which is why she is not in this episode.

I had complicated feelings about Logan leaving. I was mad at him but at the same time I missed him when he left. After he left, Natural Market was a miserable place for me to be and I didn't want to work there anymore.

quotes

matthew: "The labor deficit is getting better."
me (to rebecca): "Do you miss your friend Kellie?" (I put my arm around her)
rebecca: "Yes."
rebecca: "Not allowed in the truck."
me: "What?"
rebecca: "She is not allowed in the truck."
me: "Kellie is not allowed in the truck?"
rebecca: "Yeah."
(Later)
michelle (crying very bitterly): "I'm going to miss you all."
me (making an appreciation to logan): "I'd like to thank Logan. If it hadn't been for him I wouldn't be working here. He got me through my rough first year of college."
logan: "Thanks, B."
(We hug)

soundtrack listing

"Learn to Be Still" by The Eagles (*Hell Freezes Over* 1994)

Episode 7

---

title: **CHANGES AND TRUTH**   air date: **AUGUST 2, 2007**

---

summary

I go to Natural Market for the meeting. We are in a different room than usual. We do the usual routine and all that. I learn that I was not actually voted on when they said I was voted on. They lied to me. Now I apparently have to get voted on again and I am not going to. This is not the best meeting I have had.

notes
This is the final episode of the series because I quit the next week. I quit because the "face" was the biggest issue ever. Matthew and I had a huge fight because I still didn't know how to face. I hated it, and I resisted doing it.

quotes
matthew: "You were never voted on, Blaze."

soundtrack listing
"Ghost Story" by Sting (*Brand New Day* 1999)

"The Rose Tattoo" by David Byrne (*Rei Momo* 1989)

thanksgiving special (2006)

title: **ALL TOGETHER**   air date: **NOVEMBER 23, 2006**

cast:

blaze ginsberg: himself
mom: herself
maya: aunt
lavander: aunt
déja: aunt
bodine (bo): uncle
nana: grandmother
papa: grandfather

guest star 2006

justin: lavander's boyfriend (now ex)

summary

We all get together at Nana and Papa's house. The guest is Justin,
Lavander's boyfriend (now ex). We eat dinner; then Papa sees how I
have scabbed up a section of my hand and threatens to take drastic
action if I continue to pick at it. We go for a walk and I continue

talking about it in an obsessive way because I am worried about his drastic action. We go back to the house. We are going to play the game Mafia, but first I have soup. Then we play. I don't know exactly how to play this game, so I mess it up and get corrected by Déja. Then we play Apples to Apples, my favorite game (now ex). Later on we go home.

quotes
papa: "It's crazy to pick at something until it bleeds."
lavander (when there is a commotion going on with people arguing): "You're scaring Justin." (Puts her arms around him.)

notes
In Apples to Apples everyone gets five red cards with nouns on them. One person picks a green card with an adjective on it, and everyone puts in one of their red cards. The person with the green card chooses which noun best matches the adjective. If your red card gets picked, you win the green card. Five green cards wins the game. Apples to Apples was my favorite game until the Christmas following this Thanksgiving, when I only got one green card. I then put a ban on it for ten years. I later reduced the ban to seven years so we can play it again in 2014.

major events in 2006
I began working at Natural Market on October 29.

I started taking classes at Vista View College.

I began writing my book.

vista view college days 2 (2007)

cast:

blaze ginsberg: himself

mom: herself

ms. e: english professor
A good, patient teacher who did a great job teaching us how to write essays. When Jenny or Matt called me on my cell phone during class, she even joked about it. She cracked me up.

melissa: film professor/mom's friend
Melissa is a very nice and understanding woman. She has two children. Her son is also high functioning autistic. Melissa does not put up with certain types of bullshit from students like talking or ditching.

personal quotes: "I am not here to baby-sit. College is optional."

dante: friend
Dante is a buddy of mine. I met him around February 2007. He is very funny and he calls me "Foo" (short for "Fool"). He was in Déja's drama class in Torrey Pines High School. He is ten years older than me, and he lives with his mom. He doesn't have a job. He is planning to attend NYU after Vista View.

nora: friend (now ex)

emily: potential girlfriend/friend
Was very hot. Possibly liked me too. Younger than me by two years. Went away to college the following year and did not answer her phone when I called.

Episode List

Episode 18

title: **REWIND** air date: **JANUARY 23, 2007**

summary

It's the first day of semester number 2. I walk around the campus. I have not been here for a while. I go to English 802 again and I am worried my new teacher will be like Ms. G. But she is nothing like her at all. She tells us to free write something. When my writing was not complete, she was cool with it.

notes

My teacher's name is Ms. E this time around.

Even though the English teacher is better this time, I still am in the mode of not liking college due to the terrible things that happened the first semester. I plan to drop out and work full-time when this year is over, but Mom doesn't like that idea very much and we argue about it.

soundtrack listing

"Shine" by Hilary Duff (*Hilary Duff* 2004)

"Shower the People" by James Taylor (*In the Pocket* 1976)

"Sweet Baby James" by James Taylor (*Sweet Baby James* 1970)

Episode 19

title: **THE FIRST FILM CLASS DAY** air date: **JANUARY 25, 2007**

summary

I go to school today. I report to the lab for English and that goes pretty well. Then I have a long lunch between classes. Later on I am just dying to meet Melissa, my film teacher (and Mom's friend), and finally it's time for her class. She of course goes over the material we will go over this term. I have been worried that Lexa is enrolled in this class as well, but thankfully she is not. We begin watching *The Godfather*.

quotes

me: "I'm Blaze, Debra's son."
melissa: "Nice to meet you."

soundtrack listing

"Speed of Sound" by Coldplay (XY 2005)

This song plays because it is a very hopeful song with a big sound, and that matches the way I feel about being in this class with a teacher who is really interested in me.

Episode 20

title: **THE FIRST YOGA THIS TERM**   air date: **FEBRUARY 5, 2007**

summary

It's the first Yoga session this semester, and Linda talks about how the class will work. I am hoping to see Dava, a potential girlfriend. I have been in love with her since last month. However, Linda calls roll to see who is in the class and Dava isn't there.

notes

Dava never arrived. I was very upset at work about it.

soundtrack listing

"The Getaway" by Hilary Duff (*Hilary Duff* 2004)

Episode 20

title: **LOVEBIRD, LOVEBIRD**   air date: **FEBRUARY 7, 2007**

summary

I go to school. I go walking around before Yoga starts and I see Dava. We talk and hug. Later on we both report to class together. Linda takes roll and we get started with Savasana. I'm thinking of Dava all day, even when class is over. The next day I am at the mall with Lavander, and we get into a fight because I am being very stingy with her. She gives me two options on how to resolve this problem: I can give her gas money or I can buy her breakfast. Then she apologizes for her attitude. I tell her I am excited to go to Yoga because of Dava. She tells me to lay off having crushes on so many girls.

notes

I made up a playlist on iTunes titled "Courtesy to Dava."

Episode 21

title: **THE LADIES**   air date: **FEBRUARY 8, 2007**

summary

On a break from Film one day I go outside with my friend Andrew A. I talk to him; then my friend Nora calls me to meet up with her and her friend Emily. We go to the snack machines and chat for a while. Then on the way back to class I meet Emily officially.

notes

Nora, Emily, and I were a trio for Film class.

trivia

Fantasy events with Emily:

1. Emily and I are running away from Apples to Apples because I have hated that game since I got only one green card picked. Emily agrees with me that the game sucks. I tell her that I am blacklisting it until I am twenty-seven. She is blacklisting the game until she is fifty. We get into my car (in real life I am not driving yet—I am working on it, though).

2. I am out with Emily and Nora and I see a bus (I love buses). Nora and Emily don't want me to see it, and we get into a fight.

soundtrack listing

"Can You Hear Me?" by David Bowie (*Young Americans* 1975)

Episode 22

title: **HAPPY DENTIST DAYS**   air date: **FEBRUARY 12, 2007**

summary

Papa and I have a dentist appointment with Dr. T in downtown San Diego. We go and I look at some articles, drink tea, and watch and listen to the buses from twenty stories up. After Papa is done with his teeth, the dentist has a look at mine. There are some minor cavities discovered. We go back later to have my teeth whitened.

notes

This is the only episode shot in downtown San Diego.

I was happy that day. All the stress and problems that had been occurring during my first year of college just vanished completely, and the whole school year just stopped existing. Sadly, that nonexistence was only temporary because the school year kind of has to be over in order for it to stop existing. On the bright side, when the school year did finally end, the stress did stop existing.

The bus I heard, a 1993 New Flyer D60 articulated bus (number 1102), was very loud.

soundtrack listing
"Queen in the Black" by Stevie Wonder (*Jungle Fever* 1991)

Episode 23

title: **THE REAL LOVE**   air date: **MARCH 8, 2007**

---

summary
I am in Film. It is tense waiting for it to be over because it is usually a very long class. However, I suddenly notice that this girl Emily is very hot (as in sexy). Later on that night I suddenly just fall so deeply in love with her. I listen to "Fragile" by Sting and I think about her and pretend we did stuff in 1987 together.

notes
Emily is younger than I am by two years. She is taking one college class for credit.

trivia
I like to fantasize about doing stuff in 1987 because (1) it was the year I was born and (2) many good songs and TV shows premiered that year.

soundtrack listing
"You Are the Music in Me" by Zac Efron and Vanessa Hudgens (*High School Musical 2* 2007)

"Almost Gothic" by Steely Dan (*Two Against Nature* 2000)

"Fragile" by Sting (*Nothing Like the Sun* 1987)

"Mercy, Mercy Me" by Marvin Gaye (*What's Going On* 1971)

Episode 24

title: **I AM SURE DOWN FOR HER**   air date: **MARCH 15, 2007**

summary
I hope to see Emily today. I do and it goes nicely. In Film we are watching *Eternal Sunshine of the Spotless Mind* starring Kate Winslet and Jim Carrey. Later on Emily leaves for work.

notes
I like *Eternal Sunshine of the Spotless Mind* because all the events in the movie happen out of chronological order. Chronological order is boring. I also like the romance genre.

Episode 25

title: **LESS ATTENTION**   air date: **MARCH 22, 2007**

summary
Today in Film I am very laughy because of something my manager Matt said at work a couple of weeks ago. Nora and Emily are starting to pay less attention to me, which is a tiny bit depressing even though I don't get that badly bothered by it.

notes
Nora, Emily, and I became a false trio (meaning we separated after Film was over and they never answered any of my calls), so I now have to live with that.

soundtrack listing
"Fly Away" by Lenny Kravitz (5 1998)

Episode 26

title: **THE VISIT**   air date: **MARCH 26, 2007**

summary
Maya is taking me to visit Surrey, my old school. She and her piano quartet are going to play there today. While they get set up, I get

reunited with my old classmates and teachers. Later, it is time to watch the quartet and I do enjoy them. After they are finished, I do some more reuniting with Coach, and then I look for Mrs. L-D, but she will have to wait because we have to go. Maya takes me out for pizza, but it makes me a little depressed because I somehow associate this with still not having a girlfriend and how much I want one.

quotes
coach: "Hey, Blazer! Nice to see you."
me: "How has the bus been doing?"
coach: "Good."
me: "Is Althea still driving?"
coach: "No, there's a new guy. His name is Tony. He's real cool; you'd like him."
me: "Does the bus ever break down?"
coach: "There were some times when it went, 'gggggggg' and we didn't think it was going to start. And I thought, what would Blaze do?"
me: "I have to go."
coach: "Okay, take care."

Episode 27

title: **COLLEGE IS THE BOSS**   air date: **MARCH 27, 2007**

---

summary
I have been writing a book (*Episodes*, this memoir), and I have a great time working on it. Mom is reading it and giving me suggestions for how to make it better. Later, it unfortunately becomes time for me to do work for my History of Rock class and write my Yoga paper. I get into a fight with Mom about it. She tells me I can't go to school without finishing my paper. I call Déja and I even get into tears about it.

notes
I was also in want of a girlfriend in this episode.

Episode 28

title: **GETTING TO REALLY KNOW HER**   air date: **MARCH 29, 2007**

---

summary

I am getting ready for Film. I see Emily arriving in the building. We talk. I bring up *Raising Blaze* because I want to have more of a relationship with her and want her to know more about me. Then we go to class.

quotes

me: "My mom wrote a whole book about me. It's called *Raising Blaze*."
emily: "Cool."

Episode 29

title: **DROWNING IN THE MOVIE**   air date: **APRIL 12, 2007**

summary

In Melissa's film class we are watching *Do the Right Thing*. Emily is absent, so I only have Nora to talk to. However, I really like the movie a lot. Later on it is time to go home.

notes

Lavander buys me the movie for my twentieth birthday. It's one of her favorites too. I am now a mad Spike Lee fan.

Episode 30

title: **OUR TRUE MEANING**   air date: **APRIL 18, 2007**

summary

In Yoga I see a girl I like named Lindsey. I introduce myself and she says hi. I ask her what her name is; she tells me Lindsey is her name. We get to know each other pretty well. We even talk to each other during the guided meditation walk when we are not supposed to. At the end of the day, it is time for Déja to pick me up.

notes

Lindsey is a year younger than I am.

Lindsey has a boyfriend and she has had one for a long time. She told me this exactly one year after this episode. I do not like her anymore due to that reason and other complications.

quotes
me: "Hey."
lindsey: "Oh, hi."
me: "I'm Blaze, what's your name?"
lindsey: "I'm Lindsey."
me: "You like Yoga?"
lindsey: "Yeah."
(Later, during the walk)
me: "Do you have any brothers or sisters?"
lindsey: "I have a younger brother."
me: "I'm an only child. How much younger than you is he?"
lindsey: "Three years."
me: "You like college or do you hate it?"
lindsey: "I hate it."
me: "Me too."
me: "Ever had any of your favorite food discontinued? My favorite soup was discontinued last August."
lindsey: "One of my favorite pizzas was discontinued."

Episode 31

title: **HOLA, FAIR AMIGOS**   air date: **APRIL 19, 2007**

summary
At Vista View there is a Mexican group coming to play some music. I like that, so I eat my lunch outside and watch them perform. I try to get to know them in the middle of their performance, but when I attempt to shift the conversation into gear, a Vista View staff member tells me not to talk to them because they are busy.

notes
This was briefly a reason I did not like Vista View.

Episode 32

title: **THE KING OF THE GOOD GRADES TURNS IT DOWN** air date: **MAY 16, 2007**

summary
Déja and I have to go to Bo's house to help Nana and Papa set up Bo's

new TV. Déja and I do our usual routine of getting french fries, and then we arrive at Bo's house and a few seconds after we arrive, Nana wants to talk to me. She is proud of me because I got a good grade on my Film paper. But what turns the conversation straight to negative is that she insists I stay in college. I clearly don't like it after all the problems I have been going through. I cry a little about it, and we make amends. She gives me a hug and a dollar for a Super Lotto ticket.

notes
This is the only fight with Nana in the series.

Déja also sympathized with me today—this is her only sympathy session of the series.

I got 47 out of 48 on my Film paper.

quotes
papa: "What would you do, working full-time?"
me: "I could work at Blockbuster as a checker."
déja (during sympathy session): "These are all growing pains of life."

soundtrack listing
"Whatever It Takes" by Anita Baker (*Compositions* 1990)

Episode 33

title: **THOSE WERE THE DAYS**   air date: **MAY 18, 2007**

summary
Mom, Gabe, and I are just chilling on Sunday. I am thinking a lot about 1993 and all the events that happened that year. I even pretend that Emily was involved in one of them. I send an e-mail to Matt, making up a story about Emily and me working at Natural Market and finding that all the drinks are mysteriously gone. I then call Danny to see what's up. I think about 1993 at the same time.

notes
What happened in 1993:
1. Had to repeat kindergarten
2. Started going to Sammy's Pizza restaurant
3. Maya joined a musical group named Dream Tango

4. Déja and her friends baby-sat me regularly while Mom and Maya were at work

5. *Beavis and Butthead* premiered on TV

6. Tom Petty and the Heartbreakers released their greatest hits album, their hit "Mary Jane's Last Dance," and the music video

7. I turned six

8. Worst trip to Disneyland ever

9. Had my dreidel taken away from me by my kindergarten teacher while someone was reading a story

10. Saw "Smells Like Teen Spirit" on MTV regularly

soundtrack listing
"Cherish" by Madonna (*Like a Prayer* 1989)

Episode 34
_____

title: **YOGA FINAL**   air date: **MAY 23, 2007**
_____

summary
Today is my Yoga final. I go and do the usual routine, and I will be leading some asanas today: downward facing dog, savasana, and sitting lotus.

notes
The Yoga final was not difficult. I even enjoyed it. I ended up with an A in the class.

Episode 35
_____

title: **THE LAST DAY OF MY FIRST YEAR OF COLLEGE**   air date: **MAY 24, 2007**
_____

summary
What could possibly be better than today? The stress I have been going through now finally comes to a close. The day starts off with me eating breakfast and sending an e-mail to Matt. I go to take my English 802 final. It is embarrassingly easy—a three-year-old could master it. Mom and Maya pick me up and I go home for a while, then back to school to dictate my answers for the Film final to Melissa. Then Lavander picks me up, takes me home, and boo-ya, my first year of college is over, baby.

notes

Lavander's car was in the shop—she had a rental.

I passed all my classes, including English 802.

In my opinion, my first year of college took way too long to end.

This was basically a sequel to my last day of my sophomore year in high school. My sophomore year had also been messed up from the second day on.

goofs

Later in the day it got all cloudy and I got on Mom's nerves.

soundtrack listing

"You and the Mona Lisa" by Shawn Colvin (*A Few Small Repairs* 1996)

"Nothing's Changed" by Chris Isaak (*Heart Shaped World* 1989)

"Make It with You" by Dusty Springfield (*Dusty in Memphis* 1969)

Special
title: **CONGRATS, THIS IS A CELEBRATION**   air date: **JUNE 4, 2007**

summary

I am lying on my bed and Mom calls me to come upstairs. I have passed all my classes and this is a very happy moment. I call my friend Reilly and e-mail him to tell him the grand news. I call Matt as well. He is happy but he can't talk because his father is in the hospital with stomach problems. We go to Sammy's Pizza restaurant. It has only been five days since I was here last. I chat with Mom and Maya about how proud I should be of myself. At the same time, as a treat, I find that my hot neighbor who I am in love with maybe doesn't have a boyfriend and there are possibilities she could be my girlfriend.

Later we go home and I buy chocolate cookies for the celebration.

dance of revenge (special)

special: **2007**   release date: **OCTOBER 1, 2007**   genre: **FANTASY**
setting: **LA SCALA OPERA HOUSE IN MILAN, ITALY, SEPTEMBER 6, 2007**

ballet summary
This is a ballet of revenge. I have a somewhat dislike for Emily (the hot girl who was in my film class the previous spring) for leaving for NYU and not answering her phone. I wrote this ballet to get revenge for her in my head, making her badly in want of a boyfriend like I want a girlfriend badly. The music used was *Dance of the Hours*.

Part I: *The Blaze and His Friends Ballet*
At the crack of dawn, the iron gates open and part. We go down the hall and the curtain goes up with two other curtains following behind it. I begin watching *Sister, Sister*. When *Sister, Sister* is over, my friend Nick calls to tell me he is here (we don't hear any dialogue). He has brought two girlfriends, Kat and Dina. I bow to them and give them gifts. My two girlfriends in my counseling class (Megan and Kristine) and Megan's husband (she was apparently married off to him) call me to tell me that they're here. My friend Reilly will be attending today as well. He arrives. I bow to him and give him a little present.

My ex-boss Logan will be filming the action. In the middle of all this, Emily arrives at the opera house without an invitation and tries to apologize for never answering my calls because she was sent out of Film class for talking during the movie. She gives her age-old excuse for not answering my calls: she was busy. But Nick and I tell her that it is too late. She is heartbroken by this news and starts to cry, but I couldn't be happier about life if someone paid me. The dancing movements start right after that. I lead the ballet and everybody follows my moves. Later Emily cries hard and begins clinging for attention. Everyone gives her some sympathy, a group hug, and an "Awww, it's okay" (not meaning it, just faking it so she will shut the hell up already), but it only works temporarily. A few minutes later we head out to the back garden. Emily follows us. Her cries and clinging for attention make us uncomfortable, causing us to do two not-so-nice things:

1. Reveal the fact that we actually do not feel sympathetic for her in any way, shape, size, or format.

 2. Growl at her to stop bitching and moaning about how she was sorry for not answering my calls and how she wants a boyfriend.

We all run away from her and separate. I run away to the nearest liquor-deli to buy a lottery ticket.

Part II: *The Balndian Sisters Ballet*

The afternoon approaches as a group of twelve Italian sisters enter the garden out back. They are planning to have a feast with their mother, and then they notice Emily. One of them named Isabella chats with Emily for a minute, and Emily stops crying. They start their own ballet, and when the eldest sister, so vain about her appearance, wants to dye her hair, they help her by providing her with a different color red. She becomes even more vain and her sisters then change the color to blonde. It suits her. As the dance moves on, the eldest sister takes charge by preparing the meal for lunch.

Their mother arrives. She even joins the dance, not hungry. Later on, when it becomes closer to the end of the day, Emily becomes a little emotional again and the sisters feel nothing but sympathetic. However, their sympathy session is cut short when Isabella is really tired and wants to take a nap. The rest of the pack creates a designated resting area for her. They will come back and pick her up in one hour.

Part III: *Logan and the Boys Ballet*

As dusk approaches, Logan, his brother-in-law Dave, and some of the guys from grocery in Natural Market arrive in the back garden. Ben from Natural Market is furious that Emily gave me an indication that she liked me and then blew me off by never answering her phone when I called her. He demands an explanation for her behavior at once. Emily once again says she was busy, but this time unfortunately (for her, that is) that doesn't cut it (because Ben is on my side about pretty much everything and we've decided that anyone we do not like gets struck by a 1982 Grumman bus). He picks her up and demands she say something about her disorderly conduct toward me. She says she had her phone on vibrate and didn't feel it. Ben releases her and puts her on the bench.

Emily begins to cry. The boys all dance around Emily, and then two lovers kiss and Emily cries and clings for attention badly. After that is done, the dance movements start to become a bit unstable. The guys decide they do not really want to be here today and don't even know why they came. They start acting as if they were at work and not in the middle of a ballet. Isabella, however, stays sound asleep. Later on the boys are really over ballet and all go home.

Part IV: *The Madaricos Brothers Ballet*

Now it is the night ballet. A group of seven brothers arrive in the garden. The youngest brother, Pedro, is obsessed with finding Miss Perfect. His brothers tell him he needs to lay off a little bit. But then he sees Emily sitting on the bench, lonely. He introduces himself and they get a little romantic toward each other. Pedro is older than Emily by three months. The eldest brother, Marco, falls deeply in love with Isabella. He kneels by her chair praying to God to make her love him. She wakes and falls deeply in love with him. The rest of the brothers are disgusted and go find something else to occupy themselves with. The quartet have a little dance. The romance starts to fly.

Suddenly Emily's mom arrives at the garden wondering where her baby has been for the past twelve hours. Emily then tells her mom what happened just as I and everybody else arrive back at the garden. Emily's mom and Pedro furiously chase us down, asking for an explanation for our disorderly conduct. We run everywhere looking for a place to hide. For a minute, it looks like we got away. But then we are found again in a desperate attempt to ditch Emily's mom and her new boyfriend. After about fifteen minutes of running around the opera house in circles, we are all too dizzy to go any further and find ourselves back in the main room where it all started. Emily's mom has told our parents. Nick's father has Nick's cell phone turned off as a punishment for being mean. Emily's mom, seeing that Logan got all of her daughter's loneliness and pain on camera, snatches the videotape from Logan and takes his box-cutter and cuts the tape partly in half and then smashes the tape to smithereens with an axe. Then she randomly takes my TV set and smashes it.

The ballet ends with everybody in the ballet (except for Emily and her mother and Pedro, her new boyfriend) all hanging out in the main room with nothing to do as a punishment for our disorderly conduct.

We go back through the main hall and the gates slam shut.

The End

government offices 1 (2005)

series: **2005–**
genre: **BUSINESS**

status: **CONTINUING**

cast

blaze ginsberg: himself
mom: herself
maya: aunt
lavander: aunt
gabe: mom's boyfriend
bodine (bo): uncle
déja: aunt
nana: grandmother
papa: grandfather

guest stars

the dmv workers: themselves
lady in window at social security office 1: herself
ms. t: counselor from department of rehab
ms. s: vas (vocational assessment specialist) at pwi
mr. n: job placement specialist at pwi
mrs. t: woman from social security office

ms. b: intake worker at regional center

psychologist at regional center: herself

ms. m: caseworker at pwi

series summary

I have been going to doctors and government offices since I was five
years old. I actually was in the hospital for asthma in 1990, but I don't
remember that. I have some endocrine system issues, so I had to go to
the doctor a lot when I was younger. Now I still go but not as much.
For me, government offices—like the DMV and Social Security—have
the same vibe as doctors' offices and the hospital. Government offices
are not really my favorite places to be. They are very depressing. I go
there because of job hiring issues, to get my driver's license, my ID,
etc. In some areas it is worth it, like going to the Regional Center for
services and going to the Social Security office to get medical coverage.
On the down side, every time I leave the DMV from not passing my
driver's test, the depression sticks with me.

Episode List

Episode 1   Season 1

title: **THE DMV**   air date: **NOVEMBER 1, 2005**

summary

I have an appointment at the DMV to get an ID card. Lavander will
be taking me and Mom there. I am kind of lonely because my friends
Matt and Danny left for college in August and we are going into the
DMV, a place with a depressing atmosphere that is so 1963. On the
way there I have a conversation with Lavander about the accident on
the school bus that happened yesterday. We arrive at the DMV, and
we have to wait for a while. The DMV guy is so busy focusing on
Lavander that he puts the wrong date of birth on my ID, making me
four days younger then I am supposed to be. (We don't discover this
until my ID arrives in the mail ten days later.) When we get home I
see two buses being towed away.

notes

We were almost killed coming home by a crazy driver who cut us off.

trivia

All the desks and the gray walls and the lighting in the DMV make me think of 1963.

The day before, our bus driver was rear-ended by an SUV. It was just me on the bus and the driver. We were stuck there for a while but I wasn't hurt. The bus dispatcher called Mom to tell her about the accident.

quotes

lavander (about my accident the day before): "Did your bus driver ask you if you were okay?"
me: "No."
lavander: "She didn't even ask you?"
(At the DMV)
dmv guy (to mom, referring to lavander): "Is that your friend?"

soundtrack listing

"Now You Know" by Hilary Duff (A *Cinderella Story Soundtrack* 2004)

"So Yesterday" by Hilary Duff (*Metamorphosis* 2003)

"Tony" by Patty Griffin (*Flaming Red* 1998)

Episode 2

title: **A DEPRESSING JOL* (a.k.a. All the Government Offices)**
air date: **OCTOBER 24, 2006**

---

summary

When I need a Social Security card for my Natural Market orientation, I discover that I don't have one. We will have to go to the Social Security office to get one. Lavander comes and picks me up from Natural Market (because I can't stay there without a Social Security card) but takes me home. While I wait for Nana and Papa to come pick me and Mom up, I watch the garbage (this time there are not two guys like last time). Then Nana and Papa come to get us. Papa and I have a discussion about why it is important to have a Social Security number. We arrive at the Social Security office and I take a number, A28. It is a long time until that number, so I wait for it to be called. After about thirty minutes it is called. We get to the window and I sign

---

*JOL IS AN AFRIKAANS SLANG TERM FOR AN OUTING. I LEARNED THIS WORD FROM MY GRANDMOTHER WHO GREW UP IN SOUTH AFRICA.

paperwork for my card. I go back to Natural Market, but then there is another problem—I can't have my ID called in because of the wrong date of birth on it. We now have to go back to the DMV to get that changed. We go back to the DMV with Lavander. I take number G78 and it is also a long wait for that number to be called. Finally it is called. We tell the guy what happened. He punches a hole in my original ID and throws it in the garbage.

notes
This is the only time we go to two government offices in the same day.

quotes
papa: "Why is it important to have Social Security?"
me: "I don't know."
(At the Social Security office)
me: "That woman looks a lot like my friend Tara from school."
(Later on)
maya (over the phone): "We're going to the DMV to get your ID fixed."

trivia
Tara was a friend of mine, but, ironically, she made me feel the exact depression that I'm feeling now which is not how friends are supposed to make you feel.

soundtrack listing
"On Top of the World" by Jordan Cahill (*Stuck in the Suburbs Soundtrack* 2004)

"So Yesterday" by Hilary Duff (*Metamorphosis* 2003)

"Head over Feet" by Alanis Morissette (*Jagged Little Pill* 1995)

Episode 3

title: **REMORSE**   air date: **JANUARY 24, 2007**

summary
Déja and I are going to Scripps Hospital Rehab to visit her friend, Richard, who has just had a stroke and brain surgery. When we arrive there, I am afraid to see Richard because he has had staples in his head. But Déja assures me they have been removed. We go to see him—it's the first time

I have seen him in a while. I am happy to see him. We stay with him as he goes through musical training and other rehab for his brain.

notes

I ran into a nurse I knew from elementary school.

Richard had a stroke after he had been drinking a lot and it almost happened to him again.

I really wanted a girlfriend in this episode.

quotes

me: "Have you ever had the perfect person taken away from you?"
deja: "Hell, yeah."
richard: "I hate having a fucking pee bag."
nurse: "Oh, hi, Blaze."
me: "Do I know you?"
nurse: "I used to work at your school."

soundtrack listing

"Where Did I Go Right?" by Hilary Duff (*Metamorphosis* 2003)

"Country Road" by James Taylor (*Sweet Baby James* 1970)

Episode 4

---

title: **THE DEPARTMENT OF REHABILITATION**   air date: **MAY 7, 2007**

---

summary

We (Mom, Gabe, and I) are going to the Department of Rehab today to try to find me a new job because I have been cut down to one day a week at Natural Market and that really is not enough. We go to talk to the woman there at the front desk and then we go see Ms. T, my job counselor. Ms. T recommends that we go to the Regional Center.

quotes

mom: "Natural Market cut him down to one day a week, and they are not honest with him."
gabe: "If he doesn't want to go to school he has to get a full-time job."

soundtrack listing

"Modern Love" by David Bowie (*Let's Dance* 1983)

Episode 5

title: **THE WAR OF RICHARD COUNCIL**   air date: **MAY 2007**

summary
Mom, Maya, Déja, Nana, and I are gathering for tea and talking about Richard. He is doing bad things that can cause him to have another brain stroke. This upsets Nana a lot because when Richard had his original brain stroke it put a lot of pressure on Déja, and Nana clearly doesn't want Déja to repeat that.

quotes
nana: "If he has another stroke, nobody is going to go to Scripps again to take care of him. Because that was very stressful for you, Déja. You don't even know."
déja: "I know, I was, like, 'Richard, you're thirty years old—get a job.'"
nana: "He was not raised properly."

soundtrack listing
"Golden Years" by David Bowie (1975)

Episode 6

title: **PRAY FOR THIS TO WORK (Using My Powers To Defeat Negativity)**
air date: **MAY 14, 2007**

summary
We are going to the Social Security office because I have an appointment to see whether I can get approved for services like health coverage. Gabe will be taking us. In ten days I will be done with school. I want to work full-time instead of school because I am sick of school. However, Mom is not down for this plan at all. We arrive there and were going to wait for a number to be called. But then we realize we don't have to. I am using my magic powers to make the Social Security office waiting room as happy as June 2004 instead of the depressing dump hole the office actually is. It seems to work. June 2004 was when my sophomore year (which was fucked up since the second day) finally ended. This experience with college has been the exact same story of my sophomore year. I manage to make the usual vibe of the waiting room just disintegrate. I am doing this because for the past fifteen years my doctor's office has been associated

with school. And frankly I have quite enough of school and I'm just going to work full-time to make my life better. The lady, Mrs. T, calls us into her office. We talk and get to know each other. I do not use my powers inside this office and just try to keep it cool with the appointment. However, I get restless when the appointment takes forever to end. Later Gabe and Mom talk to me about why I should try to stay in school.

quotes

mrs. t: "He is only allowed to have $2,000 in the bank."
me: "Why?"
mrs. t: "In order to receive services, you cannot have more than $2,000 in resources."
mrs. t: "How much money do you have on you right now?"
me: "I think four dollars." (checking my wallet) "Yes, four dollars."
me (quoting michael jackson): "Cuz I'm bad, I'm bad ..."
gabe: "Working full-time is really worse than school."
mom: "I would really like you to stay in school."

soundtrack listing

"Bad" by Michael Jackson (*Bad* 1987)

"Scary Monsters" by David Bowie (*Scary Monsters* 1980)

"Weeping Wall" by David Bowie (*Low* 1977)

Episode 7

title: **PWI (Partnerships With Industry)**   air date: **MAY 15, 2007**

summary

I am going to PWI to meet my VAS (Vocational Assistance Specialist, the person who will be doing job exploration with me). Maya will be taking us there, and Nana will be going with us for the ride. Beforehand the recycling comes and I watch it. It causes Papa to not be able to get out of our driveway. When the recycling leaves we leave for PWI. I listen to "Mexico" by James Taylor on the ride up. We arrive there and talk to Ms. S, my vocational assessment specialist. We go over all the types of jobs I can have in the future. I tell her I want one with no facing required* because the face at Natural Market was the main reason I was cut down to one day a week and why that job did not work out.

*SEE ALL-STORE MEETINGS AT NATURAL MARKET FOR MORE ABOUT FACING.

notes

Ms. S and I will be taking a ride to go look for a new job starting on the 31st.

soundtrack listing

"Mexico" by James Taylor (*Gorilla* 1975)

Episode 8

title: **THE SAN DIEGO REGIONAL CENTER FOR THE DEVELOPMENTALLY DISABLED**   air date: **MAY 2007**

---

summary

I'm going to listen to a man speak about services offered at the Regional Center, and Mom will be coming in with me. I start thinking about how, back in February, I wanted a new trio of friends and I had a celebrity crush on Anais from the all-girl group Play, and how I still don't have a new trio of friends.

soundtrack listing

"Make Sure You're Sure" by Stevie Wonder (*Jungle Fever* 1991)
This song plays in many tense situations for me, like when there are work problems or mechanical failures of things like the refrigerator, which started leaking and spraying water all over everything in the kitchen late one night.

holding on:
a rough summer (2007)

release date: **MAY 28, 2007**

cast

blaze ginsberg: himself

mom: herself

maya: aunt

déja: aunt

lavander: aunt

bodine (bo): uncle

papa: grandfather

nana: grandmother

gabe: mom's boyfriend

clark a: friend

rachel: the hot neighbor/potential girlfriend

gill: buddy/neighbor

karen: cute neighbor

shelly: mother next door

svetlana: vons manager

ms. s: vas at pwi

featuring

matt: himself/buddy

melissa: herself

liam: melissa's son

zoë: melissa's daughter

jenny: friend

tessla: jenny's friend

emily: could have been girlfriend

movie summary

Scene 1: *Searching for the Perfect Summer*

It has been a very short time since my first year of college has come to a grand close. I have my first visit with Matt in months. (He was still in Irvine, but Mom did not want me to see him so I could focus more on school). We go to pick him up at the train station and chat about fantasies in the car. We hang around, and I try to get him to say things from a script I've made up but he doesn't, he just sits on my bed saying nothing. We go for a swim and act out some dialogue I've made up. Also, in addition to all that is going on, I have a crush on Rachel (our hot neighbor) and I am thinking about her a lot. I've been listening to the studio tracks released on *Hell Freezes Over* by The Eagles. The next day after Matt's visit, Nana is being brought to the house for an outing. I don't like that she's being brought over here instead of us going to pick her up, so I go for a walk to the bagel shop to chill out. I am also expecting the garbage and recycling trucks to come, but the schedule is delayed because of Memorial Day. Today Mom is going to Reed College in Portland to teach a memoir class. She'll be coming back on Saturday. Later that night, when I am watching *The Fresh Prince of Bel-Air*, I try to research the episode "The Baby Comes Out," but then something goes wrong with the Internet connection and it goes down. I go and rewire the computer and then end up messing up the mouse. The next day Déja and I are going to be spending the day together instead of her picking me up on a Wednesday, which she usually does. It goes well. We have a really good time together drinking tea, watching *Big Daddy*, and talking. I heat up some homemade soup that Mom left for me and eat. Later on we go to get a car wash because Déja's car is just filthy; then we go get french fries and talk about our experiences with the sixth grade. Later on, after Déja leaves, the recycling comes. It is late. I have been kind of hoping it would be the truck I want but it is not. But there are two trucks here again instead of just one for the second time. I watch the trucks and think about Rachel, the hot neighbor. The recycling man picks up our side's recyclables. He notices Karen, the little girl next door (Rachel's sister). He smiles and waves at her. After the trucks are done I go outside to take the cans in. Karen says hi to me. I go for a walk to the bagel shop thinking about Rachel. I talk to my homies from the bagel shop, get my two "everything" bagels, and continue thinking about Rachel. Maya comes home and then takes me out to Sammy's Pizza and I get some fries.

quotes
matt: "Blaze, what's up bro?"
me: "Not a whole lot! Nice to see you."
(The next day)
maya: "Papa is dropping Nana off."
me (angrily): "Why? I don't fucking like that!" (I leave for the bagel shop)
(When I am hanging with Déja)
me: "Was your sixth grade year good or bad?"
déja: "Uh, not good."
me: "Why is sixth grade bad?"
déja: "Because it is a big transition in your life and a lot of change."
me: "My sixth grade year was bad because I got in trouble a lot. I got suspended from recess."

Scene 2: *First Hunting for a New Job*
Ms. S, who is helping me to find a new job, comes to pick me up at the house for our first outing for a new job for me because I was cut down to only one day a week at Natural Market. We go to Del Mar Highlands and check out Ralph's, the grocery store, for the first place. We ask a produce member what the basic job description is. We then move to Rite Aid, a little shop that sells greeting cards, and then after that Ms. S takes me back home.

quotes
ms. s: "Let's go ask this produce man what the job duties are. Excuse me sir, we are doing job exploration and we want to know what the basic job duties are of working in produce?"
produce man: "You have to put produce up and make sure it's clean. The receiving guy has to do a lot of work, making sure all the orders are together."

Scene 3: *Slowly Going Downhill*

One day, after coming home from Natural Market, I get an e-mail from Matt. He doesn't format the e-mail the way I want. This upsets me, but I call him and we talk about it. I am starting to hate all the things that are giving me trouble. For example, I now intensely hate the truck that picks up our recyclables because the one I want never comes. The next day when Mom returns home she asks how everything went while she was away and we talk about that. Then I bring up our neighbor Rachel. Mom says that Rachel has a boyfriend and that she's seen them holding hands and kissing. I get so badly shocked that I nearly have a heart attack. It paralyzes me and makes me feel like I am in trouble, like it's my sixth grade year again. I call my friend David to see what is up. We talk and I go take a walk to the bagel shop. Later that night, I cry about not having a girlfriend, and I watch *Fantasia* and then have a vision of Ashley Olsen comforting me. The next day Ashley and I are kind of boyfriend and girlfriend in my mind. I am so badly messed up from Rachel having a boyfriend that I watch *Fantasia* again. I then watch some *Sleeping Beauty* and *Roseanne*.

trivia

I like Matt to put certain dates on his e-mails and refer to the things we talk about on the phone.

quotes

mom: "What happened to my iPod?"

me: "Rachel was here and she messed it up. I'm kidding."

mom: "You know, I think she has a boyfriend."

me: "What?"

mom: "I saw her with a boy outside. They were holding hands, being romantic. She was kissing him."

me: "When did you see that?"

mom: "I don't know, the other day."

me: "What day?"

mom: "I don't know, but I'm pretty sure that's her boyfriend."

me: "How old is he?"

mom: "I don't know."

Scene 4: *Very Rewarding*

The next day I talk with my friend Reilly on the phone and send him e-mails. I kind of argue with Mom about various things, and then I go for a walk. When I come home I see Rachel's brother and we chat; then

I ask him if Rachel has a boyfriend just to confirm, but he says no. That is one turnaround and I think there is still hope. I am just lying around in my room when Mom calls me upstairs to tell me I passed all my classes at Vista View. We go out for a mini-celebration to Sammy's.

Scene 5: *No Mercy*

They are having an early birthday party at the pool in our complex because Rachel's brother is leaving for college soon. I sit and chat with him. Their mother offers me cake. We chat about Rachel and then he brings up her status and tells me that she does in fact have a boyfriend. She was never a possibility after all. A few days later I am just looking at videos in YouTube of "Mysterious Theater," an old Sesame Street segment parody of the 1980 TV series, *Mystery*. Later that day we go for a formal celebration for passing all my classes. I talk to Nana and Maya about getting a present for Mom (her birthday is in four days). I get into an argument with everyone because I resist getting a specific present for Mom. I was originally going to get her an iTunes card, but she said she didn't want that and I am unwilling to spend money on a different present. Nana lectures me about this, and I tell her that I will chip in for a present.

Scene 6: *What Matt May Bring*

A week later on Father's Day I am planning to see Matt one more time before he has to hit it for college again. But a debate comes in when Nana doesn't want me and Matt to come to the beach next to her house because she doesn't want to have to worry about the two of us alone on the beach. Mom doesn't approve of the whole idea either, and the family doesn't trust me doing certain things (like driving and going in the ocean) with Matt. Mom then brings up how I could have been conserved, meaning she would still make my decisions for me even after I turned eighteen. Mom says that she didn't do that because she believes I can be mature enough to make my own decisions in the future, but she doesn't think I am quite there yet. Matt arrives. We make videos of us acting out scripts, and then Mom and Gabe take us to the beach because Mom is not comfortable with me driving with Matt since he only recently got his license. Matt and I have fun at the beach. He cracks me up by yelling, "More toilet paper!" Later on, after Gabe talks to Mom and tells her it's okay, Mom lets me and Matt go for a drive with Matt driving. I take him to my old school and show it to him. I am still thinking about the whole conserved deal. I tell Matt about how my biological father walked out on me before I was born. Matt says he is an asshole. Then we head up to the mall. Matt gets Chinese food to go and he eats it back at the house. Later we play Sorry!; he takes a nap on my bed and goes home at 8:30. The next day he calls me to tell me his drive back to his parents' house in Irvine was uneventful.

Scene 7: *Heartbreak Time at the Right Time*
About four days after getting together with Matt I find out Logan, my boss at Natural Market, is leaving. The next day at work I am very miserable. I talk with Jo, another grocery member about that, and how I want a girlfriend and I also want to have friends. Jo gives me the "be patient, it will happen" line. I then ask him about hanging out someday and he says sure. Ironically, when I ask him for his cell number he says he doesn't have one, or a home phone. I keep saying that I hate working at Natural Market. I even purposely break a salad dressing bottle when I can't find where it's supposed to go on the shelf. It turns out it has the wrong code on it, meaning we don't sell it at the store. At the end of my day, when Maya picks me up, I get in her car with a miserable attitude. At home I talk with Mom about everything, and she explains things to me and makes me feel better.

Scene 8: *Melissa's Story*
Two days after this intense turn of events I go hang out with Bo to help him out with his lawn. I am okay today. I have a crush on Candace Cameron even though she is married. I think about her while picking up sticks and moving them out of the way for Bo to mow the lawn. I am also looking forward to seeing Melissa, my film teacher/Mom's friend, for dinner. Bo takes me home and later, when Melissa is late, I go for a walk to calm down. I arrive back at the house and I see Melissa and her two cute children. When I try to say hi to Zoë, who is four years old and shy, she hides her face on her father's shoulder. We sit around the table. I eat corn and everyone else eats whatever. I suddenly start striking up a conversation with Zoë, and she wants me to read to her and bury her underneath pillows. We take it down to my room and her brother Liam (seven) is just wild. Liam is also high functioning autistic and he asks some very interesting questions. He even asks about my father. I lie to him and his sister, telling them my father is really busy and works a lot because I don't feel it is right them knowing the real story. Liam knocks all the stuff off my desk and Zoë gets Melissa, who takes Liam aside. I talk with Zoë about a punishment for Liam if he is bad again. At the end of the day, Melissa comes in and says that it is time to go.

Zoë doesn't want to leave because she has had so much fun with me.
Liam asks if I can baby-sit some day.

quotes
melissa's husband: "This is Liam and this is the cute one, Zoë. Say hi, Zoë."
melissa: "Once you get her started she won't stop."
zoë (repeated line): "Bury me again!"
zoë (another repeated line): "Read me this book. Read me this book."
liam (repeated line): "When is it time for Blaze to go?"
melissa: "Blaze is not leaving! He lives here."
(At the end of the night)
melissa: "Zoë, it's time to go, sweetie."

Scene 9: *Dreams*
One late afternoon when I am swimming at the pool I think about
how a lot of my friends have gone far away for college. Then I think
to myself that I want to go far away too, to Pacific University where Bo
went. When I come back from the pool I talk to Mom about how I
feel about the whole idea, and we talk about it and how I need to be
in order for that to happen. Mom says I need to be able to take care of
myself, manage my medications, wake myself up, and take care of my
business before I can live away from home. The next day I go to the
fair with Déja and her buddy Richard, who is basically recovered from
his brain stroke plus or minus a few things. He is still shaking a little
bit but his speech is very clear. We take a British two-story bus there.
I get a wristband so I can go on whatever rides I want when I want to
without tickets that would run out. I go on every single ride except for
Falling Star on my own. I talk with Déja about the whole girlfriend
deal. As usual, Déja tells me it will happen, be patient.

Scene 10: *Back on the Scene with Friends Finally*
One afternoon my Surrey friend Jenny calls me up and asks me if I
want to see *Ratatouille* with her and her friend Tessla. I say yes and she
says I should bring my ID. We go into the movie; I am happy I have
a new trio of friends. During the movie I keep getting worried about
getting close to them if I am leaving for college far away in a year.
The movie ends and I get Tessla's number. About five days after that,
Clark (from Surrey; see *Games 3* and *Senior Year 1*) and I have our first
outside-of-school hang out and it goes great. We play some GTA and
go driving a lot; and then Clark meets Maya, then he goes home.

Scene 11: *Number One Birthday of All Time*

I wake up in the morning and I can't believe I am twenty years old. My nose is a little backed up, so I just watch some *Full House* in bed. I start the day by opening presents. One is the *Hell Freezes Over* DVD from Mom. Déja comes over and we head for the train station because we are going to ride the Coaster downtown like we did on my fourteenth birthday. We arrive downtown and we go to Extraordinary Desserts for tea. I check my phone and I see that I have missed a call and it's from Gabe. He has left me a message wishing me a happy birthday. Dessert and tea are great. Later we go walk around downtown with the time we have before it is time to get back on the train. We look at buses and I tell everybody about what year the various buses are from. We stop at the transit store and Mom buys me an MTS (Metropolitan Transit System) mug. I see a 1991 Gillig Phantom bus and I chase after it. But then two stretch buses from 1993 arrive. They take off and are very, very loud. We start to head back to the train station. Lavander calls me to wish me happy birthday, and then we get back on the train. At home I hang out with Reilly. He and his sister and his mother will be staying for cake. Later on it's family gathering time for cake again. I have a rainbow cake (the same as my fourteenth birthday). Lavander's present to me is Spike Lee's *Do The Right Thing*. I've been wanting that movie since I liked it so much after watching it in film class. The next day I just hang with Clark and go take a ride to the mall.

quotes
me (explaining the buses): "That bus is from 1995. That bus is from 2001, that bus is from 1997, and that bus is from 2002."
maya: "How do you know so much about buses?"
me: "I looked them up online."
(At home)
me (to reilly): "They have buses a year younger than you."
reilly: "Wow, no way."
(The next day at my house)
me (hearing a weird sound from the recycling truck): "Clark, what's that noise?"
clark: "That's the recyclables going into the truck."

Scene 12: *Getting the Feeling*

Three days after my birthday we have to go to the Oceanside campus for an appointment with Ms. C, a counselor, to talk about the classes that I will be taking in the fall. Gabe is with us because I feel more comfortable with him being there. I am also going to the Del Mar races with Papa and Bo today. We arrive at the campus and we start off the conversation with what happened last time around with my English teacher not believing I've done my work and the other counselor telling me to drop out of school. Ms. C is very nice. We then get into the classes deal. Later, after we are through with that, I go to home and Papa picks me up; we go to his house and then off to the races.

Scene 13: *The Possible New Job*
One day while I am out with Ms. S and we're doing our thing, I recommend we go stop by a grocery store, Vons. We talk to a manager about the job description. A few days later I am called in for an interview with Svetlana (the manager). She is Russian. We talk about how things are going to work at this job. She is seemingly strict. Two days later when I go in to sign paperwork it takes a really long time and I keep Déja waiting in the car for a while. I have to take a drug test for the job. Svetlana puts a swab in my mouth and places it in a tube for the test. I'm a little nervous because I ate hemp cereal for breakfast and Mom says she hopes that doesn't show up as drugs. But I think I've been hired.

quotes
me (to manager): "Is there a face?"
manager: "Everybody faces their own aisle."
(With Svetlana)
svetlana (explaining policies): "If you get romantic with another employee, you must inform me."
svetlana (giving me paperwork): "Read this from top to bottom; come find me when you are done."
me: "What will happen if I don't pass my drug test? Are you going to call the police?"
svetlana (chuckles): "No, you will just not get hired."

Scene 14: *The Down Orientation*
I wake up at six o'clock in the morning and leave for the Vons orientation after eating only one fruit. I usually have two fruits for breakfast. Maya takes me. It is a long drive so I have a little while to relax in the car before I have to sit and focus for eight whole hours. We arrive there and I go inside and sit in my seat, but it is hard for me to sit still. I am wriggling, I have to get up to go to the bathroom, and I keep getting up to throw gum away. I annoy one of the other people there. At lunch I end up getting kicked out of orientation by the trainer who

tells me I am disruptive. I call Mom and I also have to call Svetlana to tell her. I have to wait for Lavander to pick me up. I look at buses while I do so. Lavander arrives and we have to go back to her house to pick up Colin (her boyfriend, now ex). I go to the bagel shop and just get bagels and talk a lot about the whole deal to my homies there. A few days later I go to talk to Claudine (one of the other managers at Vons). She says it's okay, but I never hear back from Vons to start work.

quotes

connie (the trainer, to everyone): "You don't have to walk around going (walks like Quasimodo, slurring) 'Can I help you find something? Can I help you find something?'"
(Later)
connie: "If you hurt yourself using the power tools you will get a drug test."
(Later)
connie: "Oh, Blaze, I want to talk to you. I am sending you home; you are too disruptive to the class."
me: "Please don't send me home; I won't do it again."
connie: "It's too late. You need to call your supervisor."
me: "I can't believe this shit."
jeff (connie's helper): "Walk all the way out. I don't want to hear any putdowns or profanity."
me (when I call lavander): "I was sent home from orientation. This really wasn't the right job for me."
lavander: "I'm on my way, babe. Don't worry about it. I've had that happen to me before and it will be fine."
(With Claudine)
claudine: "Don't worry about it."
me: "Do I still get hired?"
claudine: "Like I said, don't worry about it."

Scene 15: *Bus with a Broken Belt*

I am out on not such a good groove with Mom, Maya, and Nana. I am bringing everyone down because I am miserable, and they are letting me know that they don't like it. I have now pretty much had enough of the summer because of what has happened: Rachel having a boyfriend, Emily not answering her phone, getting kicked out of Vons orientation, and Logan leaving for Texas. I keep bringing everyone else down with how I dislike the vacation. But on the flip side I go back to school in two days. Later, when I am out for a swim, I call Emily and she answers her phone for a change. She is now in NYU, but then my phone loses the signal. She calls me back and we talk, and I tell her what happened in my first year of college.

quotes
emily (answering her phone): "Hello?"
me: "Hi, Emily, it's Blaze."
emily: "Hi, Blaze, what's up?"
me: "Not a whole lot. How about you?"
emily: "I'm just in NYU."
me: "What? You went away to college? When did you go?"
emily: "About five days ago. I told you I was going."
me: "I don't remember that."

movie notes
Looking back on this summer, it seems very depressing. Rachel having a boyfriend really messed things up. Aside from the races, hanging with Matt, hanging with Clark, hanging with Jenny and Tessla, and my birthday, this summer really wasn't that good. I had strongly denied it being a crappy summer until the end. Logan leaving, Rachel having a boyfriend, the cave-in at orientation (the most depressing part), and Emily never answering her phone again really made me feel like I was paying off old dues.

soundtrack listing

Scene 1
"Mexico" by James Taylor (*Gorilla* 1975)

"Barbie Girl" by Aqua (*Aquarium* 1997)

"Carry Me" by Patty Griffin (*Flaming Red* 1998)

Scene 3
"Mandolin Rain" by Bruce Hornsby (*The Way It Is* 1986)

Scene 4
"Pumpin' Up the Party" by Miley Cyrus (*Hannah Montana Soundtrack* 2006)

Scene 6
"Come Get to This" by Marvin Gaye (*Let's Get It On* 1973)

"You Can Call Me Al" by Paul Simon (*Graceland* 1986)

Scene 7
"I Wanna Be" by Emma Roberts (*Unfabulous and More* 2005)

"Never Can Say Goodbye" by The Jackson 5 (1971)

Scene 11
"Young Americans" by David Bowie (*Young Americans* 1975)

"Jungle Fever" and "If She Breaks Your Heart" by Stevie Wonder (*Jungle Fever* 1991)

"The Heart of the Matter" by Don Henley (*The End of the Innocence* 1989)

Scene 12
"Same Ole Love" by Anita Baker (*Rapture* 1986)

government offices 2 (2007)

cast
See Cast, *Government Offices 1*

Episode 9 \ Season 2

title: **ORIENTATION** air date: **JUNE 5, 2007**

---

summary
I will be going to Regional Center orientation today. The man plays a videotape of blind people and women with autistic children. Another man stands up and talks about insurance polices. In my head during the insurance talk I am calling out to my hot neighbor Rachel (as an escape) because I have also recently associated insurance with bad feelings because Mom told me that I had to take a full course load at college to keep my health insurance. Now, whenever insurance comes up in any way, I need an escape hatch in my brain.

quotes
me (in my head): "Rachel!!!!"
man: "You are required to have insurance."

Episode 10

title: **MS. B**   air date: **JULY 3, 2007**

summary

I am going to the Regional Center to meet with my Intake Worker,
Ms. B. Déja is our ride there. We wait a while for it to be time for
my appointment. Finally it is time. We all meet and get to know
each other. Mom brings up school issues in the past. Déja makes a
remark about Matt, and I scold her about it. Later when Mom and
the caseworker have to talk about something private, Déja and I
happily dismiss ourselves. Mom comes out later and tells us that I
will probably be approved for Regional Center services, like getting
a job coach. Déja then takes us home.

notes

This is Déja's second and last appearance in the series. It is also the last
episode tracing back to the early days of school.

quotes

mom: "School was an issue for Blaze. They always said to put him on
medication. In 2001 we went to the Los Angeles Diagnostic Center.
They were not helpful at all."
deja: "Matt is cuckoo."
me (gritting my teeth): "Déja!"
(Back in Déja's car)
déja: "It looks like your craziness got you approved."

Episode 11

title: **FINAL EVALUATIONS**   air date: **AUGUST 2007**

summary

Today I have my last appointment at the Regional Center to
determine whether or not I will receive services. The psychologist
who I am working with has me draw some pictures like I've done
in the past in elementary school. She asks me various questions.
Then I tell her some problems I have had, like with Tina C having
a boyfriend and Tara A backfiring at me about e-mails. I give her
the dates for all of these things. The psychologist happily writes

down the dates they occurred on. I later go shopping with Mom and Maya.

notes

I took a bathroom break in between the tests.

At first I was not too fired up about the tests and questions because they reminded me of being back in kindergarten, which was not a pleasant experience at all, but then I became cool with it.

Episode 12

title: **THE TEST**   air date: **OCTOBER 9, 2007**

summary

Bo is taking me to the DMV to take my driver's written test. We chat in the car on the way to the DMV and decide we will go to Manhattan restaurant for dinner if I pass the test. We arrive and there it is a very long line into the building. Finally we do get in the building, but a problem occurs. I need a birth certificate, but luckily my ID covers it. I sign the paperwork and then it is time for the test. I pick it up at the desk, but it takes me a while to finally get it. I take the test and feel like I know it, but unfortunately I do not pass.

notes

This is the only appearance of Bo in the series. He gave me a hard time about not passing the test.

quotes

Bo (looking over my test, laughing): "Oh my god, what do you do if you see a blind person? Honk?" (Teasing me) "Look at me—I'm honking at blind people! Donkey! You're a donkey!" (Repeated line)

Episode 13

title: **MR. N**   air date: **NOVEMBER 2007**

summary
Mom and I are going to meet Mr. N, who will be helping to get me a job and a job coach. We go to PWI to meet him; it takes a while. First we meet with Ms. M, my caseworker, and talk about Natural Market and what happened there. Then it is time to meet Mr. N. He is nice. We talk about what happened with Vons. Ironically, Vons is now the most convenient job option.

quotes
(In Ms. M's office)
mom: "In February Natural Market cut him down to one day a week, and they were never honest with him about why."
(In Mr. N's office)
mom: "At Vons where he applied, there was a lack of communication between the two managers. On the day of his orientation Blaze called me at eleven o'clock and told me he was kicked out."
mr. n: "Every three months they get a new manager at Vons."
me: "I don't want to work weekends."
mr. n: "You gotta work whenever they need you."

Episode 14

title: **TRYING AGAIN (And Still Not Passing)**   air date: **DECEMBER 26, 2007**

summary
I am going to the DMV with Gabe. We arrive there but the office is closed, so we ride around the area until it opens up. We go back to the office when it opens, and we're first in line so this time no number will be taken. I go sit down to take my test and turn off my phone. I take it back to the woman at the window. Again, I feel like I know the answers. Sadly, I end up not passing again.

notes
Mom does not appear in this episode.

quotes

me: "I called Emily and she never would answer my calls."

gabe: "Cute girls get hit on all the time, that's probably why."

gabe: "I have never seen this area before."

(Later when we are leaving the DMV)

gabe: "You gotta study the book."

me: "I thought I hit it all up in the tutorials."

gabe: "You need to invest in your own life. Jonathan* turned a twelve-hundred dollar speeding ticket into a thirty-five hundred dollar speeding ticket because he was stupid and didn't pay the bill on time. Now he has a five-year period where he can't buy a new car. Study the book, read a few pages every day, and you'll pass."

*GABE'S SON.

my crush on
sara paxton (2007)

series: **2007**   release date: **APRIL 14, 2007**

genre: **COMING OF AGE/ROMANCE**   status: **ENDED**

cast

blaze ginsberg: himself (2007)

sara paxton: herself (2007)

aquamarine: character from *aquamarine* (2007)

dina: friend (2007)

matt b: himself/executive producer (2007)

guest stars

nick: friend

mom: herself

maya: aunt

gabe: mom's boyfriend

lavander: aunt

déja: aunt

bodine (bo): uncle

nana: grandmother

papa: grandfather
logan: ex-boss.friend
gen: maya's friend
clark: friend
kat: potential girlfriend
colin: lavander's boyfriend (now ex)

Episode List
Episode 1

title: **PILOT**   air date: **APRIL 14, 2007**

summary
After having a romantic/sexy dream about swimming with Aquamarine from the movie *Aquamarine*, I seem to fall in love with Sara Paxton, the actress who plays Aquamarine. I talk about her in my e-mails to Matt. I think about her a lot. I pretend we ditch Vista View together.

notes
I sent three e-mails to Matt with Sara Paxton as the topic.

In her first appearance in my e-mails to Matt, we are a Merman and Mermaid and we are ditching Vista View. Then we have a session with Ian (my former counselor from Surrey).

I pretended I was ditching Vista View with Sara Paxton because I do not like college one little bit. The previous school year had been one of the worst school years ever, and I was planning to drop out of college and work full-time. Also, I used her as my mental shield when things were bothering me.

Episode 2

title: **I'M A PLAYA**   air date: **AUGUST 21, 2007**

summary
Very early in the morning, I am having a funny dream set in December 1993. Maya, her friend Gen, and I are at a funeral/concert. Then Matthew Cuthbert (from the movie *Anne of Green Gables*) dies. My friends Jay (from the bagel shop), Tara from Vista View, and I are talking and I am worried about death. I talk to Jay about it. I then end up going to Matthew Cuthbert's funeral. Anne of Green Gables then

dives into the grass wanting Matthew back. Then Maya, Gen, and I are packing up Gen's car, getting ready to take her home. Then I hear the beeper of one of the garbage or recycling trucks. A few seconds later I see the garbage driving away.

I am woken up from this dream by what I'm hoping is the recycling truck. I keep hearing a beeper and a low engine rumbling. I meditate and wait for it to arrive, but it does not ever end up arriving. I then fall back asleep and I wake up later and talk with Maya about *Aquamarine*. Also today I begin hating Miley Cyrus (from *Hannah Montana*). I have been pretending she was my wife on and off since the end of last March but I keep thinking negative thoughts about Miley now that I have Sara Paxton in my head. I eat my breakfast and watch the garbage. Then later on it's time to log in to Course Compass, my online math class. It is kind of a pain. In the middle of that the recycling does end up coming. I pause to watch it. After all that I am just sitting on the couch and Reilly texts me to see what's up. I tell him that I have hated Miley Cyrus since 1975 (December 11). Later in the day I go for a swim and call Logan. He answers his phone and we talk a bit.

notes

I started hating Miley because the night before I was playing videos on YouTube too loud and I got into a fight with Mom about it and I saw Miley kissing Jake (Cody Linley) on the YouTube video "Ready, Set, Don't Go" by Billy Ray Cyrus. I think it was that and the fight with Mom together which kind of messed everything up.

The sound of the truck I was hearing was from the loading dock.

This is my favorite episode of the series because I like getting up early, I got to speak to Logan on the phone, and, lastly, I was pleased to be having a crush on someone who was closer to my own age.

trivia

Gen is Maya's friend and stand partner in her orchestra.

quotes
me (waking up): "Maya, where's Mom?"
maya: "She's upstairs."
me: "What's *Aquamarine* about?"
maya: "It's a movie for twelve-year-old girls."
(Later on)
logan (on the phone): "Hey B, what's up?"

me: "Not a whole lot, you?"
logan: "Just working with my brother-in-law."
me: "Is his name Pete?"
logan: "Dave."
me: "Miley Cyrus is dead to me."
logan: "She got hit by the bus?"
me: "Yeah, she got hit on July 20, 2001."
me: "I'm in love with Sara Paxton now."
logan: "I don't know who that is."

soundtrack listing

"Connected" by Sara Paxton (2006)

"Working It Out" by Hilary Duff (*Metamorphosis* 2003)

"Lighting up the Candles" by Stevie Wonder (*Jungle Fever* 1991)

"Fire and Rain" by James Taylor (*Sweet Baby James* 1970)

"Choosey Beggar" by Smokey Robison and the Miracles (*Going to a Go-Go* 1965)

Episode 3

title: **WILD HAPPINESS**   air date: **AUGUST 22, 2007**

summary

Today I couldn't be happier. I have gotten a new trio of friends. I have been officially reunited with Nick (an old Surrey friend); I meet two girls, Megan and Kristine, outside the school library at Vista View; and I talk to them about my life. I ask them about their opinions about Miley Cyrus. They are also thumbs down on her. We have a very good conversation about life, then it is time for counseling class. I see Nick and say hello to him. Papa then picks me up and we talk about my day at school.

trivia

Counseling class helps you decide your future goals and then work on getting to them.

quotes

me: "Can I sit here?"
megan: "Sure."
me: "I'm Blaze. What are your names?"

megan: "I'm Megan."

kristine: "I'm Kristine."

me: "What classes are you taking?"

megan: "We're in Counseling."

me: "Me too."

me: "How old are you two?"

megan: "Eighteen."

kristine: "Seventeen."

me: "I'm twenty. When are your birthdays?"

megan: "August."

kristine: "October."

me: "Do you guys like Miley Cyrus?"

megan: "Nah, not really."

me: "Ever heard of Sara Paxton?"

megan: "Yeah."

me: "I have a crush on her."

megan: "You must really be into Sara Paxton."

(Later)

nick: "We should go see a movie sometime."

me: "Okay, I'll need your number."

(Nick programs his number into my phone)

papa: "How was school, boy?"

me: "School, school was wonderful. I couldn't be happier."

soundtrack listing

"Kiss the Girl" by Ashley Tisdale (2006)

Episode 4

title: **THE STORY**   air date: **AUGUST 23, 2007**

summary

I will be hanging with my friend Clark today. He arrives at my house and we chat, go for a ride, and talk about what happened with Miley Cyrus. We go to Fifteenth Street beach and I go in the water. Clark dives in as well. Later Clark gets the remote control to his dad's car wet, but luckily for him the water does not affect it. We go back to the house briefly; then we go to Elijah's. On the way there I tell him some fantasies I've made up involving Sara Paxton. At Elijah's I kind of get depressed over not really having a girlfriend.

notes

This is Clark's only appearance in the series. This is the first episode where I hang out with a friend. However, Clark is in some of Matt's e-mails to me during this period.

quotes

me (joking around): "In January 2006 Matt went and smashed a hole in Sara's air hole."

clark: "Ah. Okay, I can understand Matt doing that."

me (referring to my dream): "One day last December I was swimming with Sara. I went down underwater with her and I squeezed her and she choked."

clark: "Were you two going down for a hug?"

(At Elijah's when I get all depressed)

clark: "The longer you are without a girlfriend, the better the relationship will be when you have one."

(Later)

clark (when he is over hearing about sara's pretend air hole—repeated line): "Blaze, enough with the air hole."

soundtrack listing

"What Good Am I Without You?" by Marvin Gaye and Kim Weston (1964)

Episode 5

---

title: **SUGA PIE SARA BUNCH**   air date: **AUGUST 25, 2007**

---

summary

Nick and I are hanging out. We are on our way to the mall. On the way I sing "Suga Pie Honey Bunch" by the Four Tops in lyrics dedicated to Sara Paxton. We arrive at the mall and I buy a big bag of candy from The Candy Shoppe. On the way home from hanging with Nick, he takes me to Jack in the Box to get an orange juice. Later, I go to Maya's musical, *Westside Story*, with Mom and Gabe. The theater where Maya is playing is in Vista and I am thinking a lot of Sara Paxton on the long drive there and during the musical itself. I call Reilly to say what's up, but when he doesn't pick up I get aggro. Gabe scolds me about it.

notes
This is the only episode in this series where I call my friends and they don't pick up. I also called my friend Terri from Yoga last year. She never picked up any of my calls.

quotes
me (singing): "Suga Pie Sara Bunch, you know I love you … I can't help myself."
nick: "Ha-ha."
(Later)
nick: "How does six dollars worth of candy feel?"
me: "Good."
(Later)
me: "Why doesn't he answer his phone? Not answering is a real jerk-like thing to do."
gabe (firmly): "Hey, you know what—maybe he's busy. You can't be such a baby about it."

soundtrack listing
"Crash World" by Hilary Duff (*A Cinderella Story Soundtrack* 2004)

"Suga Pie Honey Bunch" by The Four Tops (*The Four Tops Second Album* 1965)

Episode 6

title: **AQUAMARINE**   air date: **SEPTEMBER 3, 2007**

summary
I watch *Aquamarine* on YouTube and I finally hear what Sara's talking voice sounds like. Her personality in one scene reminds me of Lavander. Her voice sounds a lot like Lavander's voice.

notes
This is the first on-screen appearance of *Aquamarine*.

Episode 7

title: **SARA IS IN THE HOUSE, BABY**   air date: **SEPTEMBER 4, 2007**

summary

At four o'clock in the morning, after crashing out on my bed without brushing my teeth or taking my meds, I wake up and go to do all that. I am thinking about how Sara's voice and personality is a lot like Lavander's. I get interrupted when I see a cricket in my room. I am worried it is a scorpion so I end up sleeping on the couch and I listen to "Here We Go Again" by Sara. I listen to the lyrics and I see how she feels about not finding the right person yet, and I compare it to me and I'm glad that someone is in my ship as well. I also have another dream, which is set in May 2004, where I get worried about death because we are talking about how Gen's eldest sister passed away and I hear a song that sounds like "One in a Million" by Miley Cyrus, but it is being sung by Bruce Springsteen and has different lyrics.

Later on, after I have been avoiding my room for so long, I get an e-mail from Matt, and in my response to it I create a fantasy scenario involving Sara Paxton's parents. I watch the full movie of *Aquamarine* in ten separate videos on YouTube. I watch and enjoy it. Sara Paxton is very cute. When I am taking my bath Matt calls me and we talk about the plans for my pretend wedding to Sara Paxton on the 29th of this month. Mom's friend Jeremy comes over. I talk to him and I am doing my English homework when the cricket reappears. Jeremy kills it.

notes

On September 5, 2004, there was a hopper bug in my bathroom and I avoided my bathroom all day until Gabe killed it. One day shy of being exactly three years later, the same thing happened.

This episode is also my favorite. This is the second of two appearances by Gen, and the second of two episodes where I sleep on the couch and get worried about death in my dream.

trivia

Fantasies about my pretend relationship with Sara Paxton:

1. I met Sara Paxton on September 29, 2001; we started dating on December 4, 2001.

2. She cheated on me in December 2003.

3. I proposed to her on May 10, 2004, and we will be getting married on September 29, 2007. Our first baby is coming in July 2008.

Information about the pretend song playing in my worrying-about-death segment:
title: "We're All Together Now" (imaginary song)
artist: Bruce Springsteen
format: CD single
recorded: 2001
released: 2001

soundtrack listing

"One in a Million" by Miley Cyrus (*Hannah Montana 2, Meet Miley Cyrus* 2007)

Episode 8

title: GIRLS, GIRLS, GIRLS (a.k.a. Tara Vs. Sara)   air date: **SEPTEMBER 10, 2007**

---

summary

Matt is on fall break from college and we are hanging out today. We are having a good time. We talk a lot about fantasies and act them out on camera. I perform "Clean Heart" by Sade with my own lyrics about how I hate Miley Cyrus and how Sara, Emma Roberts, and JoJo (from *Aquamarine*) should be against her as well.

After that we go to the pool and Matt works out. Then we take a walk to the bagel shop and we pretend I am married to Tara A* from 2001–2003. Matt and I have a very good time. Later on, at the end of the day, I take a backstage tour of Matt and his sending e-mails to me. He shows me his process—the way he sits and composes e-mails to me. I allow him to put DJ Tanner (from *Full House*) in his e-mail, which I don't usually do. Later on we wait for his aunt to pick him up and talk about why I dislike DJ.

notes

I do not permit DJ Tanner in Matt's e-mails because back in January he kept pretending that I loved her when I hated her and I still do today. This is the last episode to have anything to do with Tara from Vista View. This is the only formal appearance of Matt.

quotes

me: "If my girlfriend is older than me, I will not allow her to rest her head on my shoulder."

★SEE *KNOWING TARA.*

matt: "Blaze, your girlfriend could be thirty years older."
me: "Oh fuck you, asshole."
(We both laugh)
(Later on, when we are talking about why I don't like DJ Tanner)
me: "At least you didn't have a good year annulled and you weren't love drafted."
matt: "Are you kidding me, bro? Of course that happened. I have had good years annulled when I went off my meds. It's all right, bro, it's all part of life."

soundtrack listing
"Speed of Sound" by Coldplay (XY 2005)

"Clean Heart" by Sade (*Stronger Than Pride* 1988)

Episode 9

title: **REAL LIFE HONEY COMING THIS WAY**   air date: **SEPTEMBER 14, 2007**

summary
Nick and I are on our way to the beach. He says he will line a girlfriend up for me. I tell him I do not want her to be older; he gives me a little bit of a hard time about it, but he assures me he is joking. On the beach I have a fantasy segment. Cody Linley (Jake Ryan on *Hannah Montana*) and I are running from Miranda (the random strange girl who wanted to share my headphones with me one day recently when I was walking to the market). Later, at home, Dina (the girl Nick wants to fix me up with) calls Nick's cell phone.

notes
Dina is eighteen.

quotes
nick: "Your girlfriend is going to be seven years older than you."
me: "Nick!"
nick: "I'm kidding, she's nineteen."
nick: "She's an Italian."

Episode 10

title: **DINA TO THE RESCUE**   air date: **SEPTEMBER 15, 2007**

summary

Early in the morning: I am worried that Miranda is out to get me so I figure already having a girlfriend will save me. Miranda did say that she already has a boyfriend, but I'm so worried I keep forgetting. I haven't met Dina yet, but I imagine she looks like Sara Paxton.

notes

I meet Dina two days later. She doesn't look anything like Sara Paxton, but she does look like Déja's friend Tina, which makes me like her more than I was originally planning to. Dina, Nick, and I became a trio. Me and Mom always chat about Dina. Mom says Dina wants to have a relationship with Nick. But Nick really has no interest in her in that way; he wants to be just her friend. That is the reason why he wants me to be her boyfriend instead of him.

soundtrack listing

"Connected" by Sara Paxton (2006)

Episode 11

title: **SHE'S EVERYWHERE**   air date: **SEPTEMBER 19, 2007**

summary

I am in English 803 one morning and I show my buddy Sergio a picture of Sara Paxton I got from the Internet. He thinks she is cute as well. I think about her a lot and I learn her mother is Mexican from Answers.com.

notes

This is the second and last episode filmed at Vista View.

Episode 12

title: **REN STEVENS**   air date: **OCTOBER 4, 2007**

summary

I am kind of in love with Ren Stevens from *Even Stevens*. Things are falling apart with me and Sara because this video on YouTube said she was kissing a boy. Tonight we are going to Mom's book signing in Coronado. I am thinking of Ren Stevens constantly and have a fantasy segment going back to my seventeenth birthday. I pretend that Ren and I were singing together on my birthday.

notes

I have had a few interests in girls aside from Hilary Duff and Sara Paxton. They are:

1. Christy Carlson Romano (Ren Stevens from *Even Stevens* and Kim Possible on *Kim Possible*)
2. Tia and Tamera Mowry (from *Sister, Sister*)
3. Lalaine (Miranda on *Lizzie McGuire*)
4. Ren Stevens (character from *Even Stevens*)
5. Davida Williams (Claire Miller on *Lizzie McGuire* & Lauren on *Raise Your Voice*)
6. Lizzie McGuire (the character)

None of these ever got serious. Hilary Duff and Sara Paxton are the only ones who were really wrapped tight in my mind. I wrote a story based on how I feel.

soundtrack listing

"Little Voice" and "So Yesterday" by Hilary Duff (*Metamorphosis* 2003)

"Queen in the Black" by Stevie Wonder (*Jungle Fever* 1991)

"With Each Beat of My Heart" by Stevie Wonder (*Characters* 1987)

Episode 13

---

title: **WILDFIRES AND SARA PAXTON**   air date: **OCTOBER 22, 2007**

---

summary

There are wildfires all over San Diego today. The sky is red and ashes are raining everywhere. I will not be going to school today because of that. Escondido, Rancho Bernardo, etc. are having mandatory evacuations. The fire is even scarily heading toward us. We pack up and get ready to evacuate. Sara Paxton keeps repeatedly coming into my head, and I start associating the fires with her because both things are happening at the same time. We get in the car and we have to get gas, but the Chevron near our house is packed. At the 7-Eleven gas station, almost all the pumps are down. Finally they are working again and we get gas. It takes us a while to finally get in and get out of the gas station. Maya then offers me some of her drink. We are going to Nana and Papa's house, and if they are evacuated we will go to Maya's friends' house. However, Mom is not at all interested in going to there.

Later on, I settle down and just chill out at Nana and Papa's house. However, being chilled appears to be only temporary. There are now possibilities that Nana and Papa's house is going to be mandatory evacuated as well. We have a few backup plans. Papa keeps joking about how we should go set up a tent on the beach. We can also go to Qualcomm Stadium, we can go to a military base and all sleep on cots, or we could go to Maya's friends'. The three backup plans are scrapped. I keep getting apprehensive when the plan keeps backing up and getting canceled, and we are having a hard time putting together a plan for everybody. The plan finally is that we are going to the Candlewood Suites Hotel in Anaheim.

notes
In this episode I am thinking about Sara Paxton, but not romantically.

We were in the mandatory evacuation zone.

There was a bad wildfire in San Diego in 2003 also, but we were not evacuated that time.

soundtrack listing
"Home" by Daughtry (*Daughtry* 2006)

"Feel Good Inc." by Gorillas (*Demon Days* 2005)

"Good Enough" by Sarah McLachlan (*Fumbling Towards Ecstasy* 1993)
I kept hearing the opening part of this song, which is calm and was helping me get through the tension of the fires.

"Zeroes" by David Bowie (*Never Let Me Down* 1987)

"Ohio" by Crosby, Stills and Nash (*One Way Street* 1971)
"Ohio" is a very dramatic song about how some protestors of the Vietnam War were killed at Kent State in Ohio. There's a line about a girl lying on the ground dead. There is the same kind of drama and fear with having to leave our house and worrying about it burning to the ground.

Episode 14

title: **MY FAIR WARSHIP**   air date: **OCTOBER 24, 2007**

summary

Nick and his friend Kat come over to my house. We go down to my
room. Nick plays Grand Theft Auto and I perform songs. I get to know
Kat pretty well, and I start to like her as more than a friend. I begin
hating Sara Paxton this day because of what I have been through with
her rattling around in my head with the fires and her kissing that boy
at the club. I sing "Young Americans" by Bowie negatively directed
toward her. Later I ask Kat to dance with me and she does. After all
that, Nick, Kat, and I go on an evacuation drill, then Kat and Nick go
home. Later, I go for the ride with Bo to take Maya to the airport.

notes

Kat goes far away to college, but I don't remember where. She's very
pretty and cute and I thought she could be a potential girlfriend.

Dancing with her has a very *Cinderella* vibe.

This is the series finale of *My Crush on Sara Paxton*.

Maya is going to Saratoga, New York, to interview at a college that she
is going to attend online to finish her degree.

quotes

me: "Ever heard of Patty Griffin?"
kat: "Yeah."
kat (crying when I sing a sad song): "Ohhh."
me: "Want to dance?"
kat: "Sure."
(Later, in the car with Bo and Maya)
me: "I danced with a girl tonight."
bo: "Did your wiener stick up?"
maya: "BODINE!!!!!!!!!!!!!!!!!!!!!!!"

soundtrack listing

"Rehab" by Amy Winehouse (*Back to Black* 2006)

"Hot Thing" by Shawn Stockman (from the movie *Seventeen Again*)

"Carry Me" by Patty Griffin (*Flaming Red* 1998)

"Newborn Friend" by Seal (*Seal* 1994)

"Chemical Love" by Stevie Wonder (*Jungle Fever* 1991)

"I Go Sailing" by Stevie Wonder (*Jungle Fever* 1991)

"The Heart of the Matter" by Don Henley (*The End of the Innocence* 1989)

"Modern Love" by David Bowie (*Let's Dance* 1983)

"The Last Resort" by The Eagles (*Hotel California* 1976)

"Young Americans" by David Bowie (*Young Americans* 1975)

"My Girl Has Gone" by Smokey Robinson and the Miracles (*Going to a Go-Go* 1965)

trivia
This episode has a very long soundtrack because I am in love with Kat and that sets off a lot of music.

thanksgiving special (2007)

title: FRAGMENTED   air date: **NOVEMBER 22, 2007**

cast

blaze ginsberg: himself
mom: herself
maya: aunt
papa: grandfather
nana: grandmother
lavander: aunt
bodine (bo): uncle
déja: aunt

guest stars 2007

juan: family friend
colin: lavander's boyfriend (now ex)

summary

The night before Thanksgiving, I bake vegan chocolate chip cookies
with very little help from Mom. It's uneventful. Mom makes a coffee
cake. Maya makes pot pie and cinnamon rolls. For me, she makes

some without raisins because I don't like raisins. I'm feeling a bit weirded out from listening to Dusty Springfield's song "Make It With You" for the first time because of the way it sounds in the opening. I'm associating it with how I want a girlfriend. Also, Jenny from Surrey calls me to say hi (she's been my "best" friend since 2005).

On the morning of Thanksgiving Mom leaves early by herself because she is going to walk to Nana and Papa's house (5.2 miles away). Later, Maya and I drive to Nana and Papa's house.

It starts off okay. Our friend Juan brings Champagne. We all eat appetizers. I have brought my soups and am eating them while everyone else eats everything else. This year we will be skipping the thankful speech. Lavander and Colin leave right after this. Lavander is not feeling well, so they don't stay for dinner. Later on it is game time. Déja is in a hurry because she has to be at work at 4:30 p.m. There is a vote for Apples to Apples versus General Knowledge (a game played back on July 4th of this year). Apples to Apples wins, unfortunately. It starts off all right. But later, after not getting any cards picked, I end up backfiring and backing out of the game. I go for a little walk to let this all out. Mom gets into a fight with Bodine over the game and ends up throwing her cards at him and also backing out of the game. Later on we talk about the future holiday schedule. Nana and Papa will not be hosting Christmas next month. Nana says she does not want to host Thanksgiving next year either.

We hang around for a little while longer and then we go home. I have been so busy with school this year I haven't even been looking forward to Thanksgiving like I usually do. This year, for reasons unknown, Thanksgiving is just very empty and fragmented.

major events in 2007

I started my third semester at college (in December, I pass all my classes, including Math)

I quit Natural Market in August (since I was cut down to one day a week in February)

I will be starting work at Vons in December as a courtesy clerk. I got the job through Mr. N at PWI, and this time I will have a job coach.

I finally got a new trio of friends (Nick and Dina).

I'm still working on driving, but failed the written test twice. I have decided I need to memorize the book instead of doing the online tests and tutorials because there are questions on the test that are not in those places, like what to do about blind people and what roads have the most slippery spots.

trivia
How to play General Knowledge:
Everybody gets one piece of paper. There is one sheet with every letter of the alphabet on it. One person shuts his or her eyes and picks a random letter. There are five categories (decided on by the players) and you will have to choose something in each category that starts with the selected letter. You get ten points for each answer that nobody else has. If someone has already picked something that you chose, you only get five points for your answer. The person with the most points at the end of the game wins.

Sample categories: TV shows, songs, countries, curse words, diseases.

soundtrack listing
"Make It With You" by Dusty Springfield (*Dusty in Memphis* 1969)

"Underneath This Smile" by Hilary Duff (*Hilary Duff* 2004)

28

episodes, the book
(miniseries 2008)

miniseries: **2008**

genre: **UNIQUE ACHIEVEMENTS**

release date: **DECEMBER 18, 2007**

status: **MINISERIES**

cast

blaze ginsberg: himself

mom: herself

steve: literary agent

nancy: editor

lindsay: works with steve

gabe: mom's boyfriend

miniseries summary

I first started writing this book in February 2006. Back then I called it, "Things That Are In Syndication and Still Running." I wanted to organize the things that had been going on in my life as if they were TV series. Some things, like my crush on Hilary Duff, were still running when I first started writing. But that has now ended. Some things, like Blaze, Matt, and Danny, are in syndication. I first showed this to Mom in about March 2006. Mom really liked it, and she said it should be a book. She encouraged me to continue writing and so I took it to the next level and added more series and episodes. In the meantime, I graduated high school and started going to Vista View. I got a job at Natural Market and then it ended. I kept writing. In February 2007, Mom and I began casually working on putting the book together. It was originally called "A Memoir Database." Later it was changed to "Episodes: A Memoir." For a while we took a break from it. But we resumed in December 2007, starting with the Introduction, which is the farthest thing from easy. Mom showed the book to her friend, Steve, who is a literary agent, and he liked the book also. I finally met Steve and he is a cool guy.

Episode List
Episode 1

title: HIT THE BOOK   air date: **DECEMBER 18, 2007**

summary
I get home from work. Mom says we have work to do on the book and I am really happy to hear that. But then she says that it's the Introduction that needs to be done and I have trouble with the Introduction, but I go put my best foot forward and I e-mail it to Mom.

notes
Mom e-mailed me back saying I can do better than what I did.

soundtrack listing
"You Can Call Me Al" by Paul Simon (*Graceland* 1986)

Episode 2

title: STEVE   air date: **JANUARY 24, 2008**

summary
Mom and Gabe pick me up from work, and we go to Warwick's, a bookstore in La Jolla. It is very nice. I like Warwick's. I wander around outside and call my friends. Finally, I meet Steve and I talk to him

about certain stuff in the book. I see his colleague, Lindsay, who I met one night in November 2006 during a really bad book signing.

notes
Lindsay looks very different than she did back when I met her. Her hair is loose and she looks taller.

The book signing in November 2006 was for Mom's book *Blind Submission*. My friend Logan (from Natural Market) had promised me he was going to come for it, but he never showed up (he later said Kellie was in a grumpy mood), which upset me for the whole evening.

quotes
me (to lindsay): "I met you on November 10, 2006."
gabe: "When he was bitching and moaning about his 'girlfriend' Logan not showing up."
me: "Oh, shut up."
(Later)
me: "Am I going to have a book signing also?"
steve: "Yes."
me: "It won't be at Mysterious Galaxy, will it?"
steve: "What's wrong with Mysterious Galaxy?"
mom: "We were there for one of my book signings and it turned out to be longer than Blaze wanted so now he's boycotting the store."
me: "Can I invite celebrities to my book signing?"
steve: "Sure."

soundtrack listing
"Hey, Hey, What Can I Do?" by Led Zeppelin (1990)

Episode 3

title: **STEVE'S OFFICE**   air date: **JANUARY 25, 2008**

summary
Mom and Gabe pick me up from work at Vons and we go to Steve's office. Nancy is there. Nancy is an editor from New York who is interested in my book. We talk about the book and the arrangement of it and how we're going to split everything up. Gabe even throws in some words about my writing and how I ask him to read stuff that I wrote. I tell Nancy that there will be a series about my freshman year

of high school. All systems are a go for that idea. Meanwhile, Steve gives me two books to read. I enjoy my time at Steve's office and even see buses from below. I am really starting to get excited and happy about the book at this point.

notes
The last episode is to take place after work.

Steve is younger than Bo by eight months.

Steve's office is very 1987 (meaning I like it because I really like the year 1987).

quotes
steve: "I want you to read these books."
(Later)
me (to nancy): "What was your favorite part of the book?"
nancy: "I think *My Crush on Hilary Duff.*"
me: "Have you read *My Crush on Sara Paxton* yet?"
nancy: "I haven't had a chance to read that yet."
me: "Why do we have to cut parts of the book?"
nancy: "To help guide readers through it."

soundtrack listing
"Say OK" by Vanessa Hudgens (V 2006)

"Wake Me Up Before You Go-Go" by Wham (*Make It Big* 1984)
This song is included because it is a very happy tune.

Episode 4

title: **SOLD**   air date: **FEBRUARY 8, 2008**

---

summary
I now have a deal for the book. Nancy will be editing the book and Roaring Brook Press will be publishing it. We will be going to Sammy's restaurant with the whole family for the celebration of this wonderful turn of events. However, things don't go quite as planned. We are waiting for Papa at home, but it turns out he is already waiting for us at Sammy's. So then we leave for Sammy's and see him there and everybody is happy that I have sold my book. We talk about it a lot, and later we go home and I call my friend Dina to talk about it.

Unfortunately, things take a bad turnaround when Déja touches my iPod and then I backfire at her.

notes
Déja and I made up by talking about it and working it out.

quotes
déja: "Blaze is a big author now."
papa: "We're all very proud of him."
(When the waitress comes with the check)
everyone (pointing to me): "He gets the check!"

soundtrack listing
"Saint Agnes and the Burning Train" by Sting (*Soul Cages* 1991)
This song is very soothing even though it is kind of a sad song, melody-wise. It is an instrumental song—no lyrics. It fits the happy mood of the occasion.

Episode 5

title: **OUR DINNER WITH STEVE AND LINDSAY** air date: **FEBRUARY 16, 2008**

summary
Steve is coming over to our house for dinner tonight for a continuation of the book deal celebration. Lindsay will also be attending. Steve's girlfriend was also going to attend but she is sick, so she will not be here. Steve and Lindsay arrive with a present for me. It's Guitar Hero, and I thank them for it. Later on, I have a question about something that I feel Steve might be able to answer. It is about an animated Disney film titled *The Great Mouse Detective*. But then Steve doesn't have to answer the question because I figure out the mystery when I look on IMDB.com. I talk with Lindsay a lot about my original draft of the *Government Offices* series.

notes
The Great Mouse Detective was released in 1986. Basil Rathbone, who was credited as a cast member on IMDB, died in 1967. Basil Rathbone's roll in *The Great Mouse Detective* is from archived footage from another movie.

I also showed Steve my musical, *Girl from Out of Town*, about the girl named Kat who I fell in love with in December 2007.

We could not get Guitar Hero to work on my computer. My friend Travis and I hung out the day after this, and he couldn't work it either. Bo later took Guitar Hero to his house, and he's been playing it ever since.

quotes
me: "How was the movie released in 1986 if he died in 1967?"
steve: "Maybe they sat on it for twenty years."

trivia
Mom and Steve used to work together in 1996.

soundtrack listing
"You're Not the Man" by Sade (*Promise* 1985)

"Black Man" by Stevie Wonder (*Songs in the Key of Life* 1976)
This song is about men and women who were the first to do certain things, like walk on the North Pole and lead the Underground Railroad, and I feel it has a connection to me because I'm like the first man to get a book deal at such a young age.

Episode 6
title: **WORKING ON IT**   air date: **MARCH 17, 2008**

summary
Nancy's notes arrive. Mom and I will be getting started on the line edit as soon as I look at Nancy's notes and go through and answer every question that she asks. I am very anxious to see her comments and questions on *My Crush on Sara Paxton* but she doesn't have any. However, I then rearrange the manuscript and Mom has to put it back together. Later, Mom and I start the line edit. Mom shows me how to go through and make the changes.

notes
The book is due to be finished on September 1, 2008.

quotes
me: "Doesn't she have any questions on *My Crush on Sara Paxton*?"
mom: "Maybe not."
mom: "Uuugh, you rearranged everything."

soundtrack listing

"Kiss the Girl" by Ashley Tisdale (2006)

"Please" by Chris Isaak" (*Speak of the Devil* 1998)
There is a repeated line in this song about being killed with
questions—that is why this song is part of the soundtrack.

trivia

This is the last sentence in my book.

---

credits

Mom....Mother
Thank you for all the fun times we had editing this book and for being patient with me.

Nancy Mercado....Editor
Thank you for the way you looked at this book and saw its uniqueness.

Steve Malk....Literary Agent
Thank you for bringing this book out into the world.
Also, thank you to Lindsay Davis for all your help.

Josh...Friend
Thank you for helping push me into the grown-up world and for always listening to my stories.

Nana, Papa, Maya, Lavander, Bo, Déja, and Gabe....Family
Thank you for all your love and support and for all that you've done for me.

Mike....Friend
Thank you for all the good times you've brought to my life, especially during some rough times in sophomore year.

My Teachers...Teachers
Thank you to all the teachers who always believed in me over the years; you have really helped me a lot.

29

afterword:
my life since *episodes*

---

series: **2002–2003**

release date: **SEPTEMBER 10, 2009**

genre: **MOVIE**

status: **ENDED**

---

cast:

blaze ginsberg: himself/published author

mom: mother

maya: aunt

déja: aunt

lavander: aunt

bodine (bo): uncle

nana: grandmother

papa: grandfather

gabe: mom's boyfriend

guest stars:

clark: friend from surrey

clark's mom: herself

clark's dad: himself

louise: surrey staff member

dr. jean: educational advocate from middle school and high school

lucinda: friend from surrey

dr. r: counselor during freshman year at surrey

coach b: coach from surrey

various students from surrey: themselves

michelle: new friend

jon: michelle's husband

luis: garbage man

potential driver at waste management in training with luis: himself

isaac: recycling man

driving instructor at dmv: himself

ira: potential future boss (now ex)

sharon: ira's wife/potential future boss (now ex)

paris: friend/fairy godmother

frank: paris's husband

kristina: déja's friend

yvette: job coach (now ex)

jamie: lavander's friend

katelynn: fan/friend from san diego state

---

movie summary

On September 1, 2009, my book, *Episodes: My Life As I See It*, was officially released. At the same time, an audio version of the book was released with the actor MacLeod Andrews reading all the parts. My life changed in many different ways when the book came out. I became more popular, did a lot of interviews on radio and in person, and did a few book signings. Although I still did not find a girlfriend, I finally got my driver's license. I really like having a book out and am planning to write another one exclusively about how rough life can be with autism. Seeing the response to *Episodes* really made me want to help people who are on the spectrum by sharing my own story.

Scene 1: *First Book Signing*

It is September 10, 2009, nine days since *Episodes* was released in hardcover. Today I am having a book signing at a store called Bookworks at 7 pm. Beforehand we have a meeting with PWI (Partnerships with Industry) about my overall performance as a supermarket courtesy clerk, the job I have had since December 2007.

My job coach (now ex) Yvette and my case manager at PWI are coming to our house. I have requested today off because of my signing. Yvette and my case manager arrive and I greet them and offer them something to drink or eat while they are here, then we get into a discussion about my performance. I am doing well according to them, but there are still things I need to improve, like walking away from the checkstand in the middle of orders and other things. We then go over my goals, such as to do other things like stocking in the store. I mention that my book signing is tonight, and Yvette and my case manager are excited. Yvonne will be attending as well.

Later that night Mom helps me find something nice to wear for the signing. Déja arrives in the middle of this and is really excited and hugging me and carrying on. Her friend Kristina will also be attending. We then head over to the bookstore and I am a little nervous but then it works out really well. I get there and notice a lot of people from Surrey are there to cheer me on. When everybody is seated, a lady from Bookworks introduces Mom, then Mom gives a little talk about how proud she is of me and what an amazing book *Episodes* is. Then it is my turn to read. I read two pieces from Freshman Year, two from Senior Year, and one from the Summer 2007 movie. Everybody laughs and really enjoys it. Then I have a Q&A and many people ask questions and Yvette is in tears of joy.

Afterward, I sign copies of *Episodes* that people have bought. However, I am expecting a lot of people from my work to come, including Svetlana (who has been my boss since May). But they don't. Later, after we get home, I start having a spin-out when I tell Mom I want to go partying (in the future) with Eric who works at Dirty Dogs (the pet cleaning business next door to my work) and she says she doesn't think that would be a good idea because she says he sounds like a loser. (Eric has said many inappropriate things about girls and other things.) I talk to Gabe about it on the phone when we get home and he helps calm me down. Gabe did not come because he is out of town for business. All in all, it is a really great night.

quotes
déja (loudly): "OH MY GOSH, TONIGHT IS YOUR BIG NIGHT!!!!!!!!"
me: "I am really excited."
déja: "You should be!"

(Later, on the phone with Gabe)

gabe: "I wish I could have been there tonight. I am so proud of you."

me: "Yeah, I know, but you gotta do what you gotta do."

gabe: "Right, so your mom says you had a spin-out tonight."

me: "Yeah, because she doesn't want me to go party to meet girls."

gabe: "Look, about that . . . it's really not the place for you because of the way you process things. These people do crazy things and it would be difficult for you to have a good time. Look, Blaze, you're a lot closer to having a girlfriend than you ever were before you published a book and you should feel proud of yourself."

trivia

Video of the signing at Bookworks is on YouTube at:
http://www.youtube.com/watch?v=49uFJnjB4nQ

soundtrack listing

"While My Heart Is Still Beating," "True to Life," and "More Than This" by Roxy Music (*Avalon* 1982)

"My Eyes Don't Cry" by Stevie Wonder (*Characters* 1987)

"Love Gets Me Every Time" by Shania Twain (*Come On Over* 1997)

"Home" by Daughtry (*Daughtry* 2006)

"Love Story" by Taylor Swift (*Fearless* 2008)

"Fly" by Hilary Duff (*Hilary Duff* 2004)

"Metamorphosis" by Hilary Duff (*Metamorphosis* 2003)

"I Am Going to Get to You" by Cecile (*from Sesame Street*)

This scene has the biggest soundtrack because of how big my book is.

Scene 2: *The Surrey Signing*

On September 29, 2009, I am scheduled to have a reading at Surrey. I am a bit nervous because there is a girl there named Lily who I met in May who didn't accept me on Facebook. Mom and Maya and I are all going. We arrive in the building and the minute I see Lily I go and ask for an explanation for her lack of acceptance of me on Facebook. She says she never got my request. Later it becomes time for the reading. Then there is a Q&A and afterward I start having a spin-out because I am once again thinking about how much I want a girlfriend and I start thinking that it will never happen. I go and talk with Mr. P, the art teacher, about old times in freshman year. But then things get out of hand when the battery on my phone breaks and I can't put back in the battery and then a reporter wants to take a video and I don't want to do certain things for the camera because of OCD-related reasons. Later I go for a long walk to a shopping center called Piazza Carmel to the bagel place called Boston Bagels (now Chicago's Finest Cuisine) for two seedy twists.

trivia

I call and reserve two seedy twists at Boston Bagels because seedy twists are their most popular product and sell out easily. I also go there every week because it is a nice walk.

soundtrack listing

"Blood Money" by The Church (*Starfish* 1988)

"Try It Baby" by Marvin Gaye (*How Sweet It Is to Be Loved by You* 1964)

Scene 3: *It's a Small Autistic World After All*

One day in January 2010 a woman named Michelle contacts Mom. Michelle's six-year-old son and four-year-old daughter are high functioning autistic. We go meet her at Sammy's, a local restaurant. We introduce ourselves and Mom talks about her books and we talk about mine. Mom then brings up my ability to know what day of the week people were born on. They quiz me on some dates and Michelle is amazed. At Sammy's I am trying to make 2010 as happy as 1991 was for me and thinking that it will be the same as 1991 was. Later we load up Michelle's car and start heading for the school that her kids attend and where Mom and I will be talking about our books. We arrive there and the kids are running all over the place. Later the instructor has a hard time getting them outside. I read two pieces from Freshman Year and My Crush on Hilary Duff. It is then time for the Q&A and that goes smoothly, however, there is quite a bit of talk about me and my current girlfriend status. That makes me uncomfortable because it starts thinking that I won't have one. However, Mom did warn me that since I discussed this in the book, it would probably come up so I am not totally unprepared. Later Mom and I sign books (Mom signs copies of *Raising Blaze*, her memoir about me) and we are there for quite a while and I get restless to leave because I am very tired. Later the kids come back in and start running around the stage being all wild and their parents try to corral them. I chase Michelle's kids around and I also meet their father, Jon. He seems like a really optimistic person. Later Michelle's son follows Michelle, Mom, and me out to her car explaining his knowledge of road routes in San Diego. Like I am with buses and garbage trucks, Michelle's son is that way with routes. Mom and Michelle agree that I will come and read at the school where she teaches, called La Jolla Country Day School, in September.

quotes
mom: "Blaze can tell you what day of the week any day was on. He knows what day of the week people were born on."
michelle: "What day of the week was August 12, 1966?"
me: "Friday."
michelle: (Michelle looks it up on her iPhone.) "That's right! How did you know that?"
me: "Because it was the same day of the week in 2005 and on that day that year, that was the last reunion with my good friends Matt and Danny because they were leaving for college on the East Coast."
michelle: "Oh, wow."

(On the drive)
me: "I have this thing where I can tell what month and year a song was recorded. For example, I think that 'All Star' by Smash Mouth was recorded in February of 1999."
michelle: "What about 'Losing My Religion'?" (an R.E.M. song on the radio earlier)
me: "Spring of 1992." (This song actually came out in February 1991, but this was before I knew that.)

(At the school)
person in the audience: "Do you have a girlfriend?"
me: "No."
another person in the audience: "How would you feel about dating another autistic girl?"
me: "You know, it really wouldn't help. It would be like trying to put a fire out with gas, you know what I mean?"

trivia
At the time, I felt like 1991 was one of the best years of my life and had been fantasizing about it endlessly. At this time I started to really hate my job for various reasons.

Recording dates of songs was a long-term obsession of mine for
a while.

soundtrack listing

"The Sweet Escape" by Gwen Stefani (*The Sweet Escape* 2006)

"All Star" by Smash Mouth (*Astro Lounge* 1999)

"Losing My Religion" by R.E.M. (*Out of Time* 1991)

"Buffalo Soldier" by Bob Marley (*Confrontation* 1983)

Scene 4: *SDSU*

My day starts off super crummy on Thursday, April 22, 2010, because I
really hate my job. Papa picks me up and I drive to work (I was driving
because I had finally passed the written test on Wednesday, February
18, 2009). I talk very irrationally to Papa. He comes in to shop and
then I follow him outside to his car and I continue to talk crazy and he
gets all freaked out and calls Mom. I then miserably get through my
shift. At home Mom and I have a talk about this and then we practice
my reading but argue about my attitude. I would like to quit my job
but Mom wants me to stay until I have another job. Then we head to
San Diego State University. We continue talking about this but Mom,
however, is really over hearing my complaints. I get in the building
and start immediately looking around for pretty girls to talk to. I meet a
girl named Lindsey. Then it is time for me to read. I see a hot girl who
smiles as I read my pieces. I read two pieces from Games and one from
Vista View College Days and one from My Crush on Sara Paxton. I
then do the usual Q&A and then I officially meet the hot girl. Her
name is Katelynn. Mom and I sign books after the Q&A. As we're
starting to wrap it up, Matt calls me and I talk to him. Later Mom,
Maya, and I head home and then we talk about what I want in a
girlfriend. On the way home we stop at the market and Mom buys me
a bag of M&M's. The checker, Brandi, is really hot and is older than
me by eight and a half years but is married. I then get an idea for my
next book.

quotes
(At the store)
me: "I really hate my life. I hate the job I have and it is really ruining
my life."
papa (repeated line): "Really?"

papa (firmly): "Pull it together or I will tell your manager you can't work today."
(He calls Mom)

(At home)
mom: "What the hell, Blaze? You freaked your grandfather out?"
me: "I am sick of my job."
mom: "Papa said you hated your life."
maya: "Please try not to sound so crazy."

(At SDSU after the Q&A)
katelynn: "Hi, Blaze. I am Katelynn. I really like your book."
me: "Thank you, Katelynn."

(In the car ride to Vons)
me: "I think my next book will be about a twenty-six-year-old woman who has an affair with a fifteen-year-old freshman in high school."
mom: "That would be a good book. That kind of thing does happen sometimes."
maya: "There was this one woman who was married and she cheated on her husband with a twelve-year-old. She didn't get arrested, and the police said if she never called or saw the boy ever again she would be fine. But she then had a baby with the twelve-year-old."
me: "No way!"
maya: "Yeah."

soundtrack listing

"Why" by Annie Lennox (*Diva* 1992)

Scene 5: *La Jolla Country Day School*

On Wednesday, September 29, 2010, I am scheduled to go read at La Jolla Country Day School. Michelle picks Mom and me up. Today I am also planning to take out a major depressing vibe from 1973, run it through my head, and then retire it. I got this vibe on Fridays in March 2007 while I was working at Natural Market. I worried then that I would never find love and I was envious of people who had it. I am successful in retiring this particular vibe, at least this particular one. Michelle gives us a little tour of the school and I try really hard to make the vibe appear (even though it is notoriously depressing). I am eventually successful. I watch some kids do their thing. I read the last two episodes of My Crush on Hilary Duff and everybody appears to like it a lot. I then do a Q&A which is rather long, then I read the fifth episode from Season 1 of My Crush on Hilary Duff. Then Mom, Michelle, and I hang around and talk to Michelle about what to do about fire alarms for other kids on the autism spectrum who might have a problem with them. This is because kids on the spectrum are more sensitive to the noise. Finally, Michelle takes us home and Mom talks to her about something else that has been bugging me. I have recently blacklisted Stevie Wonder because I can't find the dates of when *Fulfillingness' First Finale* was recorded. Michelle says she will try to find the dates for us.

quotes
me (to michelle): "We need to post a law about fire alarms because kids on spectrum will bug their teachers and not want to be in class in fear of the alarm."
michelle: "Yeah, well, the one we have here is extremely loud. It beeps if something is wrong with it and a custodian looks at it."

(Back in the car)
mom: "Blaze doesn't like Stevie Wonder anymore because he can't find when *Fulfillingness' First Finale* was recorded. It was released on July 22, 1974."
michelle: "I can try to find it."
me (happily): "Thanks, Michelle, thanks a lot."
michelle: "You're welcome."

trivia
I pretend that vibes are like a fleet of buses and have engines and transmissions like buses do and run on diesel or CNG (compressed natural gas).

Vibes fueled by diesel are depressing because diesel is bad for the environment and vibes powered by CNG or hybrids are happy because CNG is an alternate fuel for diesel.

I have been actively looking for recording dates for *Fulfillingness' First Finale* since 2008 because it is a very good album and I like to know when good albums were recorded.

All units of my depressing 1973 vibe were auctioned off in November and scrapped.

When a fleet of buses retire from their Transit Authority, they go to auction and either go to another transit authority, a private owner, or a dealership that can refurbish them.

Diesel buses usually go to places such as Mexico and South America or scrap. I learned a lot of information about buses from YouTube.

In Mexico and South America they have very low vehicle emission standards, as opposed to places like California, where they are the most strict.

Fulfillingness' First Finale was recorded at Record Plant Studios in L.A. (Los Angeles), Media Sound Studios in N.Y. (New York), Westlake Audio L.A., and Electric Lady Land Studios (Electric Lady) in N.Y. Mom posted a reward offer on Facebook if anyone can find the recording dates for *Fulfillingness' First Finale*.

Scene 6: *Independence (Almost)*
On Thursday, October 7, 2010, I am not working because I have my road test. I wake up, have breakfast, and then Papa picks me up. I am a little nervous because I failed last time because I hit a curb. On the ride there we talk and I point out buses and then we arrive there and go to the desk where you are supposed to go for road tests. While we are waiting for it to be time, Papa and I practice things like where the windshield wipers and defroster are, etc. Finally it is time for my road test. The instructor tells me what to do, like, "Put on your windshield wipers, left turn signal, right turn signal, sound your horn," etc. He gets in the car and we take off. I am nervous and the test goes on for quite a while. We are driving for about twenty minutes and then finally we arrive back at the building. I pass my test. Papa is very excited and I am very happy as well. He drives us back to my house and I text everyone the grand news. I get home and Mom and Maya are very happy and then I go for a walk to the market. But Del Mar Highlands (the shopping center) is under renovation, so it is really hard to get in and out. Later, we go to Déja's house to meet everyone for ice cream as a celebration. We go there and Déja takes pictures of me and Papa together and then we go back to Déja's house and then Mom, Maya, and I go home.

quotes
papa: "So when you go with the instructor, don't talk. Focus on the road and do whatever he or she tells you."
me (noticing a bus): "That bus is from 2008."
papa: "That's great! Come on, Blaze, seriously, don't you want to pass?"
me: "Yes."

papa: "Well, you can't think about buses or you'll for sure fail."
me: "I'm not going to!"

(At the DMV later)
instructor: "Left turn signal." (I turn it on.)
instructor: "Right turn signal." (I switch it to the right.)
instructor: "Turn on your windshield wipers." (I turn them on.)
instructor: "Sound your horn." (I honk the horn.)
instructor: "Okay, we will go down the road. I will not ask you to do anything illegal or anything like that. Start the car and take a left out the driveway."
(We take off.)
instructor (repeated lines): "Go left here, go right here."
(Finally, after we have driven around a good bulk of Claremont)
instructor: "Okay, at one driveway you did rolling stops and you weren't sure if you could see totally. If you can't see completely, inch up! 11 of 15 is your score. You passed. Go to window 30!"

me (excitedly): "I passed it!"
papa: "Way to go, boy!"

(Later, on the phone with Déja)
déja (excitedly): "Oh my god, you passed it—way to go!"
me: "Yeah, I did not hit a curb this time."
déja: "Fabulous, boykie, I knew you would do it!"
me: "The vibe is very 2000."
déja: "Get out of here, 2000."

trivia
At the DMV, if you hit a curb, that is an automatic disqualification. You are allowed fifteen errors or fewer to be able to pass the road test.

Aside from 1991, 2002, and 2004, 2000 was a good year for me because my life started changing. In 2000, I got my first-ever house key and set of keys to Nana and Papa's house for my birthday. I turned thirteen and started middle school that year. Also on *Wheel of Fortune* they eliminated a specific kind of speed-up round that bothered me a lot and added Toss-Up Puzzles. At this time I wanted another year like 2000 because I hate the garbage truck that gives me the same vibe as the old wheel speed-up rounds.

soundtrack listing
"The Sheltering Sky" by King Crimson (*Discipline* 1981)

Scene 7: *The Fallbrook Special*

On January 12, 2011, I have a reading in Fallbrook to raise money to
open a library out there. Mom, Maya, Déja, and I all go and it is a long
ride and we get stuck in traffic. My friend Paris and her husband,
Frank, will be meeting us there. I met Paris back at the first *Episodes*
signing and we have been friends since she set up a tour of the NCTD
(North County Transit District) yard back in December of 2009. We
arrive there and I greet her. Then it is time for me to read and I read
Dance of Revenge. There is a quick Q&A and then we hang around
for a little while. As we prepare to leave, I talk to Frank about a couple
of NCTD buses that had some issues.

quotes
maya: "You did a good job. I am very proud of you."
déja: "Indeed! You were so cute up there." (Smooches my face.)

trivia
Paris and I talk on the phone about our experiences a lot. Paris is a
month older than Mom and lined up the NCTD tour for me because
her grandson is also on the autism spectrum and I remind her of him.
Paris had also lined up a Waste Management tour as well.

Scene 8: *Del Mar Heights Elementary School*

On January 24, 2011, I am basically wrapping up the long era of
Episodes being a new arrival. I will be going to my old elementary
school to do a reading. I am doing a reading because the school
psychologist had wanted me to come and read because a bunch of
sixth graders are struggling like I did when I was there with school
issues. Bo will be taking me and Mom there. When I arrive, the
teacher introduces me and I give a little speech. Then I read two
pieces from Senior Year, two pieces from Games, and one from My
Crush on Hilary Duff. After my reading there is a really long Q&A. As
we are getting ready to leave, the school psychologist thanks me and
tells me I will be receiving money and a thank-you card from the sixth
graders.

quotes
teacher: "Everyone, this is Blaze. He has published a book and is here
today to share with you guys."

(During the Q&A)
one kid: "Are you in college or high school?"
me: "College."
kid: "Where do you go?"
me: "Vista View."
another kid: "Who was your teacher when you came here?"
me: "Mr. Davidson."

(When Mom and I are getting ready to leave)
school psychologist: "Thanks so much for doing this. The kids really love Blaze."
mom: "No problem."
me: "Yeah, I was happy to do this. Can I do this again?"

soundtrack listing

"Saturn" and "Ebony Eyes" by Stevie Wonder (*Songs in the Key of Life* 1976)
"Saturn" is a song where the singer believes that life on Saturn would be a lot happier than on planet Earth. "Saturn" plays because I'd prefer to be going to school at Del Mar Heights and missed being a kid because I didn't have to work at a job I disliked then.

"Ebony Eyes" is a song about a girl who everyone wishes they could be and this song plays because all the kids admire me.

GO**FISH**

BLAZE GINSBERG

What did you want to be when you grew up?
I wanted to be a bunch of different things when I was a kid—a firefighter, a teacher, a garbage collector. But then I settled on wanting to be a writer.

When did you realize you wanted to be a writer?
Somewhere between eighth grade and my sophomore year in high school, I decided that writing was what I wanted to do and what made me happy.

What's your favorite childhood memory?
One of my all-time favorite childhood memories occurred in 2001. My mother had taken me out of middle school because it was a disaster for a variety of reasons. But instead of directly transferring me to another school, my mom decided to home-school me. My uncle gave me batting lessons and my aunts gave me music, drama, and handwriting lessons. My grand-father gave me math and life skills lessons, and every time I saw him, as a reward for doing a good job, he would take me for a walk to the playground of my old elementary school. All in all, I did have a happy life before this, but I did have a lot of issues with school. This is my favorite childhood memory because it was such a good experience.

As a young person, who did you look up to most?

I always looked up to my family because we are all very close and I consider my mom, my aunts, my uncle, and my grandparents to be great role models.

What was your favorite thing about school?

I always enjoyed interacting with my friends, socializing, and learning what went on in other people's lives.

What was your least favorite thing about school?

Homework and multiple-choice tests. I've always hated multiple-choice tests, because all the answers seem to me like they could be the right answers. I realize this is not how most people think about multiple-choice tests.

What were your hobbies as a kid? What are your hobbies now?

I didn't really have many hobbies as a kid because if I wasn't doing homework, I was watching TV. But now I enjoy researching buses. I'm really interested in public transportation—especially buses—and there is a lot of information out there to research.

What was your first job, and what was your "worst" job?

My first job was working at the lunch counter in my high school. I took orders and made sandwiches. It was a lot of fun. My worst job was working as a courtesy clerk in a grocery store. I hated having to corral shopping carts!

How did you celebrate publishing your first book?

I took my family out to dinner at a local restaurant and we all toasted my success!

Where do you write your books?
I wrote almost all of *Episodes* at the dining room table on my laptop computer.

What sparked your imagination for *Episodes*?
I'd been doing a lot of research on TV.com and IMDB.com, looking up various TV shows I liked to watch, and I thought it would be an interesting idea to write about my life this way—as if the things I had experienced were all TV shows with casts, plots, and dates when they first ran and ended.

The format of your book is so unique. How did you decide to write in this style?
The format is similar to the way the information is laid out on TV.com and IMDB.com so it seemed like a good way to lay out my own book.

What makes you laugh out loud?
Funny things my friends say. I think about it later and often laugh out loud. Also, my grandmother says things that make me laugh all the time—she's the funniest person I know.

What's your favorite song?
I have so many favorite songs, but one that is special to me is "Saturn" by Stevie Wonder. I feel it relates to my life somewhat because Stevie Wonder is singing about how life would be better on Saturn and how he's leaving Earth to go there and this is sometimes how I feel about my own life—being from a different type of place or wanting to be part of a better place.

What was your favorite book when you were a kid? Do you have a favorite book now?
Reading was difficult for me when I was a kid because I had

problems tracking words on the page. So I didn't read as many books as I would have liked to. But one book that I really liked a lot—the first book I really got into—was *Shiloh* by Phyllis Reynolds Naylor. I don't have a particular favorite book right now, but I do enjoy reading Shakespeare.

What's your favorite TV show or movie?
My favorite TV show of all time is the kids' show *Zoom*. But I really have many favorite TV shows and movies, too many to list.

What advice do you wish someone had given you when you were younger?
I do wish someone had helped me to interact more with other people when I was in elementary school. I was in my own world a lot of the time then, and I feel like I missed a lot of opportunities to make friends.

What should people know about you?
I would like people to know that even though I sometimes think differently than they do, I am perfectly capable of doing things. Except for my differences, I am just like everyone else, which is also true of everyone else.

What do you like best about yourself?
I think I am a nice guy and I do like that about myself.

What do you consider to be your greatest accomplishment?
Writing *Episodes*. Definitely.

SQUARE FISH

"Who needs another Pinecone?"

"Ti An's got the potential to be great," said Ashley in her prissy voice. "She's just what the Pinecones need."

We looked across the gym where Ti An was about to show Patrick what she could do on the vault. She hit the springboard with both feet, did a perfect dive roll over the horse, and came up grinning.

Patrick walked over to us, his arm around Ti An.

"Girls," he said. "I want you to meet the newest Pinecone."

I should always trust my stomach. It never lies to me. We were going to be stuck with Ti An. I didn't think she was going to be a lot of fun. In fact, I was a little worried that Ti An spelled T-R-O-U-B-L-E.

**Look for these and other books
in THE GYMNASTS series:**

THE GYMNASTS

#5 TROUBLE IN THE GYM

Elizabeth Levy

AN
APPLE
PAPERBACK

SCHOLASTIC INC.
New York Toronto London Auckland Sydney

ISBN 0-590-42194-8

Copyright © 1989 by Elizabeth Levy. All rights reserved. Published by Scholastic Inc. APPLE PAPERBACKS is a registered trademark of Scholastic Inc. THE GYMNASTS is a trademark of Scholastic Inc.

12 11 10 9 8 7 6 5 4 3 2 1   9/8 0 1 2 3 4/9

Printed in the U.S.A.   28

First Scholastic printing, May 1989

To George and Camp Aspen —
the best medicine.

Who Needs Another Pinecone?

"Lauren, stop staring," said Cindi Jockett, my best friend. Cindi's been my best friend since we were in kindergarten. She got me into gymnastics and then I quit when I was eight. Now I'm eleven. Cindi talked me into trying out for gymnastics when a new club opened in our neighborhood. I'm hooked. I go to gymnastics after school four days a week.

I couldn't take my eyes off the new girl who was talking to Patrick, our gymnastics coach. The new girl was tiny. I'm short. I'm the smallest of the Pinecones, our group at Patrick's Evergreen Gymnastics Academy, but this kid made me look like a giant. She was all skinny arms and legs. I don't think she could have been any

1

older than eight years old. But the oddest thing about her was that she was dressed in a red Atomic Amazons T-shirt and black tights. The Atomic Amazons had nearly wiped us out at the one meet we had with them. What was one of *them* doing in *our* gym? I didn't like it.

"Who is she?" I asked, trying hard not to stare.

"She's some friend of Ashley's," said Jodi. Jodi's mom is one of Patrick's assistant coaches. Patrick is careful never to make Jodi work directly with her mom, but we all know that Jodi feels pressure, just because her mom is always there. Jodi's whole family are great gymnasts. It doesn't make life very easy for Jodi.

I know what it's like to feel pressure from your family. I get it at school. My mom works for the Denver Board of Education, and my dad's a high school principal. In a way, my mom is the boss of my teachers, and all my teachers lean over backwards to try not to give me special attention. So they give me special attention by being hard on me.

The new girl saw me staring at her. "She's an Atomic Amazon," I blurted out. "What's she doing in our gym?"

"Remember, Ashley told us she had a friend who was a great gymnast who just moved into the neighborhood," said Darlene. "That's got to be her."

2

"If the new girl's a friend of Ashley's," said Jodi, "she's got to be a twerp."

I was with Jodi. I didn't like any Atomic Amazons on our turf.

Jodi, Cindi, Darlene, and I were the original Pinecones. The four of us had started at the Evergreen Gymnastics Academy at the same time. The Evergreen Gymnastics Academy sounds a lot fancier than it is. We work out in an old concrete warehouse in the suburb of Denver where I live. Patrick's our coach, and he had just opened the Academy when we joined. He didn't have many gymnasts then, and we're still not a big club.

From the beginning, Patrick called us his "Pinecones," because Pinecones grow into Evergreens. Patrick is a great coach. I'd do just about anything for him. He's serious about gymnastics, but he's funny, too. He doesn't mind if I crack jokes as long as I try hard. I love to make Patrick laugh.

For a long time, Jodi, Darlene, Cindi, and I got to work out with Patrick as our only coach, and there were no other gymnasts at our level. I guess we should have known it wouldn't last forever. I think we all hoped that there would never be any other Pinecones. I should have guessed that if a new girl came in with skills like ours, Patrick would have to put her with us. Unfortunately the first person he put with us was Ashley, and I will never think of her as a true Pinecone.

Ashley is a good gymnast, but she's so full of herself that she's a real pain. In fact, we call her Little B.I.T.: Becky-in-Training. Ashley hasn't figured out what Little B.I.T. means. Only the true Pinecones know. Becky Dyson is one of the best gymnasts at the Evergreen Academy. She competes at a higher level than the Pinecones. Unfortunately she believes that she exists at a higher level than we do. According to Becky there is nothing lower than a Pinecone. Becky lives to torment us. She's that kind of bully. Naturally Ashley admires Becky. Ashley thinks everything Becky does is golden.

If you asked me, we certainly did not need another friend of Ashley's working out with the Pinecones. It would ruin our chemistry.

Patrick glanced over at us. He noticed me staring at the new girl.

"Lauren," he called. "Give me a hand."

I trotted over. "Okay, boss, what can I do for you?" I asked.

"Lauren Baca, this is Ti An Truong," said Patrick. "Lauren, Ti An's going to start training with us. I want to see what she can do, but before I test her, I'd like you to warm her up."

"Shouldn't I warm her up, Patrick?" asked Ashley. "After all, Ti An's a little shy, and she's

4

my friend. I'm not sure we should expose her to Lauren's humor right away."

Ti An blushed. Patrick looked angry. "Ashley, I'm the one who makes the decisions around here. You go and join the other Pinecones. Lauren, make sure that Ti An is well stretched out. I'll be back to test you, Ti An, in a few minutes." Patrick smiled at Ti An. "Lauren's a good one to warm you up. She was scared stiff of being tested her first day, weren't you, Lauren? She knows what it's all about."

I grinned, feeling proud. I remembered my first day at Patrick's gym. I was sure that Patrick thought I was the weakest klutz. I really didn't have all the training of Jodi, Darlene, and Cindi.

"Remember on the first day you told me I had a lot of explosive power?" I reminded Patrick. "I love that phrase, 'explosive power.' It makes me sound like Arnold Schwarzenegger's little sister."

Ti An didn't laugh at my joke. Patrick did.

"Okay, my little powder keg, you and Ti An warm up. Ashley, come with me."

Ashley flashed me a dirty look. "Don't let Lauren scare you," she said to Ti An.

"I'm not going to scare you," I said, but Ti An looked down at her feet. She seemed shy, and I felt sorry for her.

I took Ti An through some stretches. They sure

5

were easy for her. She moved like there were no bones in her body, as if she were one of those plastic dolls that you can put in any position. She did a perfect split, then she rolled over and put her chest on the floor.

I can't do that.

She did it all without saying a word. I tried to compliment her. "Boy, are you flexible! Patrick should have had you warm *me* up."

"Do you need help?" Ti An asked in this cool voice.

I stared at her. "I was making a joke."

"Sorry," said Ti An. She blushed again. Maybe she was just nervous about being tested. Then I remembered that she was Ashley's friend. Probably Ashley had her own test for friendship. You couldn't be Ashley's friend unless you thought you were perfect.

Ti An did the rest of the warm-ups just as effortlessly and just as silently as the first set. I was more out of breath than she was after doing our push-ups. I have good upper body strength. I thought that would be one area where I could show up Ti An. But no. She had little skinny arms that looked like spaghetti, but she must have had muscles hidden in them somewhere because she did ten great push-ups, lowering her chin to the mat and keeping her body as straight as a board.

We finished just as Patrick came over to us. He had been watching us. He marked something down on his clipboard.

"Ti An's strong," I told Patrick.

"I can see that," he said. "Thanks, Lauren. I'll take over. Go join the others. You can practice your beam routine."

"So, what's she like?" Darlene asked me when I got to the beam. Ashley was up on the beam, working on her routine.

Darlene is the tallest and the oldest of the Pinecones. She's also the nicest person in the world. Darlene doesn't have a mean bone in her body, which surprises some people because her dad is Big Beef Broderick, the linesman for the Denver Broncos, and he looks mean when he's playing. But I've met Big Beef, and he's a sweetheart, too. Cindi's got four older brothers and they *love* the fact that Big Beef's daughter does gymnastics with us.

"Would you believe the new girl's perfect?" I said to Darlene. "Her name's Ti An. She's flexible and strong."

"Is she nice?" Darlene asked.

I shrugged. I had to admit that I had been all set to hate her, because she was Ashley's friend, but I didn't. There was something about Ti An that just wasn't hateful. And besides, even if she was good, I wasn't the kind of kid to hold that against her. Cindi was better than me, and she was my best friend.

I got mad at myself for thinking Ti An was a threat. I shouldn't be worried. Only creeps would hate someone because she's good. I'm not that petty.

"Out with it, Lauren," said Jodi. "What's she like?"

"She doesn't laugh. She doesn't talk. Who can tell?"

"She's too smart to talk to you," said Ashley, jumping down from the beam. "Ti An goes to my school. She's a brain."

"No one's brainier than Lauren," said Cindi, always my defender. "Lauren's in the gifted and talented program."

I hate that phrase "gifted and talented." It makes me sound like something for sale at the mall.

"Who cares about her grades?" said Jodi. "What's she like as a gymnast?" Jodi sometimes has trouble in school. Jodi's smart, but she can be lazy.

"Ti An's got the potential to be great," said Ashley in her prissy voice. "She's just what the Pinecones need."

"Who needs another Pinecone?" I asked.

"We do," said Ashley. "If we want to win."

We looked across the gym where Ti An was

about to show Patrick what she could do on the vault.

The vault is my best event. I love to run as fast as I can, hit the springboard, and jump over the leather horse. I even dream about the vault. I do perfect vaults in my dreams. So far the vaults in my dreams are much better than the ones I've done in real-life meets. In my dreams I get perfect tens. Maybe I should try sleepwalking through our next gymnastics meet.

Patrick stood at the side of the vault, ready to give Ti An a spot if she needed it. She raised her right hand in a salute. At a meet, you get points off if you do not salute the judge. Patrick likes us to make it a habit to always salute in practice, but sometimes we forget. Ti An looked as if she would never forget to salute.

She raced down the runway with a look of pure determination on her face. She hit the spring-board with both feet and did a perfect dive roll over the horse.

She came up grinning. She saw me staring at her and gave me a wave. I waved back and tried to smile. It wasn't her fault that she was good.

"She's terrific," said Jodi with a little awe in her voice.

"Maybe she'll be so good Patrick won't put her with us," said Cindi. She sounded hopeful.

I watched as Ti An showed Patrick what she

could do on the beam and the uneven bars. Ti An was good, but she wasn't doing very difficult moves. I could do more difficult vaults than she did. Cindi was better on the uneven bars. I had a sinking feeling in the pit of my stomach. I knew Ti An didn't belong in Becky's group. She wasn't good enough. But she certainly was good enough to be with us.

Patrick walked over to us, his arm around Ti An.

"Girls," he said. "I want you to meet the newest Pinecone. Ti An, meet your new teammates."

I should always trust my stomach. It never lies to me. We were going to be stuck with Ti An. I didn't think she was going to be a lot of fun. In fact, I was a little worried that Ti An spelled T-R-O-U-B-L-E.

Blonde and Perfect

Ti An had been with us a whole week, and I can't say I knew her any better than I did that first day. She hardly talked at all. She always did exactly what Patrick told her to do. She never joked around with him the way the rest of us did. Nor did she fool around with us. I had a feeling that Patrick found her a little too quiet.

He spent a lot of time with her. He never got impatient with her the way he could with me or the other Pinecones. When Patrick gets impatient with me, I know it's because he likes me and wants me to do better.

A week after Ti An had joined us, Patrick called a meeting of all the Pinecones before practice.

Jodi groaned. "I hate meetings," she whispered to me. "Anytime *any* adult calls a meeting, you can bet it means more work for kids. My mom loves to call meetings."

"What do you think Patrick wants to talk to us about?" Cindi asked.

"Maybe he's got good news," I whispered back.

"Yeah, like he's bumping Ashley up to Becky's group," whispered Cindi. "I wouldn't mind getting rid of Ashley."

"That would still leave us stuck with Ti An," I reminded Cindi.

"She's not so bad," said Darlene. "I think she's sort of cute."

"I can't figure her out," I said. "She's so quiet, and she's Ashley's friend . . . but. . . ."

"But what?" demanded Jodi.

"I don't know," I muttered. The truth was that I agreed with Darlene. Ti An was cute. She tried hard, and I couldn't help but admire her for that. But then she *was* Ashley's friend, and I did wish she'd laugh a little more. I just didn't know what to think about her.

Ti An ran to sit at Patrick's feet. Ashley sat next to her. Ti An's legs were neatly crossed, her hands folded in front of her. Ashley whispered something to her. Ti An shook her head and gazed up at Patrick.

"Okay, girls, listen up," said Patrick. "I've de-

12

cided you're ready for 'real' competition."

"What do you call the Atomic Amazons?" I asked. "Chopped liver?"

Everybody but Ti An laughed.

"I'm not calling you chopped liver," I explained to Ti An. I remembered the first day when she was wearing an Atomic Amazons T-shirt. I didn't want Ti An to think I was making fun of her.

"We had one meet with the Atomic Amazons," added Darlene. "We were slaughtered. Everybody except Cindi. She did great."

Cindi blushed. "I had a lot of help," she said.

"That meet against the Amazons was just a one-shot," said Patrick. "It didn't give you girls a chance to really test yourselves. Now I think you're ready. I've entered you in a series of four Saturday meets against clubs who have girls at your level. Becky's group will be competing, too, against girls in Class III."

"Just as long as we can avoid those Amazons," said Jodi.

"There's no avoiding them," said Patrick. "They're entered in every meet. The three clubs competing will be the Amazons, the Grandstanders, and us."

"The Grandstanders!" said Jodi. "They sound worse than the Amazons."

"They work out of the YMCA in Littleton," said Patrick. "I know their coach. She's very good.

She takes her kids very seriously."

"What if we come in last in every meet?" Cindi asked. "It'll be so humiliating."

"I don't want to hear that kind of talk," said Patrick. "It's healthy for you to compete against the best at your level."

"It's a proven fact that the Atomic Amazons do not improve my health," I said. "They make me sick."

"I don't get it," said Ti An. "I thought it was a proven fact that competition *is* healthy."

Ashley laughed. The other Pinecones giggled. I admit that I say, "It's a proven fact," all the time. Patrick teases me about it a lot. I don't mind Patrick making fun of me, or even any of the original Pinecones. But where did Ti An get the right to make fun of me?

Here she hardly says a word for a whole week, and then the first words out of her mouth are "it's a proven fact." It just didn't seem right.

Patrick winked at me. "It's a proven fact that the Pinecones need to lose their fear of the Atomic Amazons. I'm glad they have you, Ti An, on their team."

"You know, I used to work out with them," said Ti An. "They're not really Amazons. At our level, we're just as good as any of them. Darlene has beautiful lines. Cindi's a dynamo. Jodi's got all the right moves." Ti An paused as she came to me. I didn't give her a chance to continue.

"Yeah, well, then how come they outscored us in every event except for Cindi on the uneven bars?" I asked.

"You didn't have Ashley and me on your team then," said Ti An.

I couldn't believe her arrogance. The nerve of the little thing. Where did she get off talking about us like that? I looked around at Cindi, Darlene, and Jodi to see if they were just as mad as me, but they were nodding their heads as if everything Ti An was saying made perfect sense.

"We'll have our work cut out for us," said Patrick. "But I think it will be a good experience."

"Yeah," I muttered. "We'll learn to be really good losers." I hadn't realized I had spoken loud enough for Patrick to hear. I thought I had just been whispering to Cindi.

Patrick got angry. "I don't want to hear you talking like that, Lauren," he said. "That kind of attitude can infect the whole team."

"Sorry, I didn't realize I was an infectious disease." I wanted to take my words back. I sounded like such a wimpy whiner. I knew Patrick hated whiners. And I never used to whine. It was as if Ti An joining the Pinecones had turned me into something I wasn't.

Patrick stared at me thoughtfully. I was worried that he was going to get mad at me. But he didn't. He smiled at me.

"We're doing the compulsory routines for all events except the vault," he explained. "It's too boring to watch the same vault over and over. So we're allowing the gymnasts a choice."

"How about if I choose no vault?" I said.

Patrick frowned at me. "Not funny, Lauren. Vault is your best event. I've got a special one planned for you. I want you to do a layout squat vault. We've been practicing it. I just want to put some finishing touches on it. You've got a powerful takeoff. I don't think it's a vault that the other clubs will do at your level."

"Go for it, Lauren," said Jodi.

I swallowed, but I kept my mouth shut. If Patrick wasn't going to dwell on my loser crack, I wouldn't either.

A lot of gymnasts hate vaulting. Not me. I love it. You run and you jump. You fly through the air, and the goal is right there. You either make it over the horse or you mess up.

I went to the end of the runway.

"Salute me," said Patrick.

I raised my right hand.

At the end of the run I hit the springboard. The springboard combines an uphill slope and a small amount of spring. If you're not a gymnast you wouldn't know that the slope is the important factor because the whole point is to change the energy from the speed of your run into height to get you over the horse.

Vaulting is like a physics test made real.

I thought I hit the board just right. I took off. My vault was called a layout, because I was supposed to lay out above the horse, with my legs above my head before my hands made contact with the horse. The time between your takeoff and the time your hands touch the horse is called the preflight. A good preflight is one of the most important things the judges look for.

I tried to punch my hips into the air. That's not the right way. When you hit the board right, your whole body soars. My body wasn't soaring.

I stuck my hands out. Patrick grabbed my hips to get me into the right position.

I tried to tuck my legs underneath me so that I could squat on the horse, but I didn't have enough height. I ended up kind of slipping down the back of the horse and landing hard on my butt on the mat.

I heard someone laughing. I looked around. Becky was sitting on the bench with a tall, blonde girl dressed in street clothes. They were both laughing at me.

Patrick stuck out his hand to help me up.

"I goofed," I admitted.

"Do you know what you did wrong?" Patrick asked. It's his favorite question.

"I didn't go up in one piece," I said. I was really only guessing. I wasn't sure exactly what I had done wrong.

Patrick nodded enthusiastically. "Good, Lauren," he said. "That's exactly it. Go back and stand in line and try it again."

"Oh, no," groaned the girl sitting next to Becky. "I'm not sure I can bear to watch it again."

Patrick twisted around. "Becky?" he asked sharply. "Who is this? What's she doing here?"

"Sorry, Patrick," said Becky sweetly. "This is Kristen, my cousin from California. She's just visiting, but she's going to be here a whole month. She's thinking of getting into gymnastics back in California. I told her she could learn a lot by watching us work out."

Patrick nodded to Becky's cousin. "You're welcome to watch, but keep your comments to yourself, please. These girls are working very hard. They don't need any distraction."

"Lauren looked like she could use a transplant, not a distraction," said Becky, only loud enough for us to hear.

Ti An was waiting at the end of the runway.

"Oh, here comes the new girl, Kristen," Becky said to her cousin. "Watch her. Ti An is really good."

Patrick patted me on the back. "You did very well, Lauren," he said. "Now think about doing it again."

I walked slowly past the bench where Becky sat with Kristen. I watched Ti An run. She was so tiny that she looked like a little pony running along the mat.

She hit the board just right and sailed straight up, her arms above her head. She didn't have to do a layout. All she had to do was to tuck her legs up and over the vault. She balanced on the horse for a second. It was a much easier vault than mine. But she did it perfectly.

Becky's cousin clapped. She caught me looking at her and gave me a shrug.

I stood in line behind Cindi. "Are you okay?" Cindi asked. "You fell hard on that vault."

"I'm okay."

"Who's that girl with Becky?" Darlene asked.

"Her cousin from California. She said she couldn't bear to watch me again."

"Don't let her bug you," said Darlene. "Any cousin of Becky's has got to have snootiness in her genes."

"I think she looks beautiful in her jeans," said Ashley. "She's so blonde and perfect."

Darlene and I caught each other's eye and laughed. Darlene is black and I'm half Hispanic. My dad's parents were born in Mexico. Neither

Darlene nor I think that blonde is perfect.

"What's so funny?" Ashley demanded.

"Nothing," said Darlene. "Anyone as perfect as you wouldn't get it."

"I don't get it," complained Ashley.

Ti An came back from her vault. "Get what, Ashley?" Ti An asked.

"Ashley thinks that Becky's cousin is blonde and perfect," Darlene giggled.

Ti An didn't get it, either. "Well, she is, isn't she?" said Ti An, looking over at Becky and her cousin.

That little kid had a lot to learn.

Ashley started her vault. "Watch this, Ti An," she said before she took off. "I'll make Lauren's vault look like chopped liver." Ashley laughed nastily.

Ti An blushed. I realized I had turned hot in the face, too.

"How can you be friends with Ashley?" I asked Ti An.

"She's always nice to me in school," said Ti An softly. "At least she doesn't make fun of me."

"Lucky for you," I muttered.

"She's sort of different in gymnastics," admitted Ti An.

"Sure," I said sarcastically. I really didn't believe Ashley was different at school. Gymnastics doesn't make people different. Nobody could convince me that Ashley didn't love being mean and a bully. She probably liked Ti An just because Ti An was so quiet that she'd never stand up to her.

I felt a little sorry for Ti An. She might have thought she knew Ashley, but now she was meeting the real Little B.I.T. The question was, where did Ti An fit in? Was Ti An another Becky-in-training or had she just started out with the wrong crowd?

3

Turn the Page

Our first meet was a disaster for the Pinecones. I'm talking here total wipeout.

It started out badly from the beginning. Ti An was the first one up on the beam. She completely lost it. She couldn't stay up for the life of her.

The beam can do that to you. Sometimes that minute and thirty seconds on a beam seems like it's going to last forever.

I might not like Ti An, but nobody deserved a day like she was having. It was the first event in the meet; it was her first time with Patrick, and she totally blew it. She swung her legs over the beam and then sat in a V position. It's one of the easiest mounts onto the beam.

Would you believe it? Ti An's hands slipped

while her butt was still on the beam and she fell off before she was even standing.

One of the Atomic Amazons snickered.

Ti An blushed, but she got back on the beam. She hadn't taken three steps when she fell off again doing a simple waltz step.

She remounted and then fell off a third time trying to do a tuck jump.

She burst into tears. I was worried that she was going to totally lose it and refuse to finish. I've seen girls do that. Ti An wiped her cheek with the sleeve of her leotard. I've got to give her credit. Even though she couldn't stop crying, she finished her routine.

But what a disaster! The judges gave her a 3.9 and they were being generous.

As soon as her ordeal was over, she ran into a corner. I could see her shoulders shaking.

Patrick went over to comfort her.

She couldn't seem to stop crying. "Do you think we should go over and talk to her?" Darlene asked.

Patrick guided Ti An over to a bench and sat next to her, talking to her earnestly.

"I think we should let Patrick handle it," I said.

I watched the girl from the Grandstanders up on the beam. She wasn't very graceful, but at least she didn't fall off.

Then it was Darlene's turn. Normally the beam

is Darlene's best event, but maybe Ti An's dropsies were catching. Darlene fell off two times herself. She still got a 6.9, but that was the highest
score for any of us.

I fell off three times myself. It began to be almost funny. None of us could do anything right.
We couldn't figure out why.

"We're the Pinecones," I said. "We shouldn't let
one bad event throw us off."

"Ti An started it," said Jodi. "It's contagious.
One person starts falling off, and we all do."

"Yeah," said Cindi. "Ti An's good in practice,
and then she's a walking disaster in the meet.
It's embarrassing."

"Hold it," I said. "She's just a little kid. Everyone's entitled to one bad day."

"Since when are you her defender?" Jodi asked
me.

I shrugged. It just didn't seem fair to be picking
on Ti An.

Patrick and Ti An walked over to us. She still
looked shaky. I tried to smile at her. "Don't
worry, Ti An. We all fell off the beam just to make
you feel okay," I joked.

Patrick didn't like my joke. "That's not funny,
Lauren," he said. "Falling off can be contagious
for a team."

"See, I told you so," said Jodi, looking at me
triumphantly.

"The thing to do is to keep the infection under control," said Patrick. "We had one bad event. Everybody has a bad day on beam once in a while."

"How about a whole team?" I asked. "We must be setting some kind of record."

"Put it behind you," said Patrick. "Turn another page."

We tried, but we still couldn't do anything right. Jodi fell during her routine on the uneven bars. For a second I thought she was hurt. It took her several seconds to get up. But she regripped the lower bar and finished her routine.

"Do you think we're jinxed today?" Cindi asked me.

Patrick overheard her. "I don't want to hear that kind of negative talk," he said. But his voice sounded tense. The more he talked to us about controlling the contagion of falling, the more we fell.

After every disaster Patrick kept saying, "Turn the page."

Unfortunately the book for the Pinecones seemed to have been written by Stephen King. Every time we turned the page we found another chapter of *Horror Story*.

Finally it was time for the vault. I was scheduled to go after Ti An. A girl from the Atomic Amazons was going to go after me.

"Good luck," I said to Ti An.

She jumped as if I had pinched her.

"Relax," I said. "It can't get any worse."

"It's all my fault," sniffed Ti An.

"Don't be silly. We all have bad days. In fact, we all *are* having a bad day. It's not your fault."

"You don't understand," she said.

I didn't.

Besides I didn't have time to understand. I had to concentrate on my own vault. If I did my vault well, I would have a chance to make up some points. I could redeem the whole day for the Pinecones. If I could score high on my vault, I could win at least one medal for the Pinecones.

I bit my lip as I tried to picture myself doing the layout perfectly. I tried to see my body lifting high above the horse before I reached out with my hands. I saw myself tucking in at the right moment and then lifting my hands in the air as I stuck the landing.

I didn't even realize that Ti An was saluting the judge. She raced down the runway, but she misjudged her timing when she hit the board. She didn't even clear the horse.

She had a second try.

She came back down the runway.

"Turn the page," I whispered to her.

She glared at me as if I was mocking her. But

I wasn't. It was what Patrick always tells us to do when we mess up.

This time she made it. I cheered her. She blushed again. Ti An was really a blushing machine.

The judges gave her a 5.4. I thought she deserved a higher score.

The head judge nodded to me, indicating they were ready. I raised my right hand in a salute.

I charged down the runway. I hit the board just right. I kept my body straight, and my hands hit the horse. I tucked in my leg and jumped for the mats.

I put a little too much extra on my jump from the horse, and I couldn't stick my landing. I wobbled and had to take an extra step, but still it was better than anything else I had done all day.

I saluted the judges and ran back to wait for my score. Patrick held out his hand to me and gave me a low five. I'm too short and Patrick is too tall to give me a high five, so he puts his hand down next to the floor, and I slap it.

"Good vault," he said.

"I didn't stick the landing."

"You did just fine," said Patrick. "I'm proud of you. It's a much harder vault than most of the others will try."

The judges seemed to be conferring for a long

time on my score. I fidgeted with my leotard. Finally I got my score. 7.6. Patrick hugged me.

We watched the next Atomic Amazon girl salute the judge. She took off.

I couldn't believe it. She did the layout squat, too! And she didn't have to take an extra step on the landing. The judges gave her a 7.9. And then another one of the Atomic Amazons also did *my* vault. She got an 8.1. Then one of the Grandstanders got a 7.7 doing a different vault. I was out of the running.

Let me tell you, when the luck ran out for the Pinecones, it really ran out. We didn't place in one event. Zilch. Zero.

"Turn the page," said Patrick. "This was just one meet. We've got three more."

"If he says 'turn the page' one more time, I'm gonna vomit," Jodi whispered to me as we walked to the dressing room. We all felt really lousy.

"I thought at least Lauren was going to get a medal," said Darlene. "I couldn't believe it when all those Atomic Amazons copied her."

"They couldn't have copied me," I said. "They all had to practice that vault before."

"Well, it was weird," said Darlene.

I had to admit I agreed with her.

"It's like we had bad karma," said Jodi. She looked around. Ti An was behind us with Ashley.

"I think Ti An brings us bad luck."

"Cut it out," I warned her. "You know Patrick would hate that kind of talk."

"Have we ever had such a disastrous meet?" Jodi asked. "Even when we went up against the Atomic Amazons alone we did better."

"You can't blame it on Ti An," I argued.

Ti An must have heard me say her name. I saw her head jerk up. She caught my eye and then glanced quickly away.

I sighed. "I've got an idea."

"What's that?" asked Cindi. "We could use one."

"Well, you know how Patrick is always saying, 'turn the page'?"

"I think we heard it a thousand times today."

"Let's start a whole new book," I said.

Darlene, Cindi, and Jodi smiled. "I like it," said Cindi. "I like it."

"Like what?" Ti An asked shyly, as she caught up with us.

I told Ti An what I had said.

"I don't get it," she said. "Why a new book?"

"Because I don't like horror stories," I explained.

"Oh," said Ti An, but she still looked as if she didn't understand.

4

Nobody Messes
With the Pinecones

On Monday after the meet, none of us was in
a great mood, and we certainly weren't in the
mood to be teased by a non-gymnast from California. But, of course, Kristen was too insensi-
tive to see that. She had to get in her licks.

"You kids were a walking disaster at the meet,"
she said from the bench.

Patrick heard her. "Kristen," he said sharply.
"If you're going to watch our workouts, I want
you to keep your comments to yourself."

At least Kristen had the good grace to blush.

Patrick gave us a pep talk. He told us that the
only way we were going to get better was to put

Saturday's meet behind us, and to work on our routines.

All of the Pinecones would be trying different vaults. Patrick had a surprise in store for me. He wanted me to do a pike headstand vault. It's not my style. There's no run and no hurdle. You just jump from the board into a headstand on the horse and then push off with your hands. At least it might get me points for giving the judges something unexpected. I practiced it all afternoon until my head was literally spinning. By the time practice was over, I felt like my shoulders were permanently crunched around my ears. I was exhausted.

Becky's stupid cousin Kristen should have been smarter than to mess with me.

But I guess that's why I call her stupid. She was in the locker room when I got there, waiting while Becky got dressed.

"I can't believe you're really going to do that vault at the meet. It's silly-looking."

"I'd like to see you try it," I told her. Sometimes people who don't do gymnastics make me so mad. They watch gymnastics on television and think that it's so easy. It's not.

"I wouldn't do anything that made me look so foolish," said Kristen. "Of course, after Saturday, I guess you can't be more embarrassed. I was

humiliated. People thought I was your friend because I was cheering for all the Evergreens."

"Well, we're so sorry we embarrassed you," said
Cindi sarcastically.

I wasn't willing to waste sarcasm on the creep.
Kristen made me mad. I let her have it. "You
don't have any right to talk to us like that," I
shouted at her.

She gave me a dirty look. She stepped onto the
scale, fiddling with the counterweight. Patrick
makes us weigh ourselves once a week. We have
to record it in our notebooks. He doesn't want
us to lose too much weight. He doesn't have to
worry about me. I'm not exactly your typical an-
orexic gymnast. My dad says I just still have a
little baby fat on me. You'd think anybody who
works out as hard as I do wouldn't have any baby
fat left. I'm worried it's not baby fat, but pudge
that's going to stick with me when I get to be a
teenager.

Naturally Kristen was skinny, but not too
skinny. She was dressed like a Benetton ad, in
a flouncy miniskirt, tight leggings, and an over-
sized sweatshirt.

"Are you satisfied with your weight yet?" I
asked her. I had the feeling she was going to stay
on the scale forever until it finally read the weight
that she wanted.

"I'm satisfied," said Kristen, stepping off. She giggled. "Are you?"

I stepped on the scale. I couldn't believe it. Kristen had to be about six inches taller than me, but she weighed only three pounds more and that was with her clothes on. I was dressed only in my leotard.

"I never knew gymnasts could still have cellulite," said Kristen.

I looked down at myself. "What's cellulite?" I asked.

Ashley overheard us. She giggled. "Don't tell me The Brain, Lauren, doesn't know about cellulite!"

"It's a proven fact that cellulite doesn't exist," said Ti An softly. "Scientists say it's bunk."

"What is it?" I asked.

"It's fat cells, fatty," said Becky with a laugh.

I bit my lip. I would not cry in front of those twerps. But I hated them. I knew I was chunky compared to most of the other gymnasts. Kristen and Becky were just trying to humiliate me. The awful thing was they were succeeding. I felt humiliated.

"I've never heard of cellite," I admitted.

"Cell-u-lite," Kristen corrected me. "It's in all the fashion magazines. But I forgot all you pre-teens don't know about fashion."

"Speak for yourself," said Darlene. "I read *Elle*. I think it's much better than *Vogue*."

"Darlene's got more fashion in her pinkie than you do in your whole too-tall body."

"I knew what cellulite is," bragged Ashley. "And I'm only nine. Ti An knew about it and she's eight. Lauren's eleven."

Great. As if I needed to be reminded that Ti An was not only skinny and younger, she was also smart enough to know about stupid cellulite. I wished I had never picked the fight with Kristen.

"You've all got fat cells on the brain," said Jodi.

"Children," said Kristen. "I'm sorry I embarrassed you. Please don't fight on account of me."

"Don't worry, Kristen," said Becky. "The Pinecones love to argue. It's a proven fact that Lauren would rather argue than do a gymnastics trick right. She always has to discuss everything she does with Patrick. It drives Patrick wild."

"You drive Patrick wild," I shouted. "Patrick *likes* me."

"Oh, yes," drawled Becky. "I'm sure he loved the way you fouled up your vault at the meet."

"That was a very hard vault that she tried," protested Darlene. "It's harder than anything the rest of us did. Lauren's the strongest vaulter we've got. She got the highest score of any of us. It wasn't her fault all the Atomic Amazons copied her vault."

"Just like the Pinecones to blame someone else for their failure," Becky said to Kristen.

"What did you get on that vault, Lauren?" Kristen asked me. "Was it a 3.3? Or is that the number of pounds you can lift?"

I wanted to pound Kristen into the ground — headfirst. "I am so much stronger than you are, Kristen, it's a joke," I said. I admit it was kind of a lame statement, but I was mad, and it was hard to think straight.

"Lauren, you, bragging about being strong?" said Becky incredulously. "You're a hundred-twenty-pound weakling."

"I do not weigh one hundred twenty pounds!" I shouted.

"I thought all gymnasts were supposed to be strong like Becky," sneered Kristen. "Lauren *does* look like a weakling."

"Most of the Pinecones are strong," said Ashley.

"You are such a jerk," Jodi shouted at Ashley. "You certainly aren't a Pinecone. You've got the loyalty of a slug."

"Stop calling me a slug," said Ashley.

"Do these children do anything except fight?" said Kristen to Becky.

"They only fight because they're such weak excuses for gymnasts," said Becky. "It's just a cover-up."

Now I really was ready to pound both Becky and Kristen into the ground. I knew of a way to make fools out of both of them. I was so excited, I kind of hopped up and down. "Listen, little Miss California," I said. "It's a proven fact that I'm stronger than your cousin Becky. I'm stronger than ten Becky's. I can hold off ten of you."

"Child?" asked Kristen. "How old are you?"

"Eleven," I answered.

Kristen took a step closer to me. Her chin rested on my head. "I'm much taller than you. I'm strong, too. I may not do gymnastics, but I skateboard. I could squash you if I wanted."

"No way. I'm stronger than you and Becky put together." I was glad that my voice wasn't shaking. I was shaking a little inside.

Kristen turned to Becky. She twirled a finger around her ear, showing that she thought I was crazy.

Jodi, Darlene, and Cindi sidled over to me. "Lauren," Jodi whispered. "What are you getting into? You're *not* stronger than both of them."

"Don't worry about it," I whispered back. "I know what I'm doing."

"Are you sure?" asked Ti An. "Kristen may not

be very strong, but honestly, I think Becky is stronger than you are."

I gave Ti An a dirty look. "Thanks for the vote of confidence, shrimp."

Ti An looked hurt. "Sorry," she mumbled.

"Is it a trick?" Cindi asked. She knew me best. She knew when I say, "it's a proven fact," I always mean it.

"Wait and watch," I said. I sounded confident, but I wasn't sure my trick would work.

"Be careful," Darlene warned. "Kristen is not a nice person."

For Darlene those were very strong words.

"I'll make a fool out of her," I whispered.

"I hope so," whispered Ti An.

I did, too. I went over to the wall and stood facing it with my arms stretched out, and my knees bent.

"Come on, Kristen," I challenged. "Try to get me to bend my arms. Put your hands on my shoulders and push with all your might."

Cindi, Jodi, and Darlene stood to the side. I twisted my neck. I could see Kristen lock her fingers together and crack her knuckles.

I was scared. I had read about this trick in a book, but I had never actually tried it. What if it didn't work and Kristen was able to pin me against the wall like a fly? I would die of embarrassment. Maybe I should have kept my big trap shut.

Kristen put her hands on my shoulders. I felt her pushing against me, but I kept my arms straight.

"I think you need help," I said. I wasn't even sweating. I couldn't believe it. The trick was working! "Becky, your cousin isn't very strong. You stand behind her and push. Maybe the two of you can do better."

Becky came and stood behind Kristen. I felt Kristen grunt as Becky pushed with all her might. But it didn't make me bend my arms.

"The two of you are so weak," I teased. "I guess you need the Pinecones to help. Jodi, Darlene, Cindi, get behind Becky and push."

"Lauren, you'd better know what you're doing," Cindi whispered.

"No sweat," I whispered back. "Do it."

Cindi got behind Becky and pushed. Darlene put her hands on Cindi's shoulders, and Jodi got behind her. I was holding off five of them and my arms weren't even shaking. It really was a great trick.

"What about us?" whined Ashley. "Ti An and I are Pinecones, too. Don't you need us?"

"The more the merrier," I said, still keeping my arms straight. "Get behind and push. I'm still stronger than all of you."

Ashley and Ti An got on the end of the line.

Finally it was Kristen who crumbled. I could feel her hands begin to shake against my shoulders. Her elbows bent and she crashed into me. I held my ground and the line behind me fell every which way.

Kristen fell to the floor. I stepped around her and flexed my muscles. "Still wondering if I'm strong?" I asked her.

Kristen rubbed her biceps. She shook her head.

I grinned.

Becky glared at me. She held a hand out to Kristen and helped her up. "Come on, Kristen," said Becky. "Let's get out of here."

"Just remind your cousin not to mess with the Pinecones," I said to Becky's back.

"That's right," echoed Ti An. "Nobody messes with us Pinecones."

Ashley followed Kristen and Becky out of the locker room.

"Us Pinecones?" Jodi asked Ti An.

Ti An looked crushed.

I felt so good about making a fool out of Kristen, I didn't want to worry about Ti An's hurt feelings.

"Ti An's right," I said. "I did it for all the Pinecones." Ti An flashed me a grateful look.

"How did you do it?" Jodi asked. "You're

strong, but you're not stronger than all of us put together."

I licked my lips and smiled.

"Come on, Lauren," said Cindi. "Out with it. What was the gimmick?"

"Maybe Lauren really is that strong," said Ti An.

"Thank you," I said, but I was grinning at Cindi. Cindi knew me too well. She knew that there had to be a gimmick, and there was.

"I read about it in a book," I admitted. "It was one of Vicki Cobb's *Bet You Can* books. It's got lots of scientific magic stunts to pull."

"I read those books," said Ti An. "I don't remember that trick."

"It's a law of physics," I explained. "Each of you took the force of the kid directly behind you. No matter how many people pushed against me, I only had to hold off Kristen. There's no cumulative force. I picked Kristen to stand behind me because I knew I could hold her off."

"But she's six inches taller than you," said Darlene.

"Yeah, but she bragged about skateboarding. She's probably got strong legs, but I knew her arms were weak." I made a muscle and showed off my biceps. "It was no contest."

"Neat trick," said Ti An.

Just then Ashley came back into the locker

40

room. "Boy, oh boy," said Ashley. "Did you get Kristen and Becky mad! They still can't figure out how you did it."

"Good," I said, smiling.

"You proved you're no pushover," said Ti An.

"That's right," I said. "I'm nobody's pushover."

Cindi, Darlene, and Jodi grinned back at me. "Nobody messes with the Pinecones," said Cindi.

She was right. But exactly who were the Pinecones? I'd never think of Ashley as one, no matter what. But Ti An was a different fish. One moment I liked her. The next moment I didn't. I proved to Kristen and Becky that I was no pushover. But now I guess I had to prove it to myself. And maybe, just maybe, I had to prove it to Ti An.

You've Got to Act Cool

The next Saturday, our meet was in a suburb south of Denver, about an hour away. Mom was going to take us to the meet, but at the last minute she found out she had a meeting. Dad offered to do it, but I was disappointed. It's hard for me to do my best when Dad comes to the meets.

Dad is not exactly a jock. In the beginning he didn't like the idea of my doing gymnastics. Dad was worried that it would take up too much of my time. In fact, he argued against my taking classes, and I had to convince him that I could do gymnastics and still get good grades. If anything, my grades have improved since I've been doing gymnastics. It's weird. You'd think I'd be tired all the time, but I'm not.

Unfortunately Dad transferred his worries into thinking that I'm going to hurt myself. He's a little bit of a worrywart. I don't mean to complain about him. He tries to cheer me on, but he looks so anxious most of the time when he watches me do gymnastics, that it makes me nervous. He hadn't been able to go to our first meet.

"I'm sure you and the Pinecones are going to do great this time," he said. "Every team has one bad outing, and your bad one's behind you." As if we needed to be reminded about last week's disaster.

Dad picked up Cindi first and then Darlene and Jodi. "What about Ti An and Ashley?" asked Darlene, as we headed out for the thruway.

"Ashley's mom is driving them," I said.

"Did you offer to give them a ride?" Darlene asked me.

"Uh . . ." I hesitated. I hadn't exactly. It was still hard for me to think of Ti An and Ashley as real Pinecones.

"Who is Ti An?" Dad asked me. "You haven't mentioned her before."

"She's a new kid," I said. "She's only eight years old. She's a shrimp."

"Ti An? That's an interesting name," said Dad.

"She's Vietnamese," said Darlene. "But she was born here."

"That means she's American," corrected Dad.

"Uh, right," said Darlene. "Sorry."

Dad smiled at Darlene. "That's okay. I can't get my high school students to pay attention to that distinction. My nickname's Dr. Mex, and my parents are American citizens." Dad looked over at me. "Ti An sounds interesting. How come you haven't mentioned her?"

Jodi giggled.

"What's so funny?" I asked.

"Nothing," said Jodi. "It's just that I think you're a little jealous of Ti An. Before she came you were the cutest Pinecone."

"Thanks," I muttered.

"You'll always be the cutest Pinecone to me," said Dad.

"I was only teasing," said Jodi. I could tell she was worried that she had really hurt my feelings.

"It's okay," I said. "Besides, Ashley's younger than me, too, and she's cute."

"I will never think of Ashley as cute," insisted Cindi.

"Can we change the subject?" I asked.

"Uh-oh . . ." said Cindi. "Lauren's gonna get carsick at the mere mention of Ti An."

"I am not," I said. "I can get carsick on my own. Besides I'm nervous about the meet. Aren't the rest of you? What if it's another horror show?"

That shut the others up. Jodi began to bite her fingernails.

We arrived at the YMCA, where the meet was going to be held. Patrick was waiting for us in the lobby. Ti An and Ashley were already dressed in our white uniforms with the Evergreens on the front. I had to admit that Ti An did look cute.

We got dressed and joined the others out on the floor. The Atomic Amazons were already in the gym, warming up, as were the host club, The Grandstanders.

The Grandstanders all kept on their warm-up suits as they did their stretches. They didn't smile, and they didn't even look at us. They were all business.

The Amazons were huddled together in the far corner of the gym.

Patrick gathered us around him. "Okay, kids," he said. "Don't let the other clubs psyche you out. We're going to put last week's meet behind us."

"Right, turn the page," I said.

"No, Lauren. This is a whole new book."

Ti An laughed. "That's what Lauren said after the last meet."

"Well, Lauren was right, Ti An," said Patrick.

"Will you remind the judges not to read our old books?" I asked.

"Lauren," said Patrick, "no negative thoughts.

Concentrate on what you can do. Don't worry about the others. We've been working together too long and too hard to get negative. Think positive. Remember, this is a performance. Even if you don't feel it, act confident. If you act confident, the judges can't help but respect you. You've all got the skills."

"I'm so nervous I think I'm going to throw up," said Ti An.

Oh, no, I thought to myself. Was Ti An going to be one of those kids who always fouled up in competition?

"Throwing up is no way to show the judges you're confident," I said to her.

Ti An really did look a little green around the gills.

Patrick put his arm around Ti An's shoulders. "I'm glad you're nervous. It shows you're ready. Put last week's meet out of your mind."

When it was my turn to practice my vault, I saw out of the corner of my eye that the Atomic Amazons were all watching me. I wasn't going to show them the headstand vault. I wanted to save that as a surprise. I decided to do a straddle vault.

Patrick stood to the side of the horse. He didn't want to spot me unless I absolutely needed it.

I raised my right hand. Then I took off. I ran hard and I hit the board just right. My hands hit the horse and I could feel that my body was at the right angle. I split my legs. Then I landed it solid, bending my knees.

It was the best I had ever done, but of course it didn't count. I turned around and gave Patrick a low five.

Patrick shook his head at me. "Rein it in," he whispered. He looked around at the coach of the Amazons, who was watching us.

"Good vault, Lauren," Patrick whispered. "But never, never act surprised when you make a trick. You've got to act cool." But Patrick's eyes were dancing, and I could tell that he was as excited as I was that I had done it so well.

"Maybe I should do that vault instead of the headstand."

Patrick shook his head. "No, you've been practicing all week. Do the headstand. But remember to act cool."

"Act cool, act cool," I said to myself.

I didn't realize that I was talking out loud.

"What did you say?" Ti An asked.

"Act cool," I told her. I figured she needed the advice as much as I did.

Too Much Coincidence

We finished our warm-ups. The meet began. Patrick's first rule for behavior at a meet is to always know where you're supposed to be and when. "Never run around like a chicken with its head off," he says.

Normally floor exercise is the last event. But for some reason it was scheduled first, and we all thought the meet was to begin with the vault.

Suddenly we heard the announcer call out, "Lauren Baca and Ti An Truong next on floor."

Ti An and I looked at each other in a panic. We raced over to the floor mats. Patrick sighed. We heard the music. The compulsory music for our level's floor exercise is the dinkiest music you've ever heard.

I got through my exercise with no mistakes, but I didn't finish in time with the music. Ti An did a little better, but both our scores were lower than the two Grandstanders who had gone before us. Still, at least we hadn't made fools of ourselves the way we had at last Saturday's meet.

Cindi did a lot better, as did Darlene. Darlene really looked graceful, and I thought she should have scored higher than she did. But the judges seemed to be giving all the Pinecones low scores.

There were so many competitors that we had to wait a long time between events. I could feel my muscles tightening up. At least the Pinecones were doing better than last week. We were by no means cleaning up. Individually, Jodi did great on the uneven bars and got a good score, but Cindi slipped going from the low bar to the high bar. She fell on the mats. She scored in the low sixes. I didn't do much better. We were being outclassed by both the Grandstanders and the Amazons. It's no fun to go to a meet and lose, especially twice.

Becky's group was doing a lot better for the Evergreens. I heard Kristen cheering loudly after Becky's beam routine. I watched for Becky's score. She got an 8.9.

"Is that the highest score?" I asked Cindi.

Cindi shrugged. "Who cares? I'm so mad at myself. I really goofed."

"Becky's going to get a medal," said Ashley, coming back from the wall where they posted the scores.

"How are we doing?" Jodi asked.

"Lousy," said Ashley. "Can't you tell? We're third in every event so far . . . as a team. I did okay on the beam. I beat out two Atomic Amazons and three Grandstanders. But the rest of you got nothing."

"Thanks," I muttered. "We knew it."

"Well, Jodi asked me," complained Ashley.

"We still have vault," Darlene reminded us. "Lauren, just do it the way you did in practice."

"Yeah, except I'm not doing that vault. I'm doing the headstand. I didn't want the Amazons to see what I'm doing."

Just then Patrick came up to us. "I think Darlene got robbed on her score on the floor routine," I told him.

"Yeah," said Cindi. "I think the judges are marking all of us too low. I bet the judges are buddies of the Grandstanders' coach. I saw her talking to them. They were smiling and laughing."

Patrick put his hand up to stop Cindi from going any further. "No excuses. I don't want to hear that kind of talk. You girls just stay within yourselves. You're doing fine. We'll talk about what went wrong *after* the meet, not now. You still have vault in front of you."

"Yeah, just our luck, we have the worst spot in the lineup for the vault," said Jodi. "We all go first. The judges will score us low just to be on the safe side."

"Jodi," warned Patrick. "Button your lip. I want you girls just to go out there and do your best."

Jodi nodded.

"Now march over to the vault, with your heads up high," insisted Patrick. "The Pinecones are winners, not losers."

We walked past him. Patrick winked at me. "Lauren," he whispered. "Go for it."

I winked back.

When it was my turn, I could see all the Amazons and Grandstanders watching. I saluted the judge. The head judge nodded to me, indicating that she was ready.

I took a deep breath. I walked down the runway with my shoulders back. I could see some of the Grandstanders giving me a puzzled look.

They knew right away I was doing an unusual vault, because it had no run-off. I took one step onto the board and bounced up. I put my hands on the horse to balance myself and then did a headstand right onto the horse. I held the headstand for a second and then pushed against the horse with my hands. I landed right side up on both feet. I was a little off balance for my landing, but I didn't fall back and I didn't have to take an extra step.

I saluted the judge at the end of my vault. It wasn't the best I could do, but it wasn't half bad.

I waited for my score. 7.2. It was much higher than any of the other Pinecones.

We had to wait for the Grandstanders to do their vaults. None of them did a headstand, and none of them scored over a 7.1. I was winning the vault.

Then it was the Amazons turn. The first girl saluted the judge. Then she took off. But she didn't run. She walked just the way I had. I couldn't believe it. She did a headstand vault just like mine.

The judges gave her a 7.3.

Two other Amazons also did a headstand vault, and just like that I was out of the running for a medal.

I was so mad that I could hardly speak. There was the usual delay while the judges went over their final results. I knew I wasn't going to win anything. I paced around the corner of the gym.

I walked out into the corridor trying to cool myself off.

Ti An was whispering to the three Atomic Amazons who had copied my vault.

They saw me, and Ti An turned a deep red. The other Atomic Amazons started giggling.

I stared at Ti An, but she wouldn't meet my eyes. She ran back into the gym.

I followed her. What was she doing with the Atomic Amazons? Why had she looked so embarrassed when she saw me? What was she hiding? Was it just a coincidence that the Atomic Amazons had copied my vault or did we have a spy in the gym?

I didn't know the answers, but I was going to have to find out. It gave me a little bit of a creepy feeling. I didn't like suspecting one of the Pinecones, even if she wasn't an original.

7

Things Get
More Complicated

After the meet I told the Pinecones I had an announcement.

"What is it?" asked Jodi. "Next Saturday we're gonna turn into pumpkins?"

"Maybe we should call ourselves the Punkkins," said Cindi. "We can wear punk hairdos and try to scare the Amazons and the Grandstanders."

"I don't think the judges like punk," said Ashley.

"I was only kidding," said Cindi.

"This is serious," I said. "I'm calling a meeting of the Pinecones."

"Where is it?" Ashley asked.

"I meant the *original* Pinecones," I said. "We'll meet at my house."

"I don't get it," said Ti An. "Why just the original Pinecones?"

"You don't have to get it," I snapped. "I don't have to explain myself to you." I felt myself turning red. I was a little sorry that I had gotten so angry at Ti An, but if my suspicions were right, she was a grade-A creep.

"Hey, Lauren," said Cindi. "Cool it. What's going on?"

"I don't want to talk about it here," I said. "You'll have to wait for the meeting."

"She probably just wants to cry in front of her *old* friends," taunted Ashley. "I was talking to Kristen and Becky. They say the Pinecones are always sore losers."

"We aren't losers," snapped Jodi.

"What do you think it was that we did last Saturday and again today?" asked Ashley. "It sure didn't feel like winning to me."

"We tried," said Ti An. "We can't expect to win every time. Nobody wins every time."

"The Amazons do," I said. I watched Ti An closely. This time she didn't blush. She packed her leotard and gym shoes into her duffel bag. She looked up at me. "You sure you don't need me at this meeting?" she asked.

"I'm sure we don't need you," I answered. "As

I said, this is just for the original Pinecones."

"I couldn't come anyhow," said Ashley. "Kristen offered to go skateboarding with me. She's got a terrific skateboard. It cost over a hundred dollars. It was hand painted by a California artist."

"Good for her," said Darlene.

"I want to forget about gymnastics for a while," said Ashley. "It's depressing to lose all the time."

"Tell me about it," said Darlene. "We all lost."

Dad drove us back to our house. He tried to talk about the good things that had happened in the meet, but I wasn't in the mood.

"What's this about, Lauren?" Cindi asked in the car.

"Wait," I whispered. "It's a secret."

"From who?" asked Cindi, sounding annoyed. "From your dad?"

"That's okay, Lauren," said Dad. "I don't mind if you've got a secret." I've got to give Dad credit. He may not be the world's greatest cheerleader, but he does respect my privacy.

"It's not you I don't trust," I said to Dad. "It's just that what I've got to say is very upsetting."

"You sure upset Ti An," said Darlene. "She looked hurt. She's just a little kid, you know."

"Just hear me out," I said. "Wait until you listen to what I've got to tell you."

We went up to my room. I closed the door.

Darlene flopped down on my bed. Cindi and Jodi sat on the floor.

"Okay, Lauren," said Cindi. "What's the mystery? What's the big secret?"

I took a deep breath. "Well," I said. "Since Ti An's joined us, you've all seen what's happened at the first two meets." I paused.

"Yeah," joked Jodi. "We lost. So what else is new?"

"You're not going to pull that old complaint that it's Ti An's fault, are you?" Cindi asked.

"Lauren, you don't believe that stuff that she's a jinx on us?" asked Darlene.

"No, I'm not talking about bad karma or anything like that. I'm talking here about bad faith. Did anyone notice what happened to me specifically at *both* meets?"

"Yeah, Lauren, you lost, too," said Cindi. "But we're all getting better. At least we didn't lose by such a wide margin. Maybe by the fourth meet, we'll place."

"Lauren almost got a third place today on the vault," said Darlene.

"Almost," I repeated. "I don't think it was an accident that I didn't."

"What do you mean, not an accident?" asked Cindi. "You mean, somebody cheated?"

"Lauren's vault was copied by the Atomic Amazons in both meets," said Jodi, proving she's pretty smart after all. "That's a weird coincidence. Especially today. The headstand is a strange vault for one person to do. Today all the Atomic Amazons did it."

I nodded my head. I was glad that Jodi had come out with it instead of me. It made my suspicions less creepy.

"What are you guys saying?" asked Cindi. "You think the Amazons are deliberately copying Lauren's vaults?"

"Well, it's more obvious to me, because it's *my* vault that's being copied. But I think we've got a troublemaker in the gym. I don't think it's any accident that the Atomic Amazons always know what vault I'm going to do."

Darlene started to laugh. "Come off it, Lauren. You've been reading too many mysteries. The Pinecones have just had a run of bad luck. Patrick hates it when we look for excuses for not winning."

"Hold it, Darlene. I'm not looking for excuses," I argued. "Jodi pointed it out. It's just too much of a coincidence. Last Saturday, I shrugged it off as bad luck. But two Saturdays in a row!"

"Do you really think someone's spying on you and telling the Atomic Amazons what you're planning?" asked Cindi. She sounded as if she thought I was paranoid.

"Exactly," I said, nodding enthusiastically. "I'm glad you said it, not me."

"Lauren, you've got mysteries on the brain," said Darlene.

"Maybe," I said. "Maybe not. But Ti An used to take classes with the Atomic Amazons. She knows them all. And right after the meet this morning, I saw her giggling with the exact three girls that copied my vault."

Darlene sighed. "I hate things like this."

I got mad. "You sound like you think it's my fault. I'm just the victim."

"Lauren, simmer down," said Cindi. "You've got no proof that it's Ti An."

"Right," said Darlene. "Be honest; you haven't liked that little kid from the start."

I felt really hurt. My own good friends didn't believe me. I didn't say anything for a moment.

"Lauren?" said Darlene finally. "I'm sorry, but it'll tear the team apart if you accuse Ti An."

"Think about what Ti An is doing to the team," I retorted. "You say that I haven't liked Ti An. Well, I tried. She just doesn't like me. I'm the only one who the Atomic Amazons are copying. I gave her a chance. Why do you blame me?"

"I'm not blaming you," said Darlene. "It's just that I hate it when the Pinecones don't get along."

"We got along fine before Ti An joined the team."

"Lauren, are you going to tell Patrick about this?" Cindi asked. "He's not going to like it."

"I can't go to Patrick unless I have proof," I said. "Patrick might think that I'm just making excuses. I don't want him to think that."

"Great," said Darlene. "Then, you'll just let it go. There's nothing really you can do about it anyway." She sounded genuinely relieved.

I stared at her. "Let it go!" I exclaimed. "No way. I'm gonna get proof."

Cindi groaned.

"What's wrong?" I demanded.

"Nothing," said Cindi. "It's just that I know you. This is going to get a lot more complicated, isn't it?"

"Yeah," I said. "It's a proven fact that things get more complicated before they get better."

8

Every Move I Make

"How was your meeting?" Ti An asked me during practice.

This time it was me who was blushing. "Okay," I mumbled. I wondered if she knew I suspected her. We walked into the gym together.

Ti An hesitated. "Lauren," she said softly. "Can I ask you something?"

I held my breath. Was Ti An going to confess?

"Sure," I said finally.

"Do the other Pinecones like me?" she asked. Now *she* was blushing. We were like a blushing machine in the gym.

"Huh?" I muttered. "Why are you asking me?"

Ti An blushed again. She really looked pretty when she blushed. "Well, you always treat me regular, but I don't know about the others. They don't talk to me much."

I couldn't believe it. All the other Pinecones thought that I was the one who was being mean to Ti An.

"They like you," I said.

"Don't tell them I asked, will you?" Ti An whispered.

I shook my head. She ran across the gym to Patrick. I watched her. Was Ti An sorry for what she had done? Was I making the whole thing up? It would be awful if I was wrong about her.

"What were you talking to Ti An about?" Jodi asked me.

"Uh, nothing," I said, remembering my promise to Ti An. "She's just worried about our last two meets."

"Good," said Jodi. "Let her worry." Jodi put her arm around me. "The more I thought about what you said, the more I think you're right. Ti An is tipping off the Atomic Amazons. Probably she's jealous of you because you're so good at vault. We've got to think of a way to catch her at it."

It should have made me feel better to know that Jodi was on my side. But it didn't. Things were getting too complicated, even for me.

For the first hour of practice we worked on our floor routines.

Kristen came in when we were halfway through. She wrinkled up her nose at the music. Patrick was helping Ti An count out the steps.

"How can you stand to listen to that awful tune one more time?" Kristen asked me.

"We don't get to choose it," I said.

"Yeah, I can just imagine what you clowns would pick," said Kristen.

Patrick glanced over at her. I noticed that Kristen shut up as soon as she saw Patrick looking at her. She put on her Walkman.

"Lauren," said Patrick. "Get on with your conditioning. As soon as we finish with the floor routines, I want to work on everyone's vault for next week."

Cindi winked at me. "Maybe you should ask Patrick to give your vault in a secret code; that way you'll be safe."

"You don't believe me, do you?" I said. "You think I'm making it all up. Jodi believes me."

"Cool your jets, Lauren. I guess I believe you. It just sounds a little crazy, that's all."

"If it happens three times in a row, you'll have to believe me." Cindi was making me angry.

"Lauren," said Patrick. "I never said that your mouth needed conditioning. It's your body. Stop gabbing and do some push-ups."

Ashley giggled. "It's a proven fact that Lauren

never stops talking. She's got a very well-conditioned mouth."

"Why don't you learn to shut yours?" I said.

"Girls," said Patrick. He sounded exasperated. "I want you to stop this sniping."

"Yes, sir," I said to Patrick. I almost never call Patrick "sir."

"Lauren," said Patrick. "This week, you're going to do a layout straddle vault. You've practiced it before. Concentrate on body height. Instead of tucking your legs under you, split them apart, and snap them together on the rebound."

Patrick stood in back of the horse. "Give me a strong run," he said. "I'll spot you."

I ran and pushed off the board. I felt like I was diving into the horse, but Patrick held me up while I split my legs into a straddle. I jumped down onto the crash mat.

"Good!" said Patrick.

"Can I try that?" Ti An asked.

"You're not ready for it yet," said Patrick. "Ti An, you can try the layout tuck."

I walked back along the runway.

Becky was sitting on the bench, whispering to Kristen. "Good vault, shrimp," she said to me.

Trust Becky. She couldn't even give a compliment without it sounding like an insult. But I was pleased. Even she was impressed. If I could impress Becky, I was sure I'd be able to impress the judges.

"What's that vault called again?" Kristen asked. "I hate all these gymnastics terms. They're so boring."

"A layout straddle," I answered.

I watched the other Pinecones do their vaults. Finally it was my turn again.

"Try it this time without me spotting you," said Patrick. "Just remember. It's like all other layouts. Get your body higher than the horizontal before you make contact with the horse."

"Yes, sir," I said. But this time I was grinning. I did love vaulting. I wished that I could just run, jump, and never stop.

I ran full out. I hit the board perfectly and it felt like I was flying. I split my legs in the air and cleared the horse. I bent my knees to take my weight on my landing.

Patrick clapped me on the back. "That's it! Do it like that next Saturday, and I guarantee you a medal."

Ti An was watching us.

Patrick couldn't guarantee me a medal. Not if someone was telling the Atomic Amazons every move I made.

9

There's a Spy Out There

The next meet was at the Atomic Amazons club. I was psyched — ready to go into the lion's den. "I'm going to find the proof on their own turf. I'll get the villain. It's going to be chillin'," I told Cindi on the phone the night before the meet.

"We'll just call you the Rhyming Detective," said Cindi.

"I like it. I like it."

"What are you going to do *if* you get this proof?" Cindi asked.

"I'll tell Patrick what Ti An's been doing," I said. "What else?"

"He'll probably kick her out, don't you think?" Cindi's voice was soft.

I had been so concentrated on how I was going to get proof that I hadn't thought about the consequences.

"Yeah," I agreed. "I guess he will." I wished I felt happier about the idea. The idea of getting Ti An kicked out of the Evergreen Academy made me feel guilty. But then I got mad.

"It's Ti An's fault. Not mine," I argued to Cindi. "I haven't done anything wrong."

"I didn't say you did," agreed Cindi. "It's just tough. I wouldn't want to be in your shoes."

"I don't want to be in them, either," I said. "But what choice have I got?"

"None," admitted Cindi.

We hung up. Ordinarily phone calls with Cindi make me feel better. This time I only felt worse.

I was a nervous wreck by the time of the meet. Luckily my parents had an educational seminar they had to go to that Saturday. I was relieved. The last thing I wanted was any more distractions.

Jodi's mom drove all the Pinecones to the meet in her van. I was the last one to be picked up. The only seat available was next to Ti An.

I must have looked grim. Ti An picked up on it right away. "Lauren, do you feel okay?" she asked as soon as I got in.

"I'm fine," I snapped. But I didn't sound fine, not even to myself.

"Jodi's mom's been giving me lots of good advice," said Ti An. "Today I'm only going to think positive thoughts. I'm not going to let any of you down."

Jodi's mom laughed. "Ti An, sweetheart," she said. "Listen to yourself. Thinking that you're not going to let anybody down is already a negative thought."

"I'm sorry," said Ti An.

Jodi's mom reached over and patted Ti An's forearm. "And don't be sorry. You're a great little gymnast. Just go out there and have fun today. That's all anyone expects from you. You can't let anybody down."

Ti An looked over at me as if hoping for reassurance. I tried to smile.

The Atomic Amazons have the most glamorous workout space in all of Denver, maybe in all the western slope. They share their space with a health spa in a downtown skyscraper. The locker room and all the corridors are carpeted in thick pink plush. The mirrors in the locker room made us all look as skinny as Ti An.

I hurried out to the floor. I wanted to see the order of events. The vault was first. I couldn't believe it. Today was the one day that I needed time to do my spying.

Patrick came over to me as I was going over the list. "You're scheduled seventh in the vault," he said to me. "Stretch out and let's do your warm-up vaults since you're the first one out."

I looked around the gym suspiciously. Kristen was there talking to a cute boy. He was wearing a "Gymnasts have Seoul Power" T-shirt from the 1988 Olympics. Kristen saw me and deliberately turned her back to me. I didn't care. I saw Ti An come out of the dressing room. I had to follow her.

"Lauren," said Patrick impatiently, "are you listening to me? I'd like to watch you do your vault. We have time for it now."

"*I* don't have time for it," I said. I started to rush off. Patrick grabbed my forearm.

"Lauren, what's more important than preparing for this meet?" Patrick insisted.

I saw Ti An go into the corner of the gym to warm-up. Two Atomic Amazons were warming up with her. I had to get over there to hear what they were saying.

"Lauren," repeated Patrick. "I asked you a question."

I looked up at Patrick. He was very annoyed at me. I made a decision.

"I'm sorry, Patrick. But this is more important." I started to race off to the corner.

Unfortunately I forgot how much stronger Patrick is than me. He held onto me and turned me around.

"Young lady," he said, steering me to a bench. "You and I have got to talk."

I sighed and sat down on the bench, my legs dangling back and forth. My feet didn't touch the floor.

Kristen pointed at me. The boy laughed. I put my head down and watched my feet in my gymnastics shoes.

"Lauren, look at me," said Patrick. I raised my head.

"What's been going on with you?" he asked.

"Nothing," I whispered.

"It's not nothing," said Patrick. "I know you. Ordinarily you're full of enthusiasm. You're the kind of kid who thrives on competition. Even when you don't win, you always try your hardest. I never used to worry about you. I knew you had that competitive edge. You have it in your schoolwork, and you used to have it here. But the last couple meets, your mind's been a million miles away. It's a mystery to me."

I nodded. "You're right."

Patrick seemed puzzled. "What am I right about? You haven't explained anything."

"It's a mystery," I whispered.

Patrick looked exasperated. "Lauren, you're a smart girl. Use your brain. Don't tell me mumbo jumbo. I get the feeling that something very specific is bothering you. I want to know what it is."

70

"Can you keep a secret?" I said to Patrick.

Patrick nodded. "You know I can. If it's not something that I feel is dangerous or that your parents have to know about . . . I'll always try to keep a secret."

I knew that was true about Patrick. I decided to trust him. I'd tell him about my suspicions even though I didn't have proof. Maybe he'd help me figure out what to do.

"Haven't you noticed how at every meet the Atomic Amazons do the exact same vault that you've taught me?"

"I have noticed," Patrick admitted. "I thought it was a funny coincidence."

"Coincidence?" I practically choked on the word. "It's no coincidence. Someone is tipping them off." I was about to tell Patrick who I suspected when he stopped me short. He took me by the shoulders and made me face him.

"Lauren, stop right there. I don't want you to waste your time thinking up outrageous excuses like that." Patrick's blue eyes were boring into me. "Lauren, you're a gymnast, not a detective. The only way you're going to win is if you stop worrying about what the others are doing and concentrate on yourself. It's an old ballplayers saying, but it's right for gymnastics, too. You have to keep within yourself."

"How can I keep *within* myself? Somebody's

deliberately sabotaging me. The Atomic Amazons know every move I make." I was practically wailing. I must have been talking louder than I realized because Kristen and the guy she was with turned around and stared at me.

"Lauren," said Patrick, sternly, "all that talk about spies is ridiculous. Put it out of your mind and think about gymnastics. Now, let's do your warm-ups." He smiled at me, trying to take the sting out of his words. "You're a good gymnast," he said with a grin. "I don't need any detectives in my gym."

He was wrong. I could have proved that to him as soon as the first Atomic Amazon did her vault.

Naturally, it was the layout straddle vault, the one that I had been working on all week. She got a 7.8. The next Atomic Amazon did the same vault and she got a 7.6.

I shook my head at Patrick. "See," I whispered.

"Put it out of your mind, and stay within yourself," he whispered back.

I couldn't. I messed up my vault and only got a 6.6.

Patrick patted me on the back. "I know, I know," I said to him. "Turn the page."

"No, Lauren. Stay within yourself."

I looked around the gym. Ti An was talking to Ashley. Kristen was talking to the same guy. They were holding hands. Kristen was so pretty.

Naturally, she was only in Denver a couple of weeks and she already had a cute boyfriend.

I was getting so upset that I repeated Patrick's phrase to myself. "Stay within yourself," I whispered. I wanted to punch the wall. How could I stay within myself when there was a spy out there! I had to figure out a way to catch her. Patrick had made it clear. I couldn't come to him again unless I had proof positive that Ti An was out to get me. But how in the world was I going to get proof? I'd need a little help from my friends, that was for sure.

10

Operation Trap
Starts on Monday

"We've got to hand it to you, Lauren," said Darlene. "Even I'm convinced. Three strikes and she's out. Ti An's got to be tipping off the Amazons about your vault. I think we should all go to Patrick together and tell him what's been going on."

It was Sunday after the meet and the four original Pinecones were gathered at Darlene's house. It was the off-season for the Broncos, and Big Beef had fed us a carbo-loading Sunday lunch of his great spaghetti. But it hadn't been a very festive meal. Big Beef thought we were down because we had lost three meets in a row. He told us stories about teams that he had been with that hadn't won a game all season. "You think losing three in a row is depressing, try losing thirteen in a row," said Big Beef.

"Thanks, Dad, that's real encouraging," said Darlene.

"I just don't want you girls to get hung up on scoring," said Big Beef.

Cindi giggled. "I think if the Broncos' coach heard you, he'd have a fit."

"I get paid to win," said Big Beef seriously. "You girls are in it for the joy. I love going to your meets whether you win or lose. Individually, all of you had some fine moments yesterday. I've never seen this group so down in the mouth."

"Dad," said Darlene, sounding exasperated, "we don't need a pep talk. We need some more spaghetti."

We'd finished our meal and were down in Darlene's rec room, where she has a balance beam set up and other gymnastic equipment.

"Okay," said Darlene. "Does everybody agree with me? The Pinecones stick together. This is no longer just Lauren's battle. On Monday we all go to Patrick and tell him that he's got to put a stop to this."

I interrupted. "I already told Patrick, and he doesn't believe me."

"You told him about it!" Cindi exclaimed.

"I had to," I said. "At the meet yesterday, before you guys came out of the locker room, Patrick took me aside for one of his talks."

Jodi groaned. We all love Patrick, and we've all benefited from the private talks Patrick gives us, but sometimes they are hard to take.

"What was he on you about?" Jodi asked.

"He wanted to know why I hadn't been concentrating lately. I told him I couldn't concentrate because obviously someone was sabotaging me. He called me ridiculous. I didn't even get to tell him that I suspected Ti An. If I did, I think he would have gotten really angry."

"Patrick wouldn't call you ridiculous," said Cindi.

"You're right," I admitted. "He called the idea ridiculous. Same difference."

"No, it isn't," insisted Cindi.

"So now what are we going to do?" complained Darlene. "I thought we could solve it by just dumping it on Patrick's lap and letting him deal with it. He's the coach. Grown-ups should have to handle stuff like this; we shouldn't."

"I don't have the foggiest idea what to do next," I said.

"Come on," said Cindi. "You must have found out something yesterday. You were skulking around the Amazons' gym all during the meet."

I shook my head. "I didn't find out anything except that Kristen's got a boyfriend."

"Who?" asked Darlene, who is always interested in gossip. "Was he cute?"

"You probably saw him. He was wearing a 'Gymnasts Have Seoul Power' T-shirt."

"Oh, yeah, the blond," said Darlene. "He and Kristen must be attracted to each other because they look like Ken and Barbie. I saw him spotting some of the Atomic Amazons."

I stared at Darlene. "What did you say?"

"Don't you notice anything?" Darlene said. "I saw him with the Atomic Amazons. They have a lot of teenage boys who help out. He must be on the guys' team."

Of course, Darlene would notice any cute boys around, but still I shouldn't have been so blind. I prided myself on being such a great detective. I had been so sure that it was Ti An, I hadn't even realized that there was another suspect right under my nose.

"Kristen," I practically shouted. "It could be Kristen, not Ti An."

"Why do you sound so happy?" Cindi asked.

" 'Cause, don't you see? Kristen could be tipping them off through her boyfriend."

"It could be," said Darlene.

"She's sneaky enough," admitted Jodi.

"And she's a friend of Becky's," Cindi reminded us.

"Most important," I said, "Kristen doesn't like me. She's been wanting to get back at me ever since I made her look like a fool."

"But it still could be Ti An," argued Jodi. "Just because Kristen's got a boyfriend doesn't mean she's the one. There's still just as much reason to suspect Ti An."

I had to admit that Jodi had a point, but it made me depressed. I took my shoes off and hopped up on the beam. Walking a four-inch plank is good for concentration. I paced up and down the beam, trying to think. "It could be Ti An. It could be Kristen," I muttered. "I've got to come up with a plan."

Cindi groaned.

"What?" I asked.

"I just know you," said Cindi. "I know you'll come up with something incredibly elaborate. Keep it simple."

"I've got it!" I shouted. "It's brilliant, if I say so myself."

I told my plan to Jodi, Darlene, and Cindi.

Cindi grinned at me. "I've got to admit it's got possibilities," she said.

"Operation Trap starts on Monday," I announced. I could hardly wait.

Operation Trap
Is Sprung

On Monday I came into gymnastics class and told Patrick that I couldn't decide which vault I wanted to do for the last meet. I spoke in a loud voice so that Kristen could hear me from where she was sitting on the bench and Ti An could hear me from where she was warming up on the mats.

Unfortunately Patrick interrupted me before I could finish. "Lauren, I may seem old to you, but I'm not hard of hearing," he said.

"I want to practice all three of my vaults, okay?" I shouted.

Patrick gave me a puzzled look. "GOOD IDEA!" he shouted back. "Now, why are you shouting?"

"Uh, I didn't realize I was," I said. "I went to a

rock concert last night and my ears are still ringing."

"Who did you see?" Kristen asked me. "I didn't know about any rock concert in Denver."

I hate lying. I'm no good at it. "Uh, it was Cindi's brothers," I improvised. "They have a rock band. I was watching them practice."

"But you said a rock concert," corrected Kristen.

"That's because they're so good; it was just like being at a concert."

Cindi rolled her eyes up toward the ceiling. Then she grabbed me and pulled me away from Kristen. "You almost blew it," she warned me.

"I know, but I didn't know what to say."

"Cindi and Lauren," shouted Patrick. "Can you hear me? I want the Pinecones to work on their tumbling runs. Get moving!"

I grabbed Cindi's hand and we ran over to the mats to warm up. "What are we going to do when she finds out that my brothers are tone-deaf?" Cindi asked.

"We'll tell her 'Tone-Deaf' is the name of their group," I said.

"We'd better do some rolls, or Patrick's going to be on our tails," said Jodi, who was waiting for us at the mats. We did a series of forward somersaults down the mats. Ti An followed us. Ti An could really move fast. Her rolls were tight, and she bounced back up to a standing position after each one.

"You're really good," I said.

"Thanks," said Ti An. "That's how I started in gymnastics. I was only four years old and I loved to do somersaults. My mom took me to the YMCA, and I got to roll around all afternoon. I love it. I never get dizzy."

"I wish I could say that. Sometimes if I do too many somersaults in a row I get a little nauseous."

"Try breathing in the middle of the somersault," said Ti An. "It helps. My coach at the Atomic Amazons taught me that."

"Speaking of the Atomic Amazons," I said to Ti An, glad that she had given me an opening, "I've got a secret to tell you."

Ti An's whole face lit up at the idea that I trusted her. "I can keep a secret," she said earnestly, nodding her head.

"I'm going to do the layout squat vault at our meet on Saturday. I just didn't want Becky and Kristen to know what I'm doing. I think they may be tipping off the Atomic Amazons."

Ti An's eyes were shining. "You know, I wanted to get up the nerve to talk to you. I think there's something stinky going on. Three times in a row the Amazons have copied your vaults."

"I've realized that," I said softly. I couldn't trust

myself to say too much more. Could Ti An be such a good liar? I had to tell myself that she could be. I remembered a little kid in first grade who lied all the time, and even the teachers believed his lies. Just because Ti An was so tiny and young didn't mean that she couldn't lie like a trooper.

I felt much better about trying to trap Kristen. But I was a little bit scared about pulling it off. Kristen had been so swift to pick up on my lie about going to the rock concert.

I waited until after practice to try my trap out on Kristen. I lingered by the full-length mirror. I figured that was the most likely place to catch Kristen alone.

I was right. She came in and stood in front of me, fussing with the ribbons in her hair.

"What are you staring at?" she asked.

"I was just admiring your hair," I lied. That whopper Kristen found easy to believe. She smiled at me.

"Why do you wear your hair so short?" she asked me. "It makes you look even younger than you are."

I ran my hair through my short, dark brown hair. "It's a modified punk cut," I said. "At least that's what the guy who cuts it tells me."

Kristen laughed at me. "You look more like one

of Santa's elves than punk," said Kristen. "But I keep forgetting how young you are."

"I'm older than Ti An," I said.

Kristen shrugged as if I were boring her. I knew I had to get my trap in quickly.

"I think it's wonderful how often you come to our meets and watch us work out," I said.

"I don't have much else to do while I'm visiting Denver," said Kristen. "And I'm going to do gymnastics myself when I get back. I'll look good in a leotard."

With that attitude she wouldn't last three days doing the hard work of gymnastics.

"When I started," I said quickly, "I had so much trouble figuring out all the gymnastics terms. It was like learning a new language. For example, I do one vault where I tuck my legs underneath me. That's called the layout squat. But on Saturday I'll do a layout straddle vault. In the straddle I split my legs as I go over the horse. It's much harder."

Kristen turned to face me. "I heard you tell Patrick that you didn't know which vault you were going to do."

I moved a step closer to Kristen. "That was a trick," I whispered into Kristen's ear. "One of the other gymnasts is tipping off the Amazons. But you're not a gymnast. I knew I could trust you."

Kristen nodded. Boy, she must think I was dumb. She turned back to the mirror and gave herself a self-satisfied smile.

"Well, good luck," she said. " 'Bye now." She gave me a little wave.

I waved at her in the mirror. When I saw the door close, I gave myself a great big grin.

The trap was set. Ti An thought I was doing the layout squat vault. If the Atomic Amazons all did a layout squat vault, I'd know it was Ti An.

Kristen thought I was doing the layout straddle vault. If the Amazons did the straddle vault, I'd know it was Kristen.

But I would fool them all. I would practice the easiest vault of them all. The headstand vault. That's the one that I would do. I'd catch the spy, and with any luck I'd clean up on the vault event. It was time for the Pinecones to win a medal.

12

Crunch Time

We were hosting the final meet at the Evergreen Gymnastics Academy. All our parents were planning on coming. I could tell during the week that Patrick was nervous. I practiced all three of my vaults, but I paid extra attention to the fine points of the headstand vault.

By Saturday, I'd have to say that the entire Evergreen Team was a nervous wreck. There is nothing more degrading than losing on your home turf. We would have to win at least one event.

Unfortunately Becky was the only person who seemed to have a medal sewed up. The more advanced girls went first, and Becky did a spectacular routine on the beam. She came in first.

Kristen was cheering so loudly I could swear they could hear her in California. Becky also did very well on all the other events, and I was sure she had a chance for the overall award. The final tallying of the scores would have to wait until the Pinecones had their chance.

My palms were sweating as we warmed up. Ti An seemed really up for this meet. She did a perfect split. I could see the Grandstanders peeking at her in awe.

"I think Becky doing well is a good omen," Ti An said, smiling at me. "Don't you?"

"Becky's never been good luck for the Pinecones," I said.

"That was before I joined your team," said Ashley prissily. "Becky says that Ti An and I are the only Pinecones worth beans."

"That's exactly what I'd say you are worth," snapped Jodi.

"Hey gang, team spirit," I said. "Let's not fight."

Jodi stared at me. She waited until Ti An and Ashley began their practice tumbling runs before she confronted me. "Team spirit?" she questioned me. "You consider those two twerps teammates?"

"Whether we like it or not, Patrick put them with us," I said. "We've got to root for each other or we'll all lose."

Jodi winked at me. "I get it. This is all part of your trap, isn't it? You're trying to lull Ti An into thinking we don't suspect her. Then we'll snap the trap shut and she'll be off the team for good. I can't wait."

I watched Ti An finish her tumbling run. She waved to me. I started my somersaults down the mat. I remembered to breathe in the middle of the somersault the way Ti An had told me to.

I got to the end without feeling dizzy at all.

Ti An gave me a hand up. "I saw you taking deep breaths in the middle," she said shyly.

"It works," I said. "I'll try anything that works."

Ti An skipped across the gym to the beam. It was our turn to warm up. I watched her do a perfect routine. Now if only she could do it in the meet.

Then I caught myself. I was cheering for Ti An! For all I knew, she was the one who had been betraying me for weeks!

I took a deep breath and got ready to practice my own beam routine. I did it perfectly, too. I didn't fall once. Maybe the Pinecones were finally over the dropsies.

The judges rang the bell for the one touch warm-up. It means that each competitor gets one last chance on each apparatus, but if you fall once, you lose your turn.

We Pinecones amazed ourselves. We each got

to finish our routines without falling. If nothing else, the Grandstanders and the Amazons looked psyched out.

Patrick was grinning from ear to ear. "You kids were awesome in practice," he said. "Just repeat it for real, and we'll have to build a new trophy case."

"We're not the Dropsies, we're the Upsies," I sang.

"What does that mean?" asked Ashley, sounding annoyed.

"I'm not sure," I said. "But it rhymed, and it means we're winners."

"You sure are," said Patrick. "Now, the vault is first. If we can score high here, I know we'll go on to win."

My stomach did flip-flops. Jodi, Darlene, and Cindi nodded to me. It was now or never for Operation Trap.

"What's the order?" I asked Patrick.

"Since we're the host club, we go last," said Patrick. "The Atomic Amazons start. Then the Grandstanders, then us."

"Good," I said.

Patrick nodded. "This will give us a chance to know what we have to do."

Patrick didn't realize it, but he had never said truer words.

"Let's go watch the Amazons," said Jodi.

"Wait," said Ti An. "I'm coming, too."

But Jodi had already put her arm through mine. She didn't wait for Ti An.

I saw Kristen whispering to her boyfriend. They were standing with Becky.

"One more minute, and we'll know for sure," Jodi whispered to me. "I'll bet you anything they do the layout squat vault. I just know it's been Ti An who's been sabotaging you."

I chewed on my lower lip. Now that we had come down to crunch time I realized how much I didn't want it to be Ti An.

I watched the first Atomic Amazon salute the judge. Do the layout straddle, I silently begged her. Let it be Kristen.

13

It's Not Over
By a Long Shot

The first Atomic Amazon to attempt the vault ran with a look of fierce concentration on her face. She hit the board so hard it sounded like a rifle shot. She lifted her body so that her legs were way above her head when her hands hit the horse.

Now I'd know. If she tucked her legs underneath her, it would mean that it was Ti An. If she kept her legs straight and did a split to straddle the horse, it would be Kristen.

Not even the judges were watching that girl as closely as I was.

She split her legs and straddled the horse, punching hard with her hands to lift her upper body. She looked like she was jumping into a cool pool of water. Her toes were pointed and her hands were straight over her head. She made a perfect landing.

I didn't wait for the judge's score. I already knew the score.

I saw Kristen and her boyfriend standing with Becky.

I strode over to them. "Okay, you creep," I said to Kristen. "Step out into the corridor, I want to talk to you."

"Who is this?" asked Kristen's boyfriend. "The Sheriff of Evergreen Forest?"

"I'm the one who figured out what you two were doing, you worms." I put my hands on my hips. "Now, do you want to step outside, or do you want me to shout what you did in front of everyone?"

Kristen and her boyfriend held hands as we walked out into the corridor. I saw Patrick staring at us. Cindi, Darlene, and Jodi followed me.

Ti An grabbed my arm. "Where are you going? Is this a private meeting?" she asked.

"The Pinecones are about to teach Kristen another lesson," I said. "Come on along."

Kristen and her boyfriend stood with their backs to the wall. They both towered over me. I didn't care.

"You're a spy," I said to Kristen. "You've been telling your boyfriend what vault I was practicing."

"You're a dope," said Kristen.

"Kristen?" asked Becky, coming out of the gym. "Do you need my help?"

"Oh, little Lauren finally figured out what we were doing," Kristen said. "She's all upset, the poor dear."

I turned on Becky. "You knew about it, too!" I exclaimed. "I'm an Evergreen, and you let her betray me."

Becky laughed. I could have hit her. "We just wanted to teach you a lesson," she said. "I thought it was pretty funny."

Patrick came roaring out of the gym. "What's going on here?" he demanded. "You girls are up for the vault in about five minutes."

"This is more important," I said to him. "I caught the spy. Kristen has been telling the Atomic Amazons what vault I was going to do. Her boyfriend must have convinced the coach to do that vault. That's how they've been beating me."

Becky laughed at me. "They've been beating you because they're better," she said.

Patrick frowned at Becky. He looked puzzled. "Lauren, run this by me again," he said.

"Kristen and Becky thought it would be fun to

make a fool out of me," I explained. "They arranged for the Atomic Amazons at my level to always do my vault."

"Is this true, Becky?" Patrick demanded.

At least Becky was blushing. "Well, it was Kristen's idea," she whined. "Kristen and Chris became friends."

"He would be called Chris," whispered Darlene. "Kristen and Chris . . . too cute for words."

"Are you Chris?" Patrick asked. "How are you connected to the Atomic Amazons?"

"I work out there, sir," said Chris, suddenly sounding very scared. "I help spot the girls. I only suggested the vault after Kristen told me. The head coach didn't realize it was a trick on the Evergreens. But it's not really cheating. I mean, the judges still score the girls fair and square, and your girls lost."

I thought Patrick was going to punch him out.

"Young man, I'll have a talk with your coach after the meet. As for you, Kristen, I don't ever want to see you in my gym again."

"I'm going home tomorrow anyhow," said Kristen.

Becky tried to sneak back into the gym. "Becky Dyson," said Patrick. "Come back here. It's you who owe all the Pinecones an apology. Then you and I are going back into the gym and we will tell the judges that for reasons of team discipline you are disqualified from the meet."

Becky's mouth literally dropped open. "Patrick, I've won a medal," she wailed. "I've got a good chance for the overall."

"Not today, you don't," said Patrick grimly. "Maybe this forfeit will teach you a lesson that the Pinecones have already learned."

"What's that?" asked Becky sullenly.

"Team spirit is more important than any medal," said Patrick. "Now I want to hear your apology."

"If I say I'm sorry, do I really have to forfeit?" begged Becky.

"YES!" roared Patrick.

Finally Becky looked cowed. "I'm sorry, Lauren," she said.

"You should be," I said.

Patrick nodded to me. "All right, Lauren, you and the Pinecones have to pull yourselves together."

"We're okay," I said. "It's all over. I solved the mystery."

"It's not over," said Patrick. "We still have a meet to win. Becky, I want you changed and in street clothes. You can watch the rest of the meet from the stands. I'm going to talk to the judges, and then I want to come back here and talk to all of the Pinecones. This meet is not over by a long shot."

14

Was That Enough?
Was That Enough?

"What a creepy, lousy thing to do!" Ti An exclaimed. "I'd like to tar and feather Kristen."

Darlene laughed. "She'd look good in tar and feathers."

Ti An looked up at me. "You were so smart to figure it out," she said.

Now it was my turn to blush.

"I think we should declare Lauren our official Pinecone Detective," said Cindi.

I took a mock bow. "I accept. Thank you very much."

Patrick came back out into the corridor. "It's too soon for bows, Lauren. The Grandstanders are just finishing up. We're up next. I want you to do the layout straddle."

"Are you kidding? That's the vault the Atomic Amazons did. I'm going to do the headstand vault. Then the judges won't have to compare me to the Amazons."

"Lauren," said Patrick. "I'm the coach, not you. The headstand vault has a competitive rating of just 6.0. The layout straddle vault is worth nine points. You're doing the layout straddle."

"But. . . but," I stammered. "I can't do it as well as the Amazons."

Patrick grabbed me by the shoulders. "No negative thoughts," he said. "You are every bit as good as the Amazons. The only way we can win is if you do the more difficult vault. It's time for you to shift gears. You're not a detective. You're a gymnast."

I nodded my head. I swallowed hard.

"You can do it, Lauren," whispered Ti An.

"I will," I said.

We marched back into the gym. The last Grandstander was finishing her vault.

It was my turn. Patrick squatted down so that his eyes were on my level. "I want you to go full out on this one," he said. "Put everything else out of your mind. But remember, if your body is only horizontal when you hit the horse, the vault is only worth seven points. You've got to get the lift. Get your feet above your head in the pre-flight."

"I will," I promised him. "What score do I have to get to win?" I asked.

"I'll tell you afterwards," said Patrick. He stood up. "You can do it, Lauren," he said. Those were exactly Ti An's words.

The judges finished scoring the Grandstanders. The head judge nodded to me indicating that he was ready. I saluted him with my right hand held high.

Then I ran down the runway as fast and hard as I ever have. I landed on the springboard so hard that I could hear it crack. I flew through the air, and I let myself fly. My feet were way above my head. I pointed my toes and reached out for the horse. As soon as my hands hit the horse, I pushed down hard and lifted my chest. I split my legs as wide as I could. I cleared the horse. The horse seemed like it was miles below me. I pointed my toes for the landing and tried to keep the arch out of my back. I bent my knees on the landing. I landed so hard, I almost sunk to my knees, but my knees didn't touch the mat and I didn't have to take an extra step. My arms were high above my head in a V for victory.

It was the best vault I had ever done. I saluted the judges again and then ran back to Patrick. Patrick gave me a bear hug. "You were fantastic," he said to me. I could see Mom and Dad standing up.

I waited for the judges' score. "What do I need? What do I need?" I asked Patrick urgently.

"Shh," warned Patrick. The judges turned the flip card. I had gotten an 8.9, the highest score in my life.

A huge grin spread across Patrick's face.

"Was that enough? Was that enough?" I cried.

"Congratulations, Lauren," said Patrick. "You got yourself and the Pinecones a first place."

I hugged him. First place! Me! I loved it!

Detective or Gymnast? Why Not Be Both?

It was time for Ti An's beam exercise. Ti An paced in little circles.

"If she blows it again, I'll strangle her," said Cindi, who was scheduled to go after Ti An.

"She won't," I said.

Cindi grinned at me. "Now that you've gotten a medal on vault, are you guaranteeing a victory for all of us?" she asked.

"Winning's contagious," I said.

"Somebody better go tell that to Ti An," said Jodi. "She looks like she's going to be sick."

"I'll tell her," I said.

I went over to Ti An. She looked so nervous that she could barely focus on me.

"I'm up in three minutes," she wailed. "Now

that you've won a medal, everybody expects the Pinecones to do well. What if I fall a zillion times again?"

"Ti An, you're not going to fall," I said.

Ti An stared at me.

"You're going to do it just like you did in practice. You're not going to fall once."

Ti An looked up at me. I'm so short, I'm not used to anyone looking up at me.

"How do you know?" she asked.

"I took out no-fall insurance for this meet," I said.

Ti An nodded as if I wasn't making a joke. I think I really gave her confidence.

"No-fall insurance," she repeated.

"Yeah, I took it out double for you," I told her.

The announcer's voice came over the loudspeaker. "Next up on beam, Ti An Truong," he said. "Cindi Jockett next. Darlene Broderick in the hole."

"You can do it, Ti An," I said to her.

Ti An took a deep breath. She walked proudly up to the beam and saluted the judge.

I crossed every available finger. I stood next to the other Pinecones.

"I bet she's going to fall," said Ashley.

I flashed her a dirty look. "She's your friend."

"I know," said Ashley. "But I think she's the kind of girl who can't stand competition."

"I bet you you're wrong," I said. "I'm going to win a trophy for vault. I bet you my trophy that Ti An sticks her routine."

The other Pinecones stared at me. I couldn't believe what I had just said myself.

I held my breath as Ti An did a successful mount onto the beam. Ti An didn't fall once. You could almost feel the audience and the judges fall in love with her. She was a performer. She wasn't doing the most difficult routine, but she was winning everybody's heart. She finished her routine with a great dismount and saluted the judge. I finally started breathing.

Ti An ran over to us, and we gave her a Pinecone hug.

Winning is contagious. Cindi did the routine of her life, and so did Darlene, and I wasn't so bad myself. Even Ashley pulled through, but I was glad that she didn't score as high as Darlene, Cindi, or even Ti An.

By the time it was over, the Pinecones had cleaned up on beam. We had cleaned up on vault. We didn't do quite as well on floor exercise or the uneven bars. But we had won two team medals, and we were in a strong position for the overall.

We had to wait a long time for the judges to tally up the final score. I saw Becky in her street clothes sitting in the stands. She looked in a totally foul mood, and I was glad.

The four original Pinecones ended up alone for a minute. Cindi said to me, "Ti An turned out to be okay, didn't she?"

I looked over at Ti An, who was glowing.

"She's more than okay," I admitted. "I just hope she never finds out I suspected her."

"She won't," said Darlene, nudging Jodi with her elbow. "We Pinecones can keep a secret, right?"

"Right," said Jodi, but Jodi's attention was elsewhere. The judges were standing up.

They called the winners of the vault first. I had never gotten to stand on the top step as a winner. The judge handed me a trophy of a girl vaulting. It was the most beautiful thing I had ever seen. I would never have been able to give it up to Ashley if I had lost my bet about Ti An. Patrick hung a medal around my neck.

Then I went back to sit down with the Pinecones.

Ti An came in third on the beam, and Cindi and Darlene tied for first.

The Grandstanders won the uneven bars, and the Amazons swept the floor exercise.

Finally it was time for the judges to announce the team that was the overall winner.

"Third place to the Grandstanders," said the judge.

"Well, at least we're not in last place," said Cindi breathlessly.

"Second place to the Atomic Amazons," said the judge. He almost couldn't be heard because we were whooping and hollering so loud. We had won. We were in first place.

The judges called us up to collect our medals and our team trophy. It was another first for me. I had never gotten to have two medals hung around my neck. I adored it.

As Patrick hung my second medal around my neck he whispered to me, "Which would you rather be? A detective or a gymnast?"

"Why not be both?" I answered him with a big grin.